MIMESIS
INTERNATIONAL

AESTHETICS
n. 6

AESTHETICS, LITERATURE AND LIFE

Essays in honour of Jean-Pierre Cometti

Edited by
Carla Carmona and Jerrold Levinson

Part of this research and part of this editorial work were conducted while enjoying a research stay at King's College London between October 2016 and January 2017, financed by the Conserjería de Educación y Empleo of the Junta de Extremadura, Spain.

JUNTA DE EXTREMADURA
Consejería de Educación y Empleo

© 2019 – MIMESIS INTERNATIONAL (Milano – Udine)
www.mimesisinternational.com
e-mail: info@mimesisinternational.com

Book series: *Aesthetics*, n. 6

Isbn: 9788869771804

© MIM Edizioni Srl
P.I. C.F. 02419370305

TABLE OF CONTENTS

PREFACE 9
Carla Carmona and Jerrold Levinson

COMETTI ON WITTGENSTEIN AND MUSIL

COMETTI ON WITTGENSTEIN AND MUSIL 17
Jerrold Levinson

THE MAN WITHOUT QUALITIES OR THE QUESTION OF HOW
TO LIVE. IN CONVERSATION WITH JEAN-PIERRE COMETTI'S
L'HOMME EXACT 25
Carla Carmona

KAKANIAN SUITS, A CONVERSATION IN TWO PARTS BETWEEN 51
Jean-Pierre Cometti and Carla Carmona

ART, MUSIC, LITERARY CRITICISM AND THE SPIRIT OF A CULTURE

TEN THESES ON LITERARY INTERPRETATION 69
Peter Lamarque

SENTIMENTALITY AS AN AESTHETIC FLAW 87
Severin Schroeder

THE MELODY AND THE SENTENCE: WITTGENSTEIN'S
PHILOSOPHICAL INVESTIGATIONS,
CULTURALLY INTERWOVEN PERCEPTION, AND THE ANALOGY
BETWEEN MUSIC AND WORDS 99
Garry Hagberg

LITERATURE AS A KEY TO UNDERSTANDING WITTGENSTEIN

CLARIFICATION: WITTGENSTEIN'S *GEDICHTETE PHILOSOPHIE* 123
Tore Nordenstam

ART, CRAFTSMANSHIP AND PHILOSOPHICAL METHOD
ACCORDING TO WITTGENSTEIN 141
Allan Janik

WITTGENSTEIN, ETHICS AND LITERATURE. THE CASE OF
TOLSTOY'S TALE *HADJI MURAT* 157
Nicolás Sánchez Durá

ON SEEING AND ASPECTS: COMETTI, WITTGENSTEIN,
AND *DON QUIXOTE* 183
Salvador Rubio Marco

TOWARD AN ANTHROPOLOGICAL AESTHETICS. IN CONVERSATION WITH JEAN-PIERRE COMETTI

COMETTI'S LATE THOUGHTS: SOME NOTES ABOUT
CONTEMPORARY ART AND AGENCY 199
Jacques Morizot

AESTHETIC CONSUMPTIONS AND ANTHROPOLOGICAL NEEDS 215
Roberta Dreon

ON BEING ABOUT WHAT COUNTS: ART, MONEY, VALUE,
AND FIGURATIVE DISTANCE AS ARTISTIC QUALITY 237
Bertrand Rougé

EXPOSITION AND INSTALLATION: JEAN-PIERRE COMETTI
AGAINST THE COMMODIFICATION OF ART OBJECTS 269
Jean-Maurice Monnoyer

No cares for me, I'm happy as I can be, I've learned to love and to live, devil-may-care.

Même exister, cela s'apprend.
Italo Calvino

CARLA CARMONA AND JERROLD LEVINSON
PREFACE

The essays collected in the present volume discuss fundamental problems of modern and contemporary aesthetics in conversation with the French philosopher Jean-Pierre Cometti, who specialized in aesthetics, pragmatism, and Austrian philosophy, and translated Ludwig Wittgenstein, John Dewey and Robert Musil, among others, into French.

The volume, which is divided into four different parts, explores Cometti's anti-essentialist, pragmatist, and contextualist intellectual biography. The first part presents Cometti as a commentator of Wittgenstein and Musil. The following three parts respectively focus on revising the principles of art and literary criticism, while revealing the myths behind the Modernist conception of art understood widely, that is, as including music and literature, shedding light upon Wittgenstein's philosophy by means of literature and discussing contemporary art and aesthetic practices so as to propose an anthropological aesthetics.

In the opening chapter, Jerrold Levinson sketches Cometti's major contributions to the understanding of Wittgenstein and Musil by commenting on two of his books, *Philosopher avec Wittgenstein* and *L'homme exact*. Levinson observes that Cometti is effective in showing how few of those who would claim to have grasped Wittgenstein's lessons into language, meaning and mind actually absorbed those lessons. In addition, Levinson underlines the richness, subtlety, and depth of the interpretations and reflections that Cometti bequeathed us in his third monograph on Musil, which Levinson views as an example of biographical-philosophical criticism. In her chapter 'The Man Without Qualities or the Question of How to Live', Carla Carmona further examines

Cometti's insights regarding Musil's unfinished novel. Also in conversation with *L'homme exact,* Carmona addresses Musil's unique investigation of the realm of the possible and examines the ethical dimension of the novel, as well as how it relates to the inner-outer picture that was so criticized by Wittgenstein. Next, the reader encounters a conversation between Cometti and Carmona, which looks into Musil's oeuvre against the background of fin-de-siècle Vienna, by comparing his concerns with those of Egon Schiele and Wittgenstein in particular. In this context, Cometti's view that there is no such a thing as 'fin-de-siècle Vienna' comes to the fore.

In different ways, and yet converging on key points, Peter Lamarque and Severin Schroeder discuss literary criticism. Lamarque understands literary criticism as a practice, and insists that one should not extend to it features of other practices, as, for instance, features of criticism of other art forms. He also opposes the idea of 'the meaning of a literary work'. Lamarque proposes that we think of interpretation not in terms of understanding, not even in terms of meaning, but in terms of providing a perspective through which the particulars of the work can be reflected on. In Lamarque's pluralistic account, there is no single interpretation of a work, and we cannot hold all of them at the same time, but can only shift perspectives from one to another at different times. For his part, Schroeder reflects upon literary criticism's moral approach to sentimentality in literature. He shows how over the last decades there have been a number of attempts to explain sentimentality in literature as primarily a *moral* defect. In contrast, Schroeder puts forward the idea that the charge of sentimentality in literary criticism should primarily be seen as an *aesthetic* censure. Moreover, Schroeder proposes that sentimentality must be relative, first, to the cultural standards of expressing one's feelings in a given society, and secondly, to the standards of literary taste, which may allow for genres that are self-consciously stylized and artificial, both linguistically and psychologically.

Continuing the task of dispelling the myths of High Modernism, Garry Hagberg expounds Wittgenstein's conception of the work of art – that works of art and music display not only themselves, but the content and what one might call the spirit of a culture – as a way to combat the understanding of the art object as an autonomous entity closed in on itself that gained currency with High Modernism. Hagberg holds the view that for Wittgenstein, what he called 'a way of seeing' the world was in a special sense discernible both in and through a work of music: we hear the music in the culture and we hear the culture in the music. Hagberg sets Wittgenstein's views on music and language alongside each other, as providing what he thinks is the most compelling model for our culturally-interwoven understanding of both.

Tore Nordenstam's and Allan Janik's articles show the literary side of Wittgenstein's philosophy, by focusing on poetry and fiction respectively, and Nicolás Sánchez and Salvador Rubio use Tolstoi's Hadji Murat and Cervantes's Don Quixote and Sancho in order to clarify Wittgenstein's moral philosophy and his concept of seeing, seeing-as, and blindness about aspects, respectively. Nordenstam considers the *Tractatus logico-philosophicus* as a literary work of art and puts forward the idea that it belongs to the Modernist literary canon. By pointing out that in this work of Wittgenstein form and content are two sides of the same coin, he concludes that in that respect it is more like *poetry* and other forms of literature and art than standard academic contributions to the field of philosophy. Janik proposes instead *fiction* as the model for philosophy, and not poetry, and is thus inclined to challenge Wittgenstein's statement that philosophy ought to be written as a poetic composition. He enquires into the tension between art and philosophy in Wittgenstein's work, from the *Tractatus* and the Palais Stonborough to his later philosophy, in order to offer a perspicuous representation of his philosophical method. By paying special attention to Wittgenstein's philosophical style, Janik shows craftsmanship to be a *leitmotiv* in Wittgenstein's oeuvre.

Sánchez proposes the character of Hadji Murat as a lens through which to explore Wittgenstein's moral philosophy. After portraying heroism as being able to look death squarely in the face and reminding us that being heroic is a question of pathos, Sánchez considers heroism both historically and individually. Different peoples associate their pathos with different kinds of actions. The figure of Hadji Murat is presented as a key to understanding Wittgenstein's anthropological method, and the novel as containing paradigms of actions, some of which are still in circulation and others that are no longer feasible. Rubio refers to Cometti's reference in his *Ludwig Wittgenstein et la philosophie de la psychologie* to Don Quixote and Sancho's famous episode of the windmills in order to explain the Wittgensteinian concepts of *seeing, seeing-as* and *blindness about aspects*. In this way, Rubio develops Cometti's suggestion that Cervantes's *Don Quixote* illustrates and helps to dispel some philosophical confusions concerning the very diverse uses of *seeing*.

The four remaining articles share an anthropological orientation. Jacques Morizot offers a magnificent overview of Cometti's late ideas on modernity and contemporary art. The essay can be understood as an exploration of how a contemporary thinker looks at the history of modern art and its most fundamental interpretations. It discusses the delusory and ideological dimensions of the notion of aesthetic autonomy, with stops at Dada and Black Mountain College, while paying attention to Dewey's ideas developed in *Art as Experience* in relation to the latter. Morizot's essay also underscores the fundamental role that Bürger's critical and social reading of art played at a moment when formalist approaches were dominant. Roberta Dreon discusses Cometti's remark that the claim of the autonomy of art has nourished a form of false consciousness, leading to the political and practical marginalization of the arts, which are now almost completely subject to the logic of the market. The paper presents the thesis that aesthetic needs are related to the human structural dependence on a natural, and naturally social, environment. From this perspective, forms of consumption can sometimes lead to an enhancement of life and to the shared enjoyment of our interactions with the different contexts we belong to, as well as to a fruitful questioning of the present customary division of life into strict compartments.

In the next article, Bertrand Rougé engages Cometti in a discussion regarding his concept of art without properties, an idea inspired by the writings of Musil. Rougé interrogates Cometti's sociological thesis about how the aura of art today, 'the new aura', is determined by its relationship with the auras of wealth, fashion and luxury, and concludes that Cometti unfairly absolutizes the widespread notion that market value and artistic value become less and less distinguishable. Moreover, Rougé discusses whether or not art can be defined, and against Cometti's skepticism on that score, proposes that it may well be possible. Focusing on continuities rather than ruptures, he advances a modest theory and ontology of art, one inspired by rhetoric. In the volume's final article, Jean-Maurice Monnoyer portrays Cometti's *La nouvelle aura* as the culmination of his research trajectory. He sympathetically explores Cometti's idea that contemporary art overturned Walter Benjamin's forecast of the end of autographic art. But he also argues against Cometti's understanding of contemporary art as a regime of literality and underscores instead the active participation of the spectator, who makes inferences and draws conclusions regarding whether or not the installations and other works of contemporary art he encounters truly participate in the disenchantment of the world.

The diversity and freshness of these essays, as well as the vital breath they share, reflect and communicate the unique philosophical regard that was Cometti's – kaleidoscopic and free, playfully alive and enlivening, and not beholden to dualistic or reductionist attachments of any kind.

COMETTI ON WITTGENSTEIN AND MUSIL

Jerrold Levinson
COMETTI ON WITTGENSTEIN AND MUSIL[1]

I

Jean-Pierre Cometti's *Philosopher avec Wittgenstein*[2] is representative of the sort of synthetic, wide-ranging, and sympathetic-to-Anglo-American-philosophy in which, happily enough, an increasing minority of French philosophers are now engaged. The central aim of the book is not originality in the interpretation of Wittgenstein, nor is it primarily criticism of Wittgensteinian positions, but passionate and elegant defense of Wittgenstein's ultimate picture of philosophy, coupled with cautious chastisement of those who have blurred, knowingly or unknowingly, the attractive outlines of that picture. The result is a stylish essay having some of the elusive and allusive character of Wittgenstein's own thought, if none of Wittgenstein's characteristic gnomic manner of expression. One of the longer chapters of the book is devoted to Wittgenstein's aesthetic views, which recommends the book to the attention of Anglo-American aestheticians competent in French.

As regards exegesis, *Philosopher avec Wittgenstein* has the merit of drawing on a wider range of Wittgenstein's writings than are usually appealed to, in order to give a more balanced sense of what was perhaps most important to Wittgenstein as philosopher and human being. Cometti calls significantly upon texts such as

---

[1] The first part of this paper was originally published in the section of Book Notes in *Journal of Aesthetics and Art Criticism* 57, no. 4 (1999), pp. 484-485.
[2] Jean-Pierre Cometti, *Philosopher avec Wittgenstein* (Paris: Presses Universitaires de France, 1996).

the *Remarks on Frazer's Golden Bough*, the *Mixed Remarks*, the *Philosophical Grammar*, and the *Secret Notebooks*, some of which are available only in German, Italian, Spanish or French, but not English. In addition to substantial discussion of meaning, rules, language games, forms of life, and the myth of the inner – familiar topics when Wittgenstein is considered in the guise of a philosopher of mind and language – *Philosopher avec Wittgenstein* contains extended examination of Wittgenstein's views on the affinity of aesthetic and conceptual questions, on the nature and role of religious beliefs, and on the use of philosophy for transformation of self and society. These are topics often omitted or glossed over in more standard approaches to Wittgenstein as philosopher.

Cometti succeeds nicely in demonstrating the continuity of Wittgenstein's later thought, expressed across many writings and topics, putting that thought into relation with his earlier thought, though without minimizing the real differences between them. He conveys the sense in which the later thought involves radical departures from the earlier, even if some critical points of reflection, e.g., how language is far more than what is said or stated, remain constant.

Cometti is also effective in showing how many who would claim to have grasped Wittgenstein's lessons on language, meaning, and mind, and to have gone beyond them, have probably not fully absorbed those lessons, or correctly appreciated them. In this category Cometti puts Habermas and Apel, the champions of communicative rationality, Kripke, the promoter of Wittgenstein as skeptic, Hintikka, the proponent of the *Investigations* as merely the continuation of the *Tractatus*, Heidegger, the defender of philosophy's aspiration toward a pure and perfect, reality-disclosing language, and Derrida, the purveyor of language games detached from forms of life. His criticisms of all of these in favor of Wittgenstein are telling, and are predicated on judicious expositions of their positions. In addition Cometti does much to elucidate various Wittgensteinian strands in certain contemporary philosophers of pragmatist or quasi-realist persuasion, notably Rorty, Putnam, and Cavell, whom Cometti valorizes in the same measure as he chides those mentioned a moment ago.

In the chapter devoted to Wittgenstein's aesthetic views Cometti examines the *Lectures on Aesthetics* with more than usual care, while emphasizing the connections between Wittgenstein's thoughts on art, and music in particular, and his broader views on mind, language, and the human world. Of particular interest, on Cometti's portrait of Wittgenstein as aesthetician, is the scope that Wittgenstein sees, in light of his later, pragmatic conception of language, for discourse about aesthetic experience, before which silence is not, as it was in the *Tractatus*, necessarily prescribed. One's understanding of a work of art is reflected in a whole range of behaviors and capacities, verbal ones often figuring as importantly as nonverbal ones. There is extensive discussion of Wittgenstein on aspects, the connection between their emergence and the achievement of aesthetic understanding, and the crucial roles of context and comparison in getting aspects to dawn. Also central, for Cometti, is Wittgenstein's insistence on the ordinariness of aesthetic judgments, and the essential continuity between criticism of opera or painting and assessment of the cut of a dress or the meaning of a gesture. Wittgenstein's refreshing down-to-earthness on aesthetic matters is contrasted at length with Heidegger's obfuscatory otherworldliness in that regard.

The writing in *Philosopher avec Wittgenstein* is seamless throughout, moving effortlessly from one great modern to another, in generally illuminating fashion. The book is, in a sense, very true to its title: though the literary style, historical consciousness, and sectional organization is not Wittgenstein's, the motivating spirit is. It reflects a profound assimilation of Wittgenstein by a scholar of broad learning, one well placed to put Wittgenstein's later thought in context with deconstruction, analytic philosophy, Humean skepticism, and Heideggerian metaphysics, most often to Wittgenstein's advantage. Wittgenstein the exorciser of 'mental cramps' and advocate of philosophy as 'life therapy' has perhaps never had a more effective champion.

II

L'homme exact[3] is the third monograph by Cometti devoted to the Austrian novelist Robert Musil, having been preceded

---

3   Jean-Pierre Cometti, *L'Homme exact* (Paris: Seuil, 1997).

by *Robert Musil ou l'Alternative romanesque*[4] and *De 'Torless' à 'L'Homme sans qualités'*[5]. In the *L'Homme exact* (hereafter *HE*) Cometti pays further homage to Musil, his literary-philosophical hero, does Musil a great interpretive service, and most importantly, provides readers with a valuable introduction to the whole corpus of a singular writer who is still relatively unknown and underappreciated outside the German-speaking world. *HE* belongs to a curious genre, being neither straightforwardly biography nor straightforwardly intellectual criticism, but rather an intimate fusion of the two, which might be labeled literary-philosophical biography, or perhaps, biographical-philosophical criticism.

Cometti notes at the outset that Musil's readership is rather less than his recognition and reputation would lead one to expect, and one of the merits of *HE* is to give some insight as to why that might be the case. Cometti emphasizes the distinctive task Musil set for the novel, one of 'establishing possibilities' and 'constructing utopias', rather than the more common task of relating a humanly absorbing story with an easily assimilated plot. The special kind of novel at which Musil aimed, one not calculated to win the greatest number of readers, was to be a medium between science and philosophy, on the one hand, and traditional, narrative-driven literature, on the other. This, he thought, was the only form of novel capable of addressing modernity, one in which linear, cause-and-effect narration would have to be replaced by something more fluid, nuanced, and multi-dimensional, an unprecedented hybrid of the essayistic and the poetic.

Musil's early formation in science and mathematics and his first profession as an engineer, Cometti makes plain, exerted a strong influence on the conception of literature noted above, as well as giving him a lifelong taste for exactitude and logicality. But at the same time, his intimate acquaintance with those technical fields made him all the more sensitive to the dangers of a mechanical application of scientific models and methods to the realm of

---

4 Jean-Pierre Cometti, *Robert Musil ou l'Alternative romanesque* (Paris: Presses Universitaire de France, 1985).
5 Jean-Pierre Cometti, *De 'Torless' à 'L'Homme sans qualités'* (Brussels: Mardaga, 1986).

sentiment and feeling, that which was increasingly to be of utmost concern to him, and which he felt his unique form of novelistic writing was best suited to illuminate.

Cometti is instructive on significant influences on Musil's thought apart from his early scientific training, such as the philosophers Friedrich Nietzsche and Ralph Waldo Emerson, the philosopher-physicist Ernst Mach (the subject of Musil's doctoral dissertation in philosophy of science), the poets Maurice Maeterlinck and Rainer Maria Rilke, the novelists Franz Kafka and Marcel Proust, and the Gestalt psychologist Karl Stumpf. Musil's early sojourn in Brno (in the former Czechoslovakia) is also given due attention, underlining its role as the scene of Musil's first exposure to theatre, music, literary life, and romantic relationships.

Here Musil had his first intimations of an 'alternative state' of being, one he would ultimately hold to be essential to the aesthetic and the ethical dimensions of life, themselves indissociably connected. Musil saw in Gestalt psychology some potential to illuminate the nature of emotional experiences, which were not to be understood as simple effects of identifiable causes, but rather, in terms of emergent wholes with unpredictable qualities. Cometti notes a striking example of Gestaltist inspiration from this youthful period of Musil's life, where after a concert he had the vision of a woman whose silhouette would be identical or conformable to the shape or profile of a passage of music.

Cometti devotes substantial attention to Musil's early fiction, especially the novel *The Confusions of Young Torless*, in which one of Musil's characteristic themes is already front and center, that of the powerlessness of logic and reason when detached from feeling and emotion, as well as that of the necessity for a workable blueprint of human life to take account of the darkest impulses of our natures. But attention is also devoted to the works of short fiction that followed *Torless*, namely the stories 'Tonka', 'Grigia', 'The Portuguese Lady', 'The Temptation of Quiet Veronica' and 'The Perfecting of Love', as well as the play *The Enthusiasts*, on which Musil set great store. All of those writings form relevant background to the extraordinary interlacing of themes in Musil's masterpiece, *Der Mann ohne Eigenschaften,* or as it is known in French, *L'Homme sans qualités,* or as it is known in English, *The Man Without Qualities* (hereafter *MWQ*).

Cometti showcases many telling excerpts from *MWQ*, ones judiciously chosen to support his interpretation of the novel, but also ones that give a reader unfamiliar with the novel a sense of what the experience of reading the novel is like. Cometti notably finds in *MWQ* a recurrent lightness of tone or outlook, not that which Milan Kundera famously ascribed to being and held to be unbearable, but instead, that which Italo Calvino took note of in Lucretius, an attitude toward existence midway between indifference and acceptance, one touching on sublimity.

Speaking of the second, unfinished volume of *MWQ*, Cometti intriguingly reports that its overriding ambition for Musil was to relieve readers of their 'mental cramps', a project having some similarity to Wittgenstein's stated aim, in the *Philosophical Investigations*, of 'showing the fly the way out of the fly-bottle'. But what was perhaps in Musil's view the paramount purpose of imaginative literature, Cometti convincingly shows, was the cultivation of 'a sense of the possible' necessary to a just vision of human life and its aesthetic and ethical dimension, and of the sort of society in which that might best flourish.

The main project of *HE*, naturally enough, is a sensitive and contextually grounded reading of *MWQ*, to which most of Musil's life was devoted. This is achieved in part through a careful consideration of the roles played, in Musil's imaginative vision of modernity in the period immediately preceding the First World War, by the chief fictional personages of *MWQ*, most of them based loosely on real persons of Musil's acquaintance, many of them belonging to his own entourage.

These include, first and foremost, the brother and sister pair of Ulrich and Agatha, Ulrich being the exemplary 'man without qualities', or person without fixed nature, of the novel's title, and Agatha being the 'soul-mate' of Ulrich only discovered by him later in the course of the novel; the couple Walter and Clarissa, best friends of Ulrich, who partly echo and partly contest his preoccupations; and Ulrich's cousin Diotima, the host of a cultural salon that becomes the staging ground of the absurd and largely notional Parallel Campaign, aimed at countering the influence of Germany in world affairs and boosting the global image of Austria-Hungary, comically referred to also as Kakania.

These principal personages also include Arnheim, a Prussian industrialist-financier of wide influence who becomes unofficial consort of and counsel to Diotima; Count Leinsdorf, the government official charged with the nominal direction of the grandiose Parallel Campaign; General Stumm von Bordwehr, who is concerned to see that the military play a part in this grand 'project of peace', which ironically paves the way for the cataclysm of WWI; and Moosbrugger, the murderer of a prostitute who may or may not be responsible for his actions, but who inspires sympathy and even empathy on the part of some of the highly placed and morally conventional individuals of Musil's fiction.

Introducing and explicating this array of characters is Cometti's chosen way of conveying the substance and sense of Musil's main themes, such as the continual interpenetration of thought and feeling; the vacuousness of moral principles insensitive to the individuality of situations; the illusion of a substantial self; the limits of rational explanation of human behavior; the relationship between the individual and the society which surrounds him, and the deep connectedness of sensuality and spirituality.

Of special importance in Musil's worldview, as in those of his Austrian contemporaries Sigmund Freud, Arthur Schnitzler, Egon Schiele, and Stefan Zweig, and despite his explicit downplaying of this, was the role of sexual experiences in personal and moral development. As Cometti convincingly underlines, this holds true beginning with *Torless*, most obviously, then continuing through the five novellas that followed, all of which have female protagonists and sexual intrigue at their core, right through to the more intellectual-spiritual explorations of the incomplete second volume of *MWQ*.

Cometti points out with unfailing penetration the many ways in which Musil's masterwork is a novel of *dualness*: often twinning characters such as Ulrich and Agatha, or Arnheim and Diotima, or Count Leinsdorf and General Stumm; regularly alternating essayistic analyses and narrative elaborations in virtuoso fashion; emphasizing now the potential of statistical and sociological explanation of behavior, now the impotence of such to capture the elusiveness of a world and of individuals 'without qualities'; presenting, on the one hand, a surface plot of appearances and ordinary actions, and on the other hand, an underlying plot of experiences and extraordinary possibilities, ones normally covered by 'the carapace of convention'.

In bringing to a close this brief notice of *L'Homme exact*, Cometti's third and last attempt to do justice to Robert Musil and his work, I want to underline above all the richness, subtlety, and depth of the interpretations and reflections that Cometti has there bequeathed us, of which I have here been able to give only a partial and inadequate idea.

References

Jean-Pierre Cometti, *De 'Torless' à 'L'Homme sans qualités'* (Brussels: Mardaga, 1986).
—, *L'Homme exact* (Paris: Seuil, 1997).
—, *Robert Musil ou l'Alternative romanesque* (Paris: Presses Universitaire de France, 1985).
—, *Philosopher avec Wittgenstein* (Paris: Presses Universitaires de France, 1996).
Levinson, Jerrold, *Journal of Aesthetics and Art Criticism* 57, no. 4 (1999), pp. 484-485 <doi:10.2307/432165>

Carla Carmona
THE MAN WITHOUT QUALITIES OR THE QUESTION OF HOW TO LIVE
In conversation with Jean Pierre Cometti's *L'Homme exact*[1]

1. *The inner and the outer in* The Man Without Qualities

Jean Pierre Cometti explored in multiple ways the inner-outer picture that continues to exercise philosophers in the analytic and continental philosophical traditions, in spite of Ludwig Wittgenstein's well-known critique of its application to the problems of other minds and self-knowledge. Probably the most representative side of Cometti's contribution to the clarification of the picture was in the domains of our artistic and aesthetic practices. He provided us with exhaustive clarifying analyses of carefully selected individual art works, as well as with insightful comparisons of them[2].

---

[1] This paper was produced while enjoying a research stay at King's College London, financed by the Conserjería de Educación y Empleo of the Junta de Extremadura, Spain.
All translations in the present article are mine, whether from the French, in the case of Cometti's works, or from the German, in the case of *The Man Without Qualities* and other writings by Musil.
I would like to thank Jerrold Levinson for his careful reading of my paper, which has contributed to its improvement, as well as for his generous and constant company throughout this editorial journey.

[2] A selection of articles in which Cometti developed these ideas while discussing Rodin, architecture, contemporary music, and avant-garde or contemporary art, was recently published in Spanish, edited by Ricardo Ibarlucía. Those four texts, which are the result of a series of conferences that Cometti delivered in Argentina in 2010, convey very clearly his position regarding the inner-outer picture in the last years of his life, cf. Jean-Pierre Cometti, *Exterior Arte: Estética y formas de vida* (Buenos Aires: Biblos, 2014).

For instance, he used beautifully Auguste Rodin's *Inner Voice* (also known as *Meditation*) in order to show that there is no distinction between the inner and the outer in an art work, that there is no gap between the content of a work of art and its form, that speaking in terms of the content of a work of art as a separable thing does not make any sense, that it is, at any rate, outmoded and not useful. By describing the piece, Cometti showed us that interiority is not beneath the surface, that there is no distinction between the anatomy of the sculpture and its 'inner voice'[3]. He also drew our attention to the fact that the equation of exteriority and interiority could become the very method of an artist. In this regard, in relation to Robert Morris's *Box with the sound of its own making* and John Cage's *4'33"*, Cometti noted that interiority methodically (not metaphorically) consisted of exteriority, especially of the process that gave birth to the art work[4]. For Cometti there was no distinction between art and life, and he had only contempt for the concept of an aesthetic object. He availed himself of land art in order to problematize the traditional conception of the relationship between the inner and the outer and what is generally understood as the limits of a work of art, since in such art the inside and the outside are included in the art work and are no longer its limits[5].

Nonetheless, Cometti also examined minutely the later Wittgenstein's treatment of the web of fine threads interconnecting our concepts of the inner and the outer in his book *Ludwig Wittgenstein et la philosophie de la psychologie*. We find there exquisite examples, taken from literature in particular, in the chapter 'L'invention de l'intériorité', in which Cometti seems to be involved in an ongoing conversation with Robert Musil[6]. That chapter title clearly points toward Musil, since it is an expression Cometti acknowledged having borrowed from one of Musil's essays.

Cometti noted powerful parallelisms between Wittgenstein's critique of the inner-outer picture and Musil's literary explorations

---

3   Cometti, *Exterior Arte*, pp. 56-58.
4   Ibid., p. 29.
5   Ibid., p. 31.
6   Jean-Pierre Cometti, *Ludwig Wittgenstein et la philosophie de la psychologie* (Paris: Presses Universitaires de France, 2004), pp. 148-197.

of the inner man. The conception of the inner that Musil put into practice in *The Man Without Qualities (MWQ)*[7] is very close to that of the later Wittgenstein. Musil seemed to share Wittgenstein's idea that one's inner is not an object of self-knowledge, that the privilege of the first person perspective was an illusion, and that speaking in terms of 'knowing' in fact only made sense in the case of our insight into other human beings. *MWQ* portrays remarkably well the indeterminacy characteristic of the knowledge of our fellow human beings and educates and enlightens us as to how imponderable the kind of evidence that is available in that realm is. Furthermore, it questions the understanding of the inner as an object, the very idea that it is something steady and constant. Cometti also proposed that there was symmetry in terms of method between Musil's literary explorations of the inner and Wittgenstein's practice of language games[8]. Both were fictitious ways of exploring possibilities, of the inner in one case and of language in the other, in order to achieve an understanding of human beings, with a special emphasis on ways of living, forms of life, or life games. In fact, we could well describe *MWQ* as a fascinatingly diverse collection of such games.

It is thus little wonder that Cometti approached the dualistic understanding of the inner and the outer through the thorough analysis of *MWQ* that he pursued in a good number of essays and articles. The aim of this paper is to offer a modest synoptic view of Musil's extension of the possibilities of the inner in *MWQ*, and to shed light especially on its ethical dimension. I shall do this in conversation with Cometti, in particular with those ideas of his collected in his book *L'Homme exact*[9].

---

[7] I shall use Walter Fanta's recent edition of *Der Mann ohne Eigenschaften* published in six volumes by Jung und Jung between 2016 and 2018, which can also be consulted online at http://musilonline.at/musiltext/.
[8] Cometti, *Ludwig Wittgenstein et la philosophie de la psychologie*, p. 188.
[9] Jean-Pierre Cometti, *L'Homme exact: essai sur Robert Musil* (Paris: Seuil, 1997).

2. The concept of the inner man and the question of how to live

Cometti draws our attention first to Musil's reflections on the kind of knowledge that is involved in literature[10]. In *Sketch of the writer's knowledge*, Musil described literature as a domain in which exceptions prevail over the rule and facts are boundlessly variable and individual, in which facts themselves, and their combinations, 'are infinite and incalculable', a domain of 'values and valuations', of 'ethical and aesthetic relationships', of the individual, her circumstances, and her reactions in those circumstances, in such a way that every judgment, every concept, is surrounded by 'a veil of experience more subtle than the ether, by a personal arbitrariness and, a few seconds later, by the absence of any personal arbitrariness'[11]. If we extend this insight to *MWQ*, we could say that the experiences of most characters are so subjective that they become as objective as anything can be. This certainly reminds us of the passion for contradiction of the great mystics. We learn from Cometti that Musil enjoyed reading their works. Subjectivity and objectivity blend together in *MWQ*.

Against this background, Musil introduces the concept of the inner man:

> The unknown, the equalities, and the possibilities of solution have no end in advance. The task is to continue discovering new solutions, new interrelations, constellations and variables, to establish prototypes of different courses of events, seductive models of how man can be, to invent the inner man.[12]

In almost every paragraph that Cometti dedicated to *MWQ*, we find a trace of those few lines that Musil wrote in 1918. Aware of how many ideas were condensed there, Cometti tried to develop their possibilities from as many angles as possible. Musil portrayed literature as a laboratory in which there was no limit to the experimentation regarding the possibilities of being a man.

---

10 Cometti, *Ludwig Wittgenstein et la philosophie de la psychologie*, p. 149.
11 Robert Musil, 'Skizze der Erkenntnis des Dichters' (1918), in *Gesammelte Werke in neun Bänden. Essays und Reden*, ed. by Adolf Frisé (Reinbeck bei Hamburg: Rowohlt, 1978), VIII, 1025-1030 (p. 1028).
12 Musil, *Gesammelte*, VIII, 1029.

The main problem that literature ought to tackle was 'How to be a human being?', or in other words, 'How to live?'[13]. We are told that literature is able to 'establish prototypes' and 'seductive models', which do not admit only one solution[14], but an endless number of them. Thanks to them, to the constellations that will emerge in the process, to the immense variability and the many interrelations that will be encountered, the inner man can be invented, or reencountered in all its potential. Simply put, the novel provides the reader with a space in which to learn, in multiple ways, how to live, that is, how to explore the possibilities of being a subject and how to understand subjectivity[15].

Cometti contrasted the pictures of the inner man provided by philosophy with the countless number of models brought into being in literature[16]. What is the difference between a picture and a model? That the latter is aware of its nature, that is to say, the model is aware that it is *a* model, one articulation among many others of how man can be. Cometti proposed that while philosophy has a tendency to forget (and makes us forget) that its pictures of the inner man are actually mere pictures, the arts could contribute to enriching and renewing our conception of the inner without ascribing any certainty or exclusivity to the varied pictures proposed. Nevertheless, he also held that there were plenty of cases in the history of art that have gone exactly in the opposite direction, as if hand in hand with traditional conceptions in philosophy. We are told that the arts, as a result, have had a complex relationship with the inner man. Cometti understood Musil, and *MWQ* in particular, as a paradigm of the arts whose

---

13 In chapter 62, the reader is explicitly told that for Ulrich there was only one question worth thinking about (and that such a question was behind even the mathematical treatises that he wrote), the question of the right way to live.
14 The fact that Musil speaks in terms of solutions shows how much of a scientist he was. This fits well with the ideas that will be developed later regarding Musil's non-dualistic understanding of the traditional dichotomy between science (and reason) and feeling (or sentiment).
15 Musil differentiated clearly between subjectivity and subjectivism. The difference comes up explicitly in different fragments of chapter 62 of book I of *MWQ*.
16 Cometti, *Ludwig Wittgenstein et la philosophie de la psychologie*, p. 149.

main aim is to extend the possibilities of the inner by conceiving of non-exclusive prototypes and models regarding how man can be.

This kind of literature has the capacity to erase the imaginary boundaries between the inner and the outer. The metaphor regarding music that we find in chapter 38 of book I could shed light on the experimental 'space' elaborated in *MWQ*:

> Although this process was entirely real in its origin, the walls of the room disappeared, and in its place stood the golden jambs of music, this mysterious space in which I and the world, perception and feeling, inside and outside collapse into each other in the most indefinable way.[17]

MWQ could be understood as an epic examination of the idea that the inner man is context dependent. All the elements of the narrative, such as feelings, qualities, behaviors, characters and circumstances, are determined by their surroundings and to a great extent constituted by them. The possible outcomes of a given situation depend on how it interconnects with other events. Qualities as such cannot be identified because they are continuously transformed by their interactions with other qualities, and in general, by their surrounding circumstances. One could understand the idea of a man without qualities as a byproduct of this insight. Musil's comprehension of the inner man as exteriority in continuous construction lies behind his interest in investigating the realm of the possible.

3. *The investigation of the realm of the possible*

Musil's unique contribution to the extension of the possibilities of being human lies in his literary investigation of the realm of the possible. The engines of *MWQ* are triggered by exceptions. Musil was not interested in general rules, but in what is experienced by each man in particular in extremely specific circumstances. Right after his line about personal arbitrariness in *Sketch of the writer's*

---

17 Robert Musil, *Der Mann ohne Eigenschaften 1, Gesamtausgabe in 12 Bänden*, ed. by Walter Fanta (Salzburg: Jung und Jung, 2016), I, 226.

knowledge, Musil remarked on the impact that this intimate relationship with what happens has on facts: 'The facts in this domain, and therefore also their relationships, are infinite and incalculable'[18]. Facts in the realm of possibility become irregular polyhedra: what one experiences is always unique, and it depends both on the angle from which one looks at them and on what one is able to perceive of their interrelations. The outcomes of the same feeling explored from different angles are so distinct that one does not feel the right to speak of the 'same' feeling anymore. Moreover, Musil described each event with an outstanding number of exceptional details, so as to draw our attention to the fact that the same event would look completely different if we changed our perspective only slightly, that is to say, if one of those extravagant details would simply disappear. Let us journey along Musil's strategies of exploring the realm of the possible.

3.1. *The coexistence of opposites*

The strategy of combining something and its opposite was Musil's peculiar way of giving birth to what is not the case, a task apparently unachievable. That is precisely what lies behind his idea that the writer actually contributes to the invention of interiority. Musilian inners are far from solid: they are what they are and what they are not at the same time.

In *MWQ*, Musil rendered the very realm of possibility by making opposite qualities coexist in the same character, in such a way that each one of them remained a possibility, instead of appearing as if existing in fact, as if real. His characters are ensembles of numberless, alive, and often naughty possibilities, which are always in motion. Ulrich is a good example of that. He is presented as an indifferent, cold mathematician in the first book and as a fervent cavalier of love in the second book. These apparently opposing qualities are not really opposites according to Musil, for whom reason and feeling complemented each other. One is, in fact, a prolongation of the other[19]. In Cometti's words: 'the detachment

---

18 Musil, *Gesammelte Werke*, VIII, 1028.
19 I like to understand it as a journey in both directions. I often wonder how much the reader's experience would change if one started the novel with

of Ulrich, his absence of qualities [...] is what opens the way of love and prepares the break with indifference'[20].

Cometti suggests that Musil's characters are in effect openings, pure potentialities or availabilities[21]. They seem to be ready for anything that might turn up, including living their lives upside down, which in fact they often do. Observe that opposite dispositions are often united in the same personage. This is the case of Earl Leinsdorf, who in chapter 21 of book I is depicted as an aristocrat responsible for the Parallel Action, who did not pursue any political activity, or for that matter, hold any position in the court or in the state. Nonetheless, despite being 'only a patriot', Earl Leinsdorf became the centre of all the other patriots as a result of his goodwill and wealth. He had been seriously educated in religion and feudalism, and consequently believed in hierarchies, and yet his favourite line was 'all of us are socialists', and he meant it, but only in relation to the afterworld, which he imagined free of social distinctions. In chapter 24, we are told that he considered himself a religious man, but that when his professional conscience was in contradiction with his religious one, he leaned towards the former. We also know that he used to condemn this kind of behaviour publically, and that if someone had exposed him for it, he would have branded him a revolutionary, ignorant of the complexities of life.

As if this were not enough, the reader is puzzled when in chapter 37 Earl Leinsdorf prays to God for Ulrich to come, and immediately after, devotes himself to searching for him systematically[22]. One could say that, in *MWQ*, character consists in repeatedly acting out of character. This is simply how things are. The indifference that the characters in *MWQ* show when they happen to notice something unusual in their own behaviour, character, or thoughts is astonishing. The example of Earl Leinsdorf, who felt ashamed to have implored God, is an exception. But the reader does not understand his shame. After all, he was a religious man. Musil's art of contradiction consists of creating such a complex kaleidoscopic

---

      book II and then moved to book I.
20   Cometti, *L'Homme exact*, p. 127.
21   *Ibid.*, p. 44.
22   Musil, *Gesamtausgabe*, I, 222.

character that both things seem to be out of character: the imploration to God and the shame for having done it.

As a matter of fact, the coexistence of opposites extends to all elements in the novel, including circumstances. In chapter 54 of book I we are told in a short line of ten words that winter had finally come and then gone away once again[23]. While immersed in a careful reading, one has the strangest experience when one unexpectedly encounters that line. It feels as if one had journeyed through space and time without any realization of it. It is like a deep transformation that one suffered all of a sudden. In an instant, one learns that one is in winter, and immediately, without time to digest that, we are told that winter has left us behind, and we do not even know how far. In turn, neither winter nor non-winter, since we do not know in which season we are actually in, seem real. They are conveyed as mere possibilities, which are not the case anymore, and which were never very real for the reader.

Besides, the reader's attention is often drawn to the apparently contradictory dimensions of an action. Let us recall that Ulrich is portrayed as a modern man who does nothing and for whom doing nothing constitutes a titanic effort, or else as someone who tries to balance his absence of qualities by means of energy and vehemence. The reader is also exposed to his idea that a single heroic feat is minuscule in comparison to everybody's everyday actions.

Furthermore, the inhabitants of Kakania frequently abandon themselves to acting and living differently. In *L'homme exact*, we find several references to those splendid paragraphs in chapter 8 of book I of *MWQ* in which Musil portrays Kakania as a state where one enjoyed a negative freedom, expressed in the feeling that one's existence did not have any *raison d'être*. This feeling was intimately related to the fantasy of enacting other biographies, to the imagination of taking part in other events or doing something different from what one has actually done in a specific situation, to the idea that there was nothing irrevocable. We are also told that people acted differently from the way they thought, and vice versa. Action and thought, reality and possibility, thus balance each other out. Moreover, the myriad of events that cohabit in the

---

23 The German goes as follows: 'Der Winter hatte schon einmal begonnen und dann wieder aufgehört.' Musil, *Gesamtausgabe*, I, 339.

novel makes the reader feel that everything could be different: if X is doing (or thinking) Y, he could be doing (or thinking) the opposite as well, as is in fact the case at times. This intuition is summed up by the expression 'es ist passiert', which Musil defines as a privative expression that one could only find in that peculiar place that was Kakania, which was able to transform realities into words (and thoughts)[24]. In the end, no matter how many things were apparently taking place, nothing was actually happening. In this unique kind of vagueness, Kakania always remained the same.

3.2. *The equation of thought and life*

Thought and life are often equated in *MWQ*. We find an explicit formulation of this literary device in chapter 38 of book I, when we are told that Clarisse's thoughts began to flow, racing, like life itself[25].

The first instance of the equation takes place at the very beginning of the novel. First of all, we do not know who the characters that appear at first are. We are exposed to the hypothesis that they are Arnheim and Ermelinda Tuzzi, even before we are introduced to their respective roles in the novel. Nevertheless, right after that identification, in the same line, after a comma, we are told that it cannot be them, because Arnheim was at that time in Constantinople and Mrs. Tuzzi was in Bad Aussee with her husband[26]. Just like we were abandoned to non-winter, we are before two negations: non-Arhheim and non-Ermelinza Tuzzi.

Likewise, there is a lot of indetermination regarding where those 'negative' characters are. We are introduced into a city that could be like any other metropolis, and yet we are told that we could deduce from its noise that it was Kakania. The reader's experience is highly mediated: his attention is explicitly drawn to a mental operation that needs to be carried out in order to manage something as basic as situating himself. This is also an example of the intertwining of form and content that is characteristic of *MWQ*. Musil provides us with a lot of details regarding the city, which confuse us and make

---

24 *Ibid.*, I, 51.
25 *Ibid.*, I, 230.
26 *Ibid.*, I, 11.

us dizzy. Nonetheless, it is also true that those details function as noise. The accumulation of generic details generates the noise that according to the narrator is precisely what distinguishes Vienna from everywhere else. The dizziness, and consequent vagueness, thus reveals itself as a way of paradoxically situating the reader[27].

Besides, there is an atmosphere of unreality surrounding the car accident that takes place at the novel's opening. It is interesting to observe how people react to the accident. They seem to be doing things in order to help the truck driver involved in the accident, but they are actually doing nothing. We are explicitly told that it is a show, a way to mark time while they wait for the ambulance. We do not know whether the truck driver is about to die or whether he was really injured at all. Instead of a detailed description of the actual accident, we are given statistics – American ones, at that! – regarding car accidents. Furthermore, it is that imprecise, careless and unimportant accident that leads us to the house of the protagonist of the novel, Ulrich, the man without qualities. The fact that there is no connection whatsoever between the accident and Ulrich creates an aura of delusion and randomness, which permeates the whole novel from that point onwards, sometimes very deeply. As a result, we end up wondering whether the witnesses and the truck driver were actual people, whether they were somewhere at all and whether something actually did happen. There is no room for any kind of *trompe l'oeil*: it is clearly only a story inside a novel, and on purpose, one very badly told according to classical standards.

Musil's investigations into narrative possibilities contribute a great deal to the implied equation between thought and life. In fact, we often have the impression that if the scales were to tip, it would be in favor of the former. Recall that in chapter 32 of book I Ulrich disappears into the thin air of his own thoughts, and with him the narrative line, which suddenly stops. He has a flashback about an old love story that is three times as long as chapter 31, and longer than chapters 31 and 33 put together. When we return from the realm of thought to that of life, things look very different. It is an example of how the realm of thought can have a serious immediate effect on life itself. In chapter 31, Ulrich corners Bonadea

---

27   *Ibid.*, I, 10.

into an argument about Moosbrugger, who brutally raped and murdered a prostitute, that ends up exposing abruptly Bonadea's inability to justify her adultery. After such a climax, when one is reading chapter 32 for the first time, one wonders all along what is Bonadea up to. In chapter 33, we are told that she could not go on staring permanently at the ceiling and felt forced to break up with Ulrich.

As a matter of fact, Musil is continuously playing with the idea of the impossibility of a narrative line, as the very structure of the novel indicates: it is divided into two books and these into at least three parts, and a total of 161 chapters of unequal length but generally short, plus the material from the Nachlass. The impact of the structure on the experience of the reader is extraordinary. Everything that takes place acquires a character of randomness that presents itself as yet highly thought-out. What apparently happens is always subordinated to form. With this insight in mind, Musil moves backward and forward, abandoning certain events, situations and characters after they have played some role in the novel, to return to them later, or at times not at all. We are even explicitly invited to skip chapter 28 of part I in its title if we do not fancy introspection.

The relevance that the titles of the chapters have in the novel is no less than bizarre. They are minutely formulated distinct ideas that seem to propel the novel as a whole. The titles often seem more important than what actually takes place in the chapters. They give form to what happens and tell the reader what to look for in the myriad of details that she is about to encounter. At the same time, their remarkable telegraphic precision makes them so abstract that they appear as empty as the characters.

The most frequent manifestation of the equation between thought and life takes place in the character themselves, who often seem to be made out of their own thoughts and ideas, which is also conducive to the general feeling of vagueness imparted to the reader. Characters seem condemned to a peculiar form of alienation, because it is as if their own ideas possessed them, ideas that are often incoherent. If we tried to visualize a physical expression of this peculiarity, we could well imagine bodies with dislocated members, which nevertheless moved harmoniously. Clarisse is a good example of that. We do not know much about her, but we have complete access to her thoughts. Consequently, the reader identifies her with them. In addition, she expects reality to conform with her ideas, whose peculiar combination of abstraction and sensuality is able to cut people deeply. Take the following example. In chapter 14, we learn that Clarisse aimed at marrying a genius and that initially she felt that her husband Walter was one. We are also told that when she realized that he was failing to become one, she did not allow him to desist in his attempt to become what he was not, despite how painful this situation was for him[28]. As a result, Walter could be understood as a byproduct of Clarisse's ideas.

Moreover, the reader often has the impression that both Clarisse and Walter experience their own ideas rather than the world as it is. Observe this portrait of their emotions: 'The anger, the love, the happiness, the merriment and grief that Clarisse and Walter experienced in flight were not full emotions, but little more than physical shells of feelings that had been worked up into a frenzy'[29]. The same is true of qualities. We often feel that qualities are not fully incarnated in the characters. They seem not to be developed to their full potential and remain mere ideas. Musil also made room in *MWQ* for qualities that entirely lack themselves. For instance, Ulrich considers that the only explanation for the state of the world, despite the abundance of *Geist* around him, was that mind itself was devoid of mind[30]. These kinds of circumstances make the characters seem like mental experiments. They often appear to embody diverse mental experiments at the same time, and sometimes a mental experiment and its opposite, and miraculously manage to survive both quite happily.

Kakanians also have a passionate need for literary devices in their everyday lives, for metaphors and allegories in particular. This spontaneous demand is portrayed in chapter 37 as a sign of the fact that they are not completely keen on reality. We read that 'the honest, practical man of reality does not love reality or take it seriously with no holds barred', and that 'when man wants to

---

28   Ibid., I, 81.
29   Ibid., I, 225.
30   Ibid., I, 244.

raise something, he needs a metaphor'[31]. The topic discussed in the chapter is the metaphor of the 'Austrian Year', in opposition to an 'Austrian Century', which sums up Earl Leinsdorf insights concerning the nation, including the Parallel Campaign. The reader learns that the metaphor had an overwhelming effect on the people, including Earl Leinsdorf himself, thanks to its vagueness. We are told that a poetic symbol involves a certain kind of imprecision that has the capacity to raise and magnify the spirit.

The subtle correspondence between the novel and Musil's biography also contributes to the equation between thought and life. Cometti studied in detail Musil's use of biographical elements in his literary works. Nonetheless, there are no strict identifications between his characters and himself or the people that he encountered in his life. The characters in *MWQ* simultaneously share elements of Musil's biography, or of his partners, acquaintances, or friends, or of the women he loved in particular. Characters from different novels also share qualities. Claudine (the protagonist in the novella *The perfecting of a love*[32]) and Agathe (Ulrich's twin sister) share qualities of Martha, Musil's wife[33]. Cometti spoke of a 'web of correspondences', of qualities, extracted from his personal life, that permeated all his oeuvre and that went beyond its limits, in such a way that it is not the biography that writes the novel, but the other way around. It is the novel that writes Musil's life, that confers on it its meaning[34]. In other words, it is his writings that organize and explain his biography. As a result, the ordinary relationship between biography and literature is inverted. In fact, Cometti expressed indirectly that Musil's oeuvre was a condition of possibility for his own biography[35]. I agree with Cometti that Musil wrote not only in order to extend the limits of what is possible, but also to find solutions to his own life and to make sense of it.

The fact that Musil aimed to provide mankind with a catalogue of types of characters of his time also explains why he turned to real life. In this method of his, we encounter again the paradox

---

31   *Ibid.*, I, 217-218.
32   Musil, *Gesammelte Werke*, VI.
33   Cometti, *L'Homme exact*, p. 56.
34   *Ibid.*, p. 59.
35   *Ibid.*, p. 60.

of the equation of objectivity and subjectivity that I already identified as typical of *MWQ*: the psychological types of an epoch are extracted from private, unique lives. And this is the other side of the indifference that the characters continuously manifest, as well as of their impersonal feelings or qualities. It is no coincidence that Musil also borrowed qualities and other biographical details from people whose lives barely touched him. In that manner, he equated qualities that were dear to him and those that were not, contributing with that set of equivalences to the catalogue of types that he was after by means of the depersonalization of his own biography in the novel.

3.3. *Writing with rubble*

Cometti told us that *MWQ* seems to be built with rubble[36]. He uses this expression while discussing the idea that the things that happen in it do not have an eventful character, that they are mere simulacra. The Parallel Campaign is the idea of an action, and not a clear one. The Moosbrugger case is mere sensationalism. The car accident that opens the novel is presented as an abstract statistical framework. Cometti used the term 'non-event' to refer to such instances and invited us to understand them as parodies[37]. According to his interpretation, the novel was a constant parody that somehow created a blurred picture of consistency at the same time that it made sure that nobody – and that applies to both characters and readers – is ever sure whether something has actually taken place, and in the case that it did happen, what meaning it could have.

Characters are also built with rubble. Cometti spoke of a Musilian art of the creation of characters that entails their own principle of decomposition[38]. The great Musilian irony, as we are explicitly told in the title of chapter 39 of book I, is that a man without qualities calls for a world of qualities without man. We are told that Ulrich's qualities had more to do with one another than with him, and that they did not seem closer to him than to anybody

---

36   *Ibid.*, p. 81.
37   *Ibid.*, p. 124.
38   *Ibid.*, p. 62.

else who also happened to possess them. In fact, once the reader is fully immersed in the novel, qualities seem equally close to all characters, whether these have manifested them or not. We learn that there is only a difference in attitude between identifying with one's own experiences and qualities and distancing oneself from them[39]. Consequently, the novel is swarming with interchangeable qualities that adhere only accidentally to the characters[40], which explains why certain characters possess the same qualities. Cometti proposed that the parallels between the characters could be understood as *trompe l'oeil*, which create a certain form of lightness that blurred the contours of the real and the possible, thus contributing to the fundamental aim of the novel[41].

In the early stages of the novel, it is odd for the reader to find in a character a quality that we associate with another. Such resemblances repeatedly question all the characters involved. The reader is placed in unexpected points of view and forced to look at the characters as if for the first time; that is to say, the illusory layer of permanence with which we are accustomed when we relate to other human beings, or that we picture ourselves having, is diluted.

Let me stress that Musil *builds* with rubble. He was right in understanding his literary method as constructive[42]. Cometti reminds us that despite having inside them an ever-live grenade, Musilian characters are, after all, characters, even without having one. In chapter 39 of book I, we are explicitly told that 'Ulrich had to admit with a smile that he was a character after all, even without having one'[43]. The novel prevents us from imagining the characters differently. They are not mere amalgams of qualities that could have been configured in another way[44]. The characters are like works in progress. They are not identical with their qualities and might sometimes feel a certain kind of alienation as a result of such lack of exact correspondence[45]. They accept further qualities, even

---

39   Musil, *Gesamtausgabe*, I, 234.
40   Cometti, *L'Homme exact*, p. 61.
41   Ibid., pp. 121-122.
42   Constructiveness was what according to Musil differentiated his writings from those of Marcel Proust or James Joyce.
43   Musil, *Gesamtausgabe*, I, 237.
44   Cometti, *L'Homme exact*, p. 61.
45   Musil, *Gesamtausgabe*, I, 237.

qualities that seem to be in contradiction with the ones that they already have. The reader also feels that one of their qualities might suddenly collapse like a star. Nonetheless, the reader recognizes them despite their 'infradetermination'.

Alienation manifests itself in the form of a peculiar emptiness. It is no coincidence that Walter asserted to Clarisse that Ulrich was empty, and that it was precisely his emptiness that she admired in him[46]. Interrogated by a puzzled Clarisse about what being a man without qualities meant, Walter exclaimed in response 'absolutely nothing'[47]. This has to do with Ulrich's incapacity to articulate what he really was[48]. Perhaps he could point toward this or that quality or behavior, but little more. Any attempt would be partial as a result of the nature of Musil's character construction. His characters are always unfinished. They always admit change. No character incarnates the paradox better than Ulrich: all the personal that there is in him is the result of an impersonality that manifests his indeterminacy, and that is precisely what makes of him a man without qualities[49].

Another consistent man without qualities is the Emperor, who can be understood as an incarnation of the idea that we are before a world of experiences without the person who experiences them[50]. We are told that many books were written on the many things that he did, but we do not hear of any of them in particular. The Emperor is as empty as everyone else, which explains why many Kakanians, even some of those involved in the Parallel Campaign, felt that he had never existed. The Emperor, like that Parallel Campaign, takes the form of a black hole: it condenses so many things that it ends up swallowing up its own qualities and what surrounds them.

The indetermination of the Parallel Campaign also contributes to the general atmosphere of vagueness. Cometti depicted it as 'one of the most absurd and funniest things ever imagined by a novelist'[51]. Picture a crusade whose goal was never fully defined, which inspired a whole nation, and which enchanted foreigners.

---

46 Ibid., I, 97-98.
47 Ibid., I, 99.
48 Ibid., I, 237.
49 Cometti, *L'Homme exact*, p. 81.
50 Musil, *Gesamtausgabe*, I, 236.
51 Cometti, *L'Homme exact*, p. 81.

We have lots of information regarding what happens in the meetings where the (possible) actions are discussed, and yet we only know that it is supposed to be a certain form of celebration of the seventy-year reign of the Emperor but sometimes we are not positive about it and consider that it might be a complot to overthrow him. The characters themselves are asked whether they have in mind anything in particular and their answers are often negative. For instance, Diotima, after describing the Parallel Campaign as the largest and most important project ever imagined, tells Ulrich that she does not have anything specific in mind because there are so many good options that it is difficult to choose one of them. Diotima is also presented as an incarnation of the Parallel Campaign that is ready to swallow Ulrich up. Nonetheless, the reader sometimes feels that Diotima herself has been swallowed up by the event. In general, the characters seem to be swallowed up by the things in which they get involved, and ultimately by the general atmosphere of vagueness that pervades the novel.

The remarks gathered in the previous section regarding the structure of *MWQ* could be understood as instances of Musil's mastery of building with rubble. The book seems to deny its own status as a novel. The reader is given so many details about each character and her circumstances, and so worries that at times it feels as if one was before a disorderly combination of short stories and novellas. In this regard, Cometti advanced that the fact that there is no sense of the narrative is a correlate of the absence of qualities[52]. As a result, he continued, the narrative becomes more fundamental: the fact that the individual is empty, a vacuum that cannot narrate itself coherently, makes its articulation more urgent. The inductive humility of Musil's articulation is paradoxically heroic. Cometti described it as a complex network of factors that intersect in disorderly fashion and get lost in infinity[53].

---

52   *Ibid.*, 108. Cometti explored this idea in relation to Musil's conception of history in Jean-Pierre Cometti, *Musil philosophe. L'utopie de l'essayisme* (Paris: Seuil, 2001), p. 36.
53   Cometti, *L'Homme exact*, p. 105.

3.4. *Blurring by means of being exact*

In chapter 44 of book I, a secondary character, Soliman, looks through the keyhole of the main door to Diotima's drawing room, and his eyes come to rest on a lot of details: a piece of white paper, a nose, a shadow, a ring... It is a good metaphor of the effect that the exactness of the details in *MWQ* has on the reader. Reading the novel is like looking through the keyhole of a majestic palace in ruins. Like Soliman, the reader encounters life splintered into fragments. It is never possible to attain a comprehensive view of the whole novel. It reminds me of Honoré Balzac's *The Unknown Masterpiece*, in which the great master Frenhofer shows to his friends, after much request on their part, what he considers his masterpiece, a painting of a female nude on which he had been working for the last ten years. According to his claims, the painting is so perfect that the figure looks alive. When he uncovers the painting, his friends see nothing. Only after coming closer to the painting are they able to discern in a corner of the canvas the tip of a bare foot that emerged from the prevailing chaos of color. The elaborated and thought-out details that the reader encounters in *MWQ* have the same effect on us that the lively tip of the bare foot in Frenhofer's unknown masterpiece has on his painter friends.

There is a paradoxical relationship between accuracy and indeterminacy that permeates the whole novel and generates a widespread atmosphere of likelihood. For instance, qualities are random and impersonal, on the one hand, and function as stigmas that leave an indelible trace on their bearers, on the other hand. It is little wonder that the novel presents itself as a utopia of exact living. We find an explicit reference to the utopia of exactness in the title of chapter 61 of book I, in which Musil explains what he means by 'utopia'. The reader learns that utopias are possibilities that are intertwined with their circumstances in such a way that these simply do not allow them to become realities[54]. In the same paragraph, utopias are also portrayed as experiments in which the possible alteration of an element and the effects it would produce on that composite phenomenon that we call life are observed. In the case of the utopia of exactness, the observed element is exactness

---

54   Musil, *Gesamtausgabe*, I, 392.

itself. What one finds out is that exactness has the exceptional effect of blurring everything that it touches. It is the case of the exact man, in whom exactness works as a fire that cleansed him of any other quality. Beyond being exact, everything else in him remains indefinite.

Musil opposed the exact man and morality. Firstly, the exact is the opposite of the general. In *MWQ* the exact is expressed in the form of details that are as tangible and unique as possible, which escape the application of general rules, and as a result, the tentacles of morality. Secondly, the indefiniteness that characterises the exact man challenges 'the firm set of conditions of the inner, which are guaranteed by morality'[55]. We also learn in the same longish line of chapter 61 about the effect that the vagueness associated with the exact has on the realm of feeling: it transforms distinct passions into something like a primeval fire of goodness. It is only when we get to this chapter that we understand what Musil meant when he wrote in chapter 3 of book I that Ulrich's father is moved by universal impulses and general reasons. He is an exception to the model of the man without qualities, the counterexample in the experiment of the utopia of exactness, a representative of morality.

There is also imprecision regarding how one relates to one's qualities. In chapter 13, we are told that Ulrich felt further removed than ever before from what he had really wanted to be, and that he was never clear about what that was. Chapter 40 adds that all qualities remained equally far from him and that he was equally indifferent to all of them, whether he had made them his own or not. Such indifference imprecisely forced him to live against himself, which turns the novel into an immense experimental site that lacks direction[56].

The reader also learns in chapter 13 that Ulrich saw in himself all the qualities favored by his times, but that he had simply lost the capacity to apply them, and that in order to remedy it, he resolved to take a one-year leave of absence from his life[57]. I still remember that when I read that line for the first time I had to stop and ask myself what it meant to take a leave of absence from one's life. It

---

55 Ibid., I, 392.
56 Ibid., I, 239.
57 Ibid., I, 72.

is no coincidence that it is supposed to last for one year. It cannot be understood as a simple pause. It is a true experiment in the realm of possibility. It is an invitation to imagine other lives and to seriously play at living differently by means of the exploration of the possibilities that fortuitously arise.

Observe that after only a few pages, in chapter 16, Ulrich has the feeling that his qualities are not those that the times legitimize. That idea seems to contradict what we were told in chapter 13, that he had all the qualities favored by his times except one, that of earning one's living. This feeling of his is a consequence of his examination of a couple of pictures from a magazine in which a famous tennis player and a champion swimmer are portrayed with plenty of qualities applauded by the times (toward which Ulrich felt only contempt). Such qualities appeared to him as something that one simply had to accept, as one accepts skyscrapers or electricity. The comparison has a powerful effect. Those qualities of the times acquire a very concrete reality. As a result, Ulrich's own qualities, which are not as tangible, suffer an increase in vagueness.

3.5. *Operating with the sense of possibility*

The concept of a man without qualities is intimately related to the concept of the sense of possibility, which is defined in chapter 4 as the ability to conceive that everything could also be in another way. The reader is trained in thinking about everything that is not the case but that could well be, and in valuing equally what is and what is not[58]. The sense of possibility should not be conceived as a denial of reality. On the contrary, it understands reality as a problem, as a fiction, as something yet to be invented, which explains why Musil made sure that his chef d'oeuvre mediated between himself and his biography.

We are told at the end of chapter 4 of book I that a man without qualities applies the sense of possibility to himself and does not have a sense of reality even regarding his own self. As the reader digests the novel, she feels compelled to operate with the sense of possibility with regard to her understanding of the fiction. Only the reader who operates with the sense of possibility stops having

---

58   Ibid., I, 20.

the feeling that nothing takes place in the novel and realizes that there is nothing to be found beyond the exploration of the realm of the possible. If the reader operates with the sense of reality, she cannot help but expect something more solid behind the many things that appear to her as mirages. Only the reader who operates with the sense of possibility realizes that what we see is not external evidence of something hidden that has to be disclosed. She also grows in awareness of the fact that there is no unique answer to the question of how to live. The countless life games that she has in her mind's eye reveal themselves as a myriad of non-exclusive and unpredictable ways of living.

MWQ is above all an invitation to apply the sense of possibility to one's life. The narrative is only an excuse to awaken the reader to the realm of possibility. The steady picture of life that we usually have should be abandoned. In chapter 62 of book I it is formulated as living hypothetically[59]. Someone who lives hypothetically has the insight that everything is revocable. We learn that she lives with the suspicion that the given order of things is not as solid as it pretends to be. Every single thing reveals itself to her as undergoing an invisible ongoing transformation. We are explicitly told that the present is no more than a hypothesis that has not yet been surmounted. Ulrich's guarded scientific attitude toward facts, his effort to avoid drawing premature conclusions in his life, as well as his hesitance to make something of himself, are explained in these terms. Like Ulrich, paraphrasing Musil, the reader feels compelled to understand herself differently, to be open to everything that may enrich her inwardly and to go through life like a stride, free to move in every direction, from equilibrium to equilibrium, but always in motion.

It is no coincidence that immediately after these insightful remarks about living hypothetically, Musil introduced his concept of essay. We learn that an essay explores something from many sides without wholly encompassing it, because otherwise it would lose its scope and be reduced to a concept. We also learn that this is how Ulrich handles his own life because he is aware that everything, including the value of moral actions, depends on its surrounding circumstances, which are constituted now one way,

---

59   *Ibid.*, I, 397-398.

now another. It is this essayistic attitude that the reader is urged to develop as a means to make of her life a never-ending essay. In other words, the reader is urged to write her own life as a discursive exploration.

We are also invited to stop looking for reasons and causes in our lives, which configure a picture of reality too stable. *MWQ* is not structured either linearly or causally. Cometti brilliantly argued that Musil abandons the idea of a cause and uses instead the idea of a motive, that is to say, that from the real that responds to one's feelings, which can be reconciled with the most personal side of oneself[60]. Abandoning causal explanation makes room for living differently. Musil is after a lived (felt) life. In this regard, we could say that the purpose of the novel is ultimately ethical, and that Musil wanted to free us from the bounds inherent in the inner-outer picture.

4. *The ethics of the lived life: on feeling one's life*

All the formal aspects and literary devices that have come up regarding the way the novel is structured and written share the common goal of extending the possibilities of feeling. We learn from Cometti that Musil thought that the conventional devices of fiction seemed too coarse and rigid to be able to trace the subtle threads of feeling[61]. He also drew our attention to the impact that the interactions between ethics and morality[62] have on the

---

60 Cometti explained that what really matters to the characters in *MWQ* is the realm of significance, which is structured in a chain of motives. This explains how Musil's characters relate to each other. Behind their behaviors there are never reasons or causes, but feelings. That is precisely why it is so difficult to predict how his characters are going to behave, and why they sometimes focus their attention on the most random things. Cometti drew our attention to a paragraph in book II of *MWQ* in which Ulrich describes to Agathe how a landscape painter finds a motive in nature (*L'Homme exact*, pp. 48-49). The painter sees it and identifies it. One could say, à la Wittgenstein, that something clicks.
61 Cometti, *L'Homme exact*, p. 107.
62 Cometti studied in detail the relationship between ethics and morality in Musil's oeuvre. Musil believed that morality (which is described in chapter 62 of book I of *MWQ* as a senile form of a system of energies that originally

architecture of the novel. The realm of feeling coincides with the ethical life. Living ethically for Musil involved living free from the unhelpfully generic guidelines of morality. It was a life of the singular, of the infinitesimal[63], of feeling, and it meant leaving the abstract, the conceptual, in other words, morality, behind. Truth is not addressed in that domain, which focuses on circumstances as constitutive motives of feeling. Cometti expressed it beautifully: there is a plurality of ways of living, which depend on individual circumstances, and all of these provide feelings with skeletons and personal meanings[64]. For Musil, morality was of no use regarding the non-causal intricacies of everyday life. To render this idea vivid, he continuously makes the moral order (and the reader) face situations that cannot be resolved in any binding and general way. As a result, the reader gradually gets used to the diverse kinds of ways of being in the novel, and ends up considering her own life as a Heraclitian range of possibilities. Ultimately, she feels the need to enter 'the other state': to make her life really her own by means of her active participation in it. In order to help the reader in her venture, Musil immerses himself in the task of drawing alternative maps of human emotion.

Cometti examined Musil's understanding of his utopia of the exact living as a diagnosis of his times and of its contradictions[65]. For Musil, the most fundamental contradiction was that science described a world in dissolution that is veiled by a morality of another era, which inappropriately ties them together. One

---

was charged with feeling) was constituted by dead thoughts and ethics by *pensées vivantes*. The former meant regulating one's life according to impersonal rules; the latter meant responding to one's life as a painter does to a motive. Cometti put it quite simply: the question is not anymore what we ought to do, but rather, what I want to be (*L'Homme exact*, p. 54). For further analysis of Musil's concept of *pensées vivantes*, cf. Jean-Pierre Cometti, 'Pensées vivantes et forms de vie', *Robert Musil. Colloque dirigé par Jean-Pierre Cometti* (Paris: Editions Royaumont, 1986), pp. 146-165.

63 Cometti referred to the infinitesimal to account for those details that are not captured by the untrained everyday gaze, which remain as sediment in the ordinary. In this regard, Musil trains the reader in an alternative way of looking, Jean-Pierre Cometti, *Robert Musil: De 'Torless' à 'L'Homme sans qualités'* (Brussels: Mardaga, 1986), pp. 138-139.
64 Cometti, *L'Homme exact*, p. 53.
65 Ibid., p. 82.

could say that Musil understood that the role of literature was to untie the unsuitable ribbons of morality. We learn from science that there are no stable types. Literature could no longer ignore it. In fact, this is precisely what literature should explore. Musil sought an alliance between science and literature, as if literature could deepen the scientific vision of the world by exploring other narrative possibilities. Ulrich, the man without qualities par excellence, reveals himself as both a symptom of his times and one of its solutions. After all, Ulrich, the exact man, enters 'the other state', incarnated in the apparition in his life of his twin sister, Agathe, thus embodying reason and feeling. Constantly engaged in the impossibility of narrating his own life, and as a result of that task, an experimenter and at the same time a writer, Ulrich unites content and form in his very persona[66].

By means of constant parodying, *MWQ* manages to overcome the insurmountable disjunctions established by modernity. As Cometti explained in relation to the dualism between reason and feeling, one could say that Musil tried to rid the spirit of its mental cramps by integrating in the essence of the novel the tensions of such crucial modern fractures[67]. There is indeed much yet to learn from Musil's playful prototypes regarding the question of how to live.

References

Cometti, Jean-Pierre, *Exterior Arte: Estética y formas de vida* (Buenos Aires: Biblos, 2014).
—, *L'Homme exact: essai sur Robert Musil* (Paris: Seuil, 1997).
—, *Ludwig Wittgenstein et la philosophie de la psychologie* (Paris: Presses Universitaires de France, 2004).
—, *Musil philosophe. L'utopie de l'essayisme* (Paris: Seuil, 2001).
—, 'Pensées vivantes et forms de vie', in *Robert Musil. Colloque dirigé par Jean-Pierre Cometti* (Paris: Editions Royaumont, 1986), pp. 146-165.

---

66 Villö Huszai, '"Agathe ist wirklich da" order: Wie von einem epistemologisch zweifel-haften Gefühl erzählen?', *Musil. Ironie, Satire, falsche Gefühle*, ed. by Kevin Mulligan and Armin Westerhoof (Paderborn: mentis Verlag, 2009), pp. 187-207 (p. 206).
67 Cometti, *L'Homme exact*, p. 146.

—, *Robert Musil: De 'Torless' à 'L'Homme sans qualités'* (Brussels: Mardaga, 1986).

Huszai, Villö, '"Agathe ist wirklich da" order: Wie von einem epistemologisch zweifel-haften Gefühl erzählen?', *Musil. Ironie, Satire, falsche Gefühle*, ed. by Kevin Mulligan and Armin Westerhoof (Paderborn: mentis Verlag, 2009), pp. 187-207.

Musil, Robert, *Der Mann ohne Eigenschaften 1-6, Gesamtausgabe in 12 Bänden*, ed. by Walter Fanta (Salzburg: Jung und Jung, 2016-2018).

—, 'Skizze der Erkenntnis des Dichters' (1918), in *Gesammelte Werke in neun Bänden. Essays und Reden*, ed. by Adolf Frisé (Reinbeck bei Hamburg: Rowohlt, 1978), VIII, 1025-1030.

KAKANIAN SUITS
A conversation in two parts between Jean-Pierre Cometti and Carla Carmona

I. *Clarisse as a depiction by Egon Schiele*[1]

Carla Carmona (CC). Would you agree that Robert Musil's thoughts on being a character without having one on the basis of the outstanding and yet common existential problems of Ulrich, the main character in *The Man without Qualities (MWQ)*[2], qualified precisely by the fact that he has no qualities, is somehow very Wittgensteinian? For instance, take his comparison between a man without qualities and a set of qualities without a man, or his statement that the difference between identifying oneself with one's own experiences and qualities and distancing oneself from them consists only of a difference in attitude, a deliberate decision in favor of a particular perspective as valid as any other one. Ulrich felt that the qualities he had achieved during his life had to do more with each other than with him, that they belonged as much to the rest of their bearers.

However, this was not one of Schiele's certainties. He was very attached to the romantic idea of genius, and felt that there was a connection between the authentic artist, the genius, and the divine. The painter wrote most of his poems against that background, and depicted himself as a reminiscent martyr in many of his canvases and drawings, such as when he portrayed himself as St. Sebastian. Do you think that the difference in attitude between Schiele, Musil, and even Wittgenstein in this matter has something to do with the

---

1 This conversation was published in *Egon Schiele Jahrbuch*, 1 (2011), pp. 224-227.
2 Robert Musil, *Der Mann ohne Eigenschaften 1-6, Gesamtausgabe in 12 Bänden*, ed. by Walter Fanta (Salzburg: Jung und Jung, 2016-2018).

fact that Schiele died just before the First World War ended, that is, that he still lived in what Stefan Zweig termed the 'Golden Age of Security', or in its immediate ruins? When do you think that Musil changed his views to those reflected in *MWQ*?

Jean-Pierre Cometti (JPC). As you know, there are commentators who consider that Musil and Wittgenstein are very close. I always felt something like that. But the difficulty appears when you try to state explicitly what they share, what we could really consider as common between them. I feel that Wittgenstein would not have liked a novel like *MWQ*. I don't have any evidence of this (he probably did not read it), but we do know what he liked, that being very classical works, especially in novels (think of Gottfried Keller, and also that Wittgenstein preferred poetry to novels). Of course, they shared an interest in logic and science. However, in Wittgenstein this concern is closely related to two of his convictions: that logic is not a way of knowing, and that language does not enable us to reach what allows that language make sense. On such matters, he is very close to Schopenhauer. As a thinker, Musil was rather a positivist: he was always thinking of how we could deal with ethics or esthetics like we do with mathematics or physics.

Things are very different from Wittgenstein's perspective. What I mean is that there is something very romanticist in Wittgenstein which is alien to Musil. Perhaps you do not agree with this interpretation, because Musil took a lot of time for questions such as that of the *andere Zustand*, which is related to romanticism. But you must remember two things: first, that it is a 'thought experiment' and, secondly, that for Musil a very important point was the gap dug between intellect and feeling by modern thought – and romanticism. It is exactly what Wittgenstein presupposes in his *Tractatus*[3].

The situation is certainly different in Wittgenstein's second philosophy. From this point of view, the concept of a man without qualities could be considered as an exceptional thought experiment, but what might it mean? Perhaps such a concept (for

---

3   Ludwig Wittgenstein, *Tractatus Logico-Philosophicus* (London: Routledge & Kegan Paul, 1922).

both Musil and Wittgenstein this time) could be understood as a reflection of the conditions of the very world described by Musil in his novel, and which is also the world that Wittgenstein was speaking about when he referred to the modern world in the preface to his *Philosophical Remarks*[4]. However, there is still a big difference. The way in which Musil speaks of such a world is ironical. He never felt any nostalgia. On the contrary, Wittgenstein shared a *Viennese symptom:* the feeling you can find in Zweig's *The World of Yesterday*[5] (*Die Welt von Gestern*). It's no coincidence that, while Wittgenstein was influenced by Spengler or Weininger, Musil hated what they represented. Schiele and Wittgenstein are on the same side: the side of the typical world that Musil takes rather as an experience, the experience of a failure in history.

There is something strange with Musil in this respect. I think that he did not like very much either music or painting. He never took into consideration the Viennese artists living at the time, whose names, at least, he certainly knew, and perhaps their work. And nevertheless, he draws extraordinary portraits of Clarisse and Walter, both madly in love with the music of Wagner. I would like to make a point about Schiele in relation to this. If you want to get an idea of what Clarisse looked like, the best you can do is to look at Schiele's paintings.

CC. And yet, how can we understand Wittgenstein's notion of genius in this context? Do you think that Musil agreed with Wittgenstein's view, as well as with his identification between ethics and aesthetics, so prominent in fin-de-siècle Vienna?

JPC. The point is that, where Wittgenstein takes the romantic notion of Genius as an evidence, Musil makes it a specific problem, and understands it as the expression of a mythology. You probably remember the chapter in Musil's novel in which Ulrich 'discovers' that a racehorse can have genius. In a world of 'qualities without a man' the very notion of genius collapses. Of course, the question is

---

4   Ludwig Wittgenstein, *Philosophical Remarks*, ed. by Rush Rhess, trans. by Raymond Hargreaves and Roger White (Chicago: University of Chicago Press, 1980).
5   Stefan Zweig, *The World of Yesterday*, trans. by Anthea Bell (Nebraska: University of Nebraska, 2013).

'and what about art?', and the answer is the following: the only art that we are able to conceive is an 'art without qualities'[6]. Such an art is based on 'ways of doing', like 'language games' in Wittgenstein's *Investigations*[7]. Such a vision involves dropping the romantic images that hold us captive. It also means that, from a certain point of view, ethics and aesthetics are one and the same. In the earlier Wittgenstein, ethics and aesthetics are the same, because they are outside the world; for Musil, the reason is different: what you *feel* and what you *do* while making art (in writing, for instance), what people are able to feel or understand when dealing with art, belongs to their life and is related to their ways of living. The only question of ethics is (as suggested in *MWQ*): how do we live, and how can our lives be better, more free, more lovable?

CC. In your book *Robert Musil: De 'Törless' à 'L'Homme sans qualités*'[8], you proposed that *MWQ* is governed by two different forces, that of history and that of ethics (as opposed to morality), which complement each other. Do you think that one of the reasons for Wittgenstein's early remarks on ethics sounding so metaphysical is that he did not take history into consideration? Nevertheless, even Wittgenstein's early philosophy meets Musil's idea in *MWQ* that *'le bien et le mal sont des valeurs fonctionnelles'*.

JPC. This book is unfortunately too far from my mind. What I would say now is that ethics – as I have just presented it – is the main issue in the second part of *MWQ*. But one must always keep in mind that it is a novel, a fiction, i.e. a 'thought experiment'. In other words, if there is one thing that Musil is wondering about in this part of the novel, it is how life and humankind would be if we were able to love (ourselves and other selves) differently, beyond the understanding of the self as ego-centered.

But another question (correlative of the first one) must be asked: Ulrich and Agathe live without any substantial link to the

---

6   On this concept, see Jean-Pierre Cometti, *L'art sans qualités* (Tours: Farrago, 1999).
7   Ludwig Wittgenstein, *Philosophical Investigations*, trans. by G. E. M. Anscombe (Oxford: Blackwell, 1953).
8   Jean-Pierre Cometti, *Robert Musil: De 'Torless' à 'L'Homme sans qualités'* (Brussels: Mardaga, 1986).

surrounding world. They are living in a utopia. They should create, invent a way to restore such a relation in agreement with their hypothetical[9] life. No one can ignore history. The problem with history – from an ethical point of view – is that it runs without making any differences. From this point of view, the way it goes is indifferent. How to really live what we live? That is the question, and this question applies equally to history and to life. Musil does not separate these two issues. On the contrary, Wittgenstein separates them. He seems interested mainly in the first one. This can explain why Wittgenstein gives to good and evil a rather metaphysical and religious meaning, often in a Kierkegaardian vein. However, everything is not so cut and dry because Wittgenstein's ideas in the *Philosophical Investigations* – derived from concepts like 'language games' or 'forms of life' – are open to other possibilities.

CC. Schiele's pictorial syntax is very rich in all kinds of resources. One of the most paradigmatic ones is his use of details. There are paintings in which one can admire colorful flowers scattered in landscapes depicted from a point so high in the sky that it would be impossible to even imagine them. And yet they are there, so present that the composition is practically called into question. At times Schiele's figures are subordinated to one of their extremities, whether a whole leg or just an elbow, which stands up while the rest of the figure is alienated. Musil's idea of qualities possessing men comes to mind. In Schiele's art, especially in his non-allegorical canvases and in his drawings, the notion of a figure as a whole does not exist. Everything is fragmented. When figures, objects and structures are allowed in the composition, they are fragmented. When they are not, as in his landscapes, the impossibility of having something framed, and for that matter, under control, is presented. This is highlighted by Schiele's use of parallelisms and repetitions in his art of pictorial composition. Furthermore, Schiele's eccentric self-portraits, such as his famous *Seated Male Nude (Self-Portrait)* from 1910, today in the Leopold Museum in Vienna, makes me think of the 'Parallel Campaign' around which *MWQ* evolves. Could you give us a picture of Musil's later syntax?

---

9   Chapter 62 of book I of MWQ is devoted to the concept of 'living hypothetically'.

JPC. Very interesting. It is probably the best focal point for comparing their works. There are also lots of details in MWQ, and these details – especially when they belong to characters – correspond to what Musil called 'qualities', that is, 'properties' that we usually relate to the self. However, it is an illusion to think that they belong substantially to the self, which does not own them (contrary to what is suggested by the German word 'Eigenschaft' or the French word 'propriété'), and they can be related to different 'egos'. That is the reason why one can find such qualities in separate states, as if they were floating in the air, and also why the same quality can be common to very different characters. For instance, going back to the novel, Ulrich and General Stumm von Bordwehr share some attitudes or sometimes tend to the same kind of reflections, which at first glance seem very strange. There is, between them, what Wittgenstein referred to as 'family resemblances'. This way of relating the elements of the 'plot' is typical of Musil's writing. It is closely related to his concept of *Eigenschaftslosigkeit*. It is also one of the main aspects of his irony. Let me observe that this is a philosophical point. One cannot build a book upon the concept of *Eigenschaftslosigkeit* without expecting any consequences on the way in which it has been built. In this case, the result is the inability to use the traditional sense of the narrative. Note that in chapter 122, Ulrich discovers that he has lost 'the sense of narrative order'.

CC. Yes, he faces the impossibility of threading all that has occurred on a single thread, of putting all the events of one's life in chronological order...

JPC. Exactly.

CC. Which story or metaphor of the many in MWQ would you choose to illustrate fin-de-siècle Vienna?

JPC. Certainly and without hesitation: the metaphor of the camel. I am thinking of the passage – at the beginning of the novel – where Musil describes Kakania. In Kakania, history runs at the pace of the pitch of a camel.

CC. When it is not clear what is up or down, what goes forward or backward...

JPC. Yes, Musil formulated it as 'always the same story' (*seinesgleichen geschieht*). This is very significant for several reasons, particularly for understanding the situation where, whatever you do, nothing can change. Ulrich's decision to live 'hypothetically' is directly connected to this state of affairs. In other words, if you want to take it this way, it is an ironical version of the notion of 'the end of history', perhaps of 'postmodernism'.

CC. Just by looking at Schiele's paintings, could you compare him with any of the characters in *MWQ*? Can you think of any correspondence between one of the stories or metaphors in the novel and his art?

JPC. As I have already suggested, the character who comes immediately to my mind is Clarisse. But there are others like Gerda, and maybe Hans Sepp. This is related to the problem of syntax in the sense you spoke of. These characters are particularly 'dislocated'. In their case, the problem of the self arises dramatically – though in several ways. It is different in Ulrich's case, because the way he deals with this problem is not *existential* but *intellectual* and *hypothetical*, that is, as if it were an experiment. Although *MWQ* is sometimes full of emotion and sensuality (particularly in the second part of the novel), Musil is a very cerebral writer. Those aspects of the novel that make room for comparisons with Schiele's artistic inspiration are mainly related to his description of 'fin-de-siècle' Vienna.

CC. Does Schiele's conviction that *'Alles ist lebend tot'* ('everything is living dead') say anything to you in relationship to *MWQ* or to Musil's literary practice? And his belief in the idea that all beings are equal?

JPC. It is hard to say. Two parallels come to mind. First, the fact that the picture of Kakania in the novel is that of a world 'lebend tot' in a certain sense. This is related to the way in which everything happens in a world where all is equal and makes no difference. It is in this sense that Musil spoke of history as 'spectral'. Secondly, the fact that 'qualities' are the only thing that gives us the certainty of being unique in the universe. How unique could be a man without qualities? It seems to me that both Musil and Schiele – each in his own way – worked hard to weaken this representation.

CC. If you were asked to choose three figures, or the work of three people, to help us understand *MWQ*, who would they be, and, briefly, why?

JPC. One is tempted to think of other writers, perhaps of Dostoyevsky, for instance, or writers that Musil appreciated, or typical writers of the Viennese atmosphere. But the way Musil came to literature is very particular. I think it is mainly related to his intellectual questioning. Ernst Mach had without any doubt an impact on him – at least at the beginning – and he certainly helps to understand several points in Musil's thought and work. I would be tempted to say the same of psychology, particularly in the field of feelings, and, of course, of *Gestaltpsychology*, to which Musil gave great importance. Why? According to Musil, the main problem arising in the modern world was that of the divisions of the mind. And it is also important, from this point of view, to understand why Musil thought that philosophy was not on the right track to overcoming these problems. Perhaps he understood literature as an opportunity to deal with these problems in a different way, and with other tools, such as fiction.

CC. Do you think that there is anything in common between Musil's move from *Törless* to *MWQ* in relation to what language can express and what it cannot, and that of Wittgenstein from the *Tractatus* to the *Philosophical Investigations*?

JPC. I am afraid I cannot answer this question with all the attention it deserves. Like in the *Tractatus*, silence plays an important role in *Törless*. From this point of view, the end of the novel is interesting: the young Törless leaves the school with his mother, busy with his thoughts, and when she asks him what the matter is, he only says, 'Nothing, just an idea!'. However, if we compare this first novel with *MWQ*, things are different. In the latter, silence and 'the sense of the hidden' are connected with attitudes and ways of believing typical of people who, like Diotima, are dreaming of a world of pure spirits, where souls need no bodies to communicate. In the meantime, everything has been relativized. The problems, in Wittgenstein, are not exactly the same, but between the *Tractatus* and the *Philosophical Investigations*, the problem of language has changed considerably. I think that, like in Musil, the problem has been relativized, because Wittgenstein then sees the problem from the point of view of 'language games', and this means that the bounds we have to consider are those of *these* games, and not of *the* language as such.

CC. Do you have any suggestions for future researchers on fin-de-siècle Vienna?

JPC. This is a field which proved to be very attractive several years ago. Fin-de-siècle Vienna was fashionable. It did not last. Now, what could attract a young researcher to these topics? There is a picture of Vienna that acquired much success, the picture of a world in which a lot of discoveries were made, an intellectual and artistic world very rich and dense, where everyone was acquainted with everyone. This is certainly surprising, but not true. The truth is that Musil seemed to be unaware of Wittgenstein, Schönberg or Klimt, and Wittgenstein unaware of Musil; Freud seemed to have no idea of Wittgenstein or Musil, and so on. Why? How could this be? How could all of these innovative writers and thinkers be so ignorant of their own time, in such a 'little world'? Is it right? Must we think that the place where they lived was not significant enough for them so as to command their attention? I am not so sure that what we have learnt of that Vienna does not need to be reconsidered.

II. *Schiele, Musil and the Experience of War*[10]

CC. I have always found very peculiar the traces that World War I left on Egon Schiele's art. He depicted Austrian soldiers and Russian prisoners in a very detached way. In fact, those depictions could serve as good illustrations of Wittgenstein's notion of 'the perspective from eternity'. Both soldiers and prisoners are treated with respect, dressed in their respective uniforms against an empty background. Schiele also portrayed a few military buildings from the outside plus storage and study rooms which provided the army with all kinds of tools and liquor. He was dreaming of a mausoleum just before he died. His intentions were not completely clear, but it seems that he meant to worship not a particular person but the dead as a whole. He had done several sketches that show that he was planning to put an opened sarcophagus of ivory and gold in the middle, with a mummy inside. Who the mummy was did not matter to him. It was also a temple for art, and for his art. Some of his paintings were supposed to surround it: monument-like paintings.

However, he lived a very different war within himself. He was tormented in a way in the same vein as Wittgenstein. One could say that, above all, Wittgenstein suffered the war within himself, and that he used it for his own development as a human being. Do you think that this would also apply to Musil? How are these war times reflected in Musil's writings?

JPC. The way Musil lived World War I was thoroughly different. Musil was an officer – first, he had been a student in a military school for several years –, but it was not his own choice, and I think that, unlike Wittgenstein, he never took any heroic attitude during the war. He depicts the war in a short story called 'Ein Soldat erzählt' ('A Soldier's Tale'). The protagonist's lack of involvement in what takes place around him and to him is striking. He tells his story without any kind of exaltation, but rather with a feeling of a sudden cataclysm, even when 'flying arrows' arise in the sky and go through his body ('the baptism of fire').

---

10   Carla Carmona and Jean-Pierre Cometti, Schiele, Musil and the Experience of War *Egon Schiele Jahrbuch*, 2/3 (2014), pp. 286-289.

CC. That Musilian image of the soldier and the arrows reminds me of Schiele's self-portrait as Saint Sebastian. There is no exaltation in his self-portrait either, even if there are quite a few flying arrows around the figure. The detachment of the figure is outstanding. It seems to be beyond its circumstances. In fact, it is not clear whether the arrows actually go through the figure or not. But in Schiele's case, this kind of attitude has religious connotations. I mean 'religious' in a Wittgensteinian way, it is an attitude that has a very powerful ethical dimension.

JPC. I believe that Musil's attitude was quite different. For instance, he never understood the war as an opportunity to 'test' himself, in a religious sense, like Wittgenstein did. However, what I believe to be important about that period for his work and worldview is that he began to perceive and understand then what he called 'the significance of circumstances' for so-called 'human nature'. He held the view that our ways of acting and reacting are unpredictable, and that our substance is 'colloidal'. There is no life without 'form', but that form is not achieved once and for all. That is why there are disturbing proximities between certain states of mind or experiences, like those of madness, sexuality, mysticism, aesthetic experience, or criminality. Musil calls our attention to those correspondences all the way through *MWQ*. All those states are expressions of the 'Other state' and they argue in favor of what he called the 'theorem of human amorphism' in his important essay *Der deutsche Mensch als Symptom*[11], where the idea that the human being is both able to eat human flesh and to build cathedrals plays the role of a leitmotiv.

CC. The metaphor of our colloidal substance is very useful to understand the concept of 'a man without qualities' and that of 'the character of the inhabitants of a country'. While describing Kakania, Musil writes:

> For the inhabitant of a country has at least nine characters: a professional, a national, a civic, a class, a geographic, a sexual, a conscious, an unconscious, and possibly even a private character to

---

11   Robert Musil, *Der deutsche Mensch als Symptom* (Berlin: Rowohlt, 1967).

boot. He unites them in himself, but they dissolve him, so that he is really nothing more than a small basin hollowed out by these many streamlets that trickle into it and drain out of it again, to join other such rills in filling some other basin. Which is why every inhabitant of the earth also has a tenth character that is nothing else than the passive fantasy of spaces yet unfilled. This permits a person all but one thing: to take seriously what his at least nine other characters do and what happens to them; in other words, it prevents precisely what should be his true fulfillment.[12]

I think that this is intimately connected to the concept of 'the sense of possibility'. Do you think that 'the sense of possibility' applies also to the qualities of an individual in *MWQ*? Does Ulrich act? I understand that action is closer to possibility than to reality, or at least as close to one as to the other. When he acts, he always considers many possibilities, to the point that at times the reader doubts what he actually ended up doing. One could say that this last statement could be applied to the whole book. One sometimes has to read a chapter a couple of times to grasp what actually happened, to identify the possibility that prevails.

JPC. From this point of view, the experience of war was, no doubt, very important for Musil. We have to remind ourselves that *MWQ* begins just one year before the declaration of war, and that everything in the novel asks to be grasped in light of this background. Musil's intellectual attitude is also intimately related to his experience of this context. His contribution to the Congress of Writers in Paris – in the thirties, just before World War II – is also a significant expression of the mistrust that both the times and the blindness of most people inspired in him. In this regard, MWQ can be considered as a way of describing the fundamental symptoms of a coming catastrophe. What seems to be a farce – the famous 'Parallel Campaign' – is actually a portrayal of a drama that is building up in the atmosphere of general irresponsibility. The

---

12   For the original, see Robert Musil, *Der Mann ohne Eigenschaften 1, Gesamtausgabe in 12 Bänden*, ed. by Walter Fanta (Salzburg: Jung und Jung, 2016), pp. 50-51. This version corresponds to Sophie Wilkins and Burton Pike's translation (Robert Musil, *The Man Without Qualities* (London: Picador, 1995), p. 30.

fact is that this intellectual context of ideas (think of Spengler, Klages, etc.) was certainly the breeding ground of ideologies that precipitated the world into the war and its horrors. Musil was particularly aware of this state of things. The only question is whether this is enough to justify his kind of 'apolitism', his skepticism, and his way of behaving selfishly during World War II, when, after having left Austria, a few years before dying, he tried to negotiate the measures that he had wrongly heard that would affect his writings in Hitler's Germany.

CC. And what do you think of the main characters in *MWQ* in relation to Musil's attitude towards the war? Ulrich had also a military past. It is presented early in the novel in a very random way. It was one of his attempts to become a great man and he used it to seduce civilian women till the day he was militarily scolded for it. Furthermore, he did not even know what a great man was. He wanted to become a general because his idol was Napoleon. He wanted to become both a general and a tyrant. However, he never revealed his desire of that to anybody.

I am also thinking of General Stumm. It seems that he got to his profession because he was never able to take anything else seriously enough. In fact, he did not pursue his chosen profession that way. He was not talented for the military, he hated horses and everything surrounding them, especially the circles of men and their conversations. After having avoided love and its disorders for a very long time, he decided to marry in order to fulfill his ideal of the 'married officer', but he realizes that his first options were truer to his character. He starts thinking then of other women, and that is where Diotima enters his life. The representative of the Ministry of War in the Parallel Campaign devotes himself to finding the ultimate expression of peace so as to satisfy his unrequited love.

Perhaps the most military of all the characters in the novel is Arnheim, the man with qualities, even though he does not have that quality in particular, that is, that of belonging to the military. In a similar way, he could talk about everything, like an encyclopedia, with the capacity to say nothing. Then we have Clarisse, who could be understood as the only real soldier in the whole story, fighting Walter's music and life as it came. What about

Bonadea? An unconscious soldier of the sensual, as one might put it in Schopenhauerian terms?

JPC. I confess that I never thought of the characters in *MWQ* that way. I find it very interesting, but I believe that the impact that Musil's attitude towards the war left on his characters has something to do with the fact that Diotima, Arnheim, Stumm, and so on – as is implied by the very concept of a 'man without qualities' – are only an aggregate of qualities – like the self in Mach's *Analysis of Sensations*[13]. We can perceive military features in Arnheim's behavior or thoughts, and even in Diotima's or Stumm's, and at the same time contrasting aspects, and they can be sometimes very surprising. And this is precisely one of the things that make this novel so different from any other type of *Bildungsroman*. All characters are immersed in a plural and undetermined world, and this plurality is also within them; their self is plural. This is also what makes Ulrich, as a character, so different from Julien Sorel, for example, in Stendhal's novel *The Red and the Black*. It seems to me that the influence that the experience of war had on Musil's writings cannot be dissociated from this state of things. As Musil put it in *Deutsche Mensch als Symptom*, man is a 'morally colloidal substance', he changes according to circumstances; he needs a spine, and this means that when such a condition fails or when the aged become too old to do the job, the possibility of war arises. In *MWQ*, the 'Parallel Campaign' and war compete, and it is clear that the former is not able to fulfill all the needs that are at stake. It might be useful to remember at this point what Hegel thought of war. He understood it as a necessity that takes place when the social whole is dissolving. But Musil is not Hegel. The question is not to take into account the sense of history, since there is none, but to know what it would mean for it to have a sense. Think of this question: why do we not invent History, or why do we not make history?

CC. Well, that is a difficult question. I would say that history has only a human sense, and that human beings, in fact, invent

---

13 Ernst Mach, *The Analysis of Sensations, and the Relation of the Physical to the Psychical,* trans. by. C. M. Williams and Sydney Waterlow (London: The Open Court Publishing Company, 1914).

and make history. It is clear that we make stories out of what takes place around us and that we opt for a couple of those stories and call that history. Probably Musil wanted to make all this evident. After all, his characters are trying very hard to make history. That is the objective of the 'Parallel Campaign', even if it does not get them anywhere. There is nothing that constitutes itself as History in *MWQ*, because for Musil all human stories have the same value. He tries to make evident how eager we are to institutionalize and prioritize our own storytelling.

JPC. It is clear that history depends on the different ways we tell stories. These ways are not only concerned with the past and what we remember of it. They also have consequences on the future and our ability to think over it. In a certain sense, to 'tell' history is a way of saying something about the future. When Musil said that we should invent history, what he meant is perhaps something like this: history is not something already made, like a temporal 'readymade'. We should make it because there is not such a thing that some god or some *ananke* has already planned. It is our responsibility, and this responsibility commits us in the present. However, the different characters in *MWQ* do not play any part in the 'telling' of history from this point of view, since they live in a post-modern dream *avant la lettre* where history has lost its meaning and its reality. This is another way to understand Musil's notion of the 'sense of possibility': when the field of possibilities closes itself and no possibility can change anything. 'No future', this is the last word of the story, which means: war!

References

Carmona, Carla and Jean-Pierre Cometti, 'Clarisse as a Depiction by Schiele', *Egon Schiele Jahrbuch*, 1 (2011), pp. 224-227.
—, 'Schiele, Musil and the Experience of War', *Egon Schiele Jahrbuch*, 2/3 (2014), pp. 286-289.
Cometti, Jean-Pierre, *L'art sans qualités* (Tours: Farrago, 1999).
—, *Robert Musil: De 'Torless' à 'L'Homme sans qualités'* (Brussels: Mardaga, 1986).

Mach, Ernst, *The Analysis of Sensations, and the Relation of the Physical to the Psychical*, trans. by. C. M. Williams and Sydney Waterlow (London: The Open Court Publishing Company, 1914).
Musil, Robert, *Der Mann ohne Eigenschaften 1-6, Gesamtausgabe in 12 Bänden*, ed. by Walter Fanta (Salzburg: Jung und Jung, 2016-2018).
—, *Der deutsche Mensch als Symptom* (Berlin: Rowohlt, 1967).
—, *The Man Without Qualities*, trans. by Sophie Wilkins and Burton Pike (London: Picador, 1995).
Zweig, Stefan, *The World of Yesterday*, trans. by Anthea Bell (Nebraska: University of Nebraska, 2013).
Wittgenstein, Ludwig, *Philosophical Investigactions*, trans. by G. E. M. Anscombe (Oxford: Blackwell, 1953).
—, *Philosophical Remarks*, ed. by Rush Rhess, trans. by Raymond Hargreaves and Roger White (Chicago: University of Chicago Press, 1980).
—, *Tractatus Logico-Philosophicus* (London: Routledge & Kegan Paul, 1922).

ART, MUSIC, LITERARY CRITICISM
AND THE SPIRIT OF A CULTURE

Peter Lamarque
TEN THESES ON LITERARY INTERPRETATION

When I speak of 'literary interpretation' I mean commentary of the following kind:

> If Heathcliff exploits Hareton culturally and economically, he nevertheless feels a certain rough-and-ready *rapport* with him. The contradiction Heathcliff embodies, then, is brought home in the fact that he combines Heights violence with Grange methods to gain power over both properties; and this means that while he is economically progressive he is culturally outdated. He represents a turbulent form of capitalist aggression which must historically be civilised – blended with spiritual values, as it will be in the case of his surrogate Hareton. The terms into which the novel casts this imperative are those of the need to refine, in the person of Hareton, the old yeoman class; but since Hareton's achievement of the Grange is an ironic consequence of Heathcliff's own activity, there is a sense in which it is the capitalist drive symbolised by Heathcliff which must submit to spiritual cultivation.[1]

> At the penultimate moment in the play, Lear seems very large indeed. He has seen through the self-delusion of 'masculine' definitions of the human, and has endured his 'feminine' suffering. He remains 'masculine': he does not drown in guilt, he retains will, he retains prowess enough to kill Cordelia's killer. He remains 'feminine' in that he renounces power-in-the-world, and desires only felicity, love, harmony. He has achieved full humanness. But this achievement required Cordelia. His 'madness' in the field outside Dover is not really madness at all: it is thwarted wholeness, perception of the delusions in society without a complementary

---

1   Terry Eagleton, *Myths of Power: A Marxist Study of the Brontës* (London: Macmillan, 2nd ed. 1988), pp. 115-116.

fullness of pleasure in other things. Without Cordelia, Lear would remain in bitter cynicism. Thus, the play suggests (again) that a chaste constant woman is necessary to transform a legitimate man into an integrated man.[2]

'Do not fear Baas': the four words come from nowhere, or from the darkness of my pre-poem anticipation, unannounced, unlocated, unidentified; before I take them in as a statement, they brush against me in the dark as the physical signal of another human presence. Yet when I understand them as a meaningful sequence, they offer reassurance, seeming to know in advance the alarm that they will cause, and offer to allay it even as they produce it. [...] Somewhere in the background, further complicating the tonality, hovers the angelic utterance, 'Fear not'. But it is not reassuring to have one's fears predicted, mapped out, at least not by the source of those fears. I have been seen, and seen through, while I remain in the dark. [...] [E]ach time I speak [the words in the poem] I have to choose a particular tone, setting a limit to the range of nuances that play across them. [...] This remains true of the following lines. 'It's just that I appeared': words of explanation and comfort, yet conveying the alarm of an encounter with an apparition, emerging suddenly out of nowhere – the nowhere that people of 'other' races inhabit in a racist culture. 'And our faces met': what could be simpler and more calming. Yet at the same time there is something disturbing about the notion of faces, rather than people, meeting.[3]

There are notable differences in the passages. One refers to a novel, *Wuthering Heights*, one to a play, *King Lear*, and the third to a short lyric poem, 'The Actual Dialogue' by Mongane Wally Serote. They belong to different schools of literary criticism: to Marxism, feminism and what Derek Attridge, in a different context, calls 'minimal interpretation' of a broadly humanistic kind[4]. And they focus on different kinds of aspects of the works they discuss: the social and cultural differences between characters,

---

2   Marilyn French, from *Shakespeare's Division of Experience* (1982), repr. in *Shakespearian Tragedy*, ed. by John Drakakis (London: Longman, 1992), p. 256.
3   Derek Attridge, *The Singularity of Literature* (London: Routledge, 2004), pp. 115-116.
4   Derek Attridge and Henry Staten, *The Craft of Poetry: Dialogues on minimal interpretation* (London: Routledge, 2015).

the psychological state of a character, and the effect of a line in a poem. But I believe that the similarities between the passages far outweigh the differences. They are all recognizable as instances of literary criticism of a familiar kind, they all relate particularities to wider themes, and they all offer perspectives on the works in question which enlarge a reader's appreciation of the works and suggest interesting ways of thinking about the works that might not be obvious on an initial or superficial reading. I take them to be paradigmatic of literary interpretation.

Now let's see what more can be said of commentary of this kind. I will list ten theses about such interpretation, all of which I endorse but several of which I recognize as controversial.

1. *Forms of interpretation are governed by the objects of interpretation*

This I take to be an absolutely basic principle of interpretation. Interpretation has different aims and follows different procedures and conventions according to the domains of its application. Interpretation in the sciences and social sciences, in psychoanalysis, in the political sphere, in theology, in the law, in forensic investigation, in archaeology, and in literary criticism cannot be assumed to have the same aims or follow the same conventions. The practices are different. There is a fundamental dependence relation between the mode of interpretation and the objects of interpretation, so much so that interpretation cannot proceed without some prior determination of the kind of thing being interpreted.

There are two important consequences of this principle. The first is that what I have to say about literary interpretation will not automatically transfer to other applications and indeed is very unlikely to be relevant elsewhere (although there are strong commonalities across the arts). The objects of interpretation in this case are works of literature and I take it as an unargued postulate of the discussion that literary works, under the relevant conception, count as works of art, so literary interpretation is a species of artistic interpretation. I won't agonize over the term 'literature'; I will not attempt to define the term and I have no need to do so. In this context I simply mean novels, plays, poems, and short stories (or strictly a subclass of these) and I exclude biographies, histories, works of philosophy, and other modes of narrative. I acknowledge the existence of borderline cases here but they will make no difference to what I have to say about interpretation. I aim to characterise a paradigmatic species of commentary about literary works, as illustrated earlier, which I take to be familiar and commonplace in literary circles. More precisely I take interpretation of this kind to be a core mode of apprehension in a practice of literature which is normative or broadly rule-governed. In characterising literary interpretation I am at least partially characterising a practice.

The second point connects to the first: it should not be assumed that forms of interpretation grounded in other practices and applied in different domains will be transferable to works of literature. It is a common mistake in this discussion to assume that transferability is possible and appropriate: for example, that what applies to other quite distinct modes of communication will apply also to literature.

2. *The phrase 'the meaning of a work of literature' makes little sense and is unhelpful (it should be avoided)*

Over and over we hear it said that the aim of literary interpretation is to find the meaning of a literary work. The vacuity of the phrase shows, I believe, how radically misconceived is much discussion of interpretation applied to works of literature. Note that it is not the singularity implied by the definite article that creates the problem; the phrase 'a meaning of a literary work' is no better. The first hint that something is wrong comes when we ask how we might complete sentences that start, for example, 'the meaning of *Pride and Prejudice* is ____' or '*The Mayor of Casterbridge* means ____'. The oddity is not just with literary works. It is doubtful that there is such a thing as the meaning of Hume's *Treatise*.

One defence of 'the meaning of a work of literature' might go like this. Works of literature are made up of component sentences; each sentence has a meaning (determined, say, by its truth-conditions); so the meaning of the whole work is simply a compound of the meanings of its component sentences. But this will not do the trick. The meaning arrived at through this route is textual meaning but textual meaning is not identical to work meaning because a work is not identical to its constitutive text. Two tokens of type-identical texts might be distinct works. More to the point literary interpretation is not the recovery of textual meaning.

Here Monroe Beardsley's important distinction between explication and interpretation must be acknowledged. Explication is the investigation of verbal or sentential meaning. This is an integral and important part of literary critical enquiry, pursuing unusual, idiomatic usages as well as connotations and symbolism notably in poetry. But interpretation, in the conception that interests me, as illustrated in the examples, has a different role. It applies not at a sentential or verbal level but to whole works or substantial passages and arguably it is not *meaning* in any literal sense that it reveals but, as we shall see, something more like thematic significance, or valued experience.

The rejection of 'the meaning of a work of literature' in Thesis 2 rests not just on the somewhat glib point about English usage, the oddity of speaking in this way, but on something much deeper: the difference between a text and a work and the difference between explication and interpretation. If we want to grasp what interpretation is in this context, then we had better abandon talk of 'the meaning of a work of literature'.

3. *No appeal to 'utterance meaning' or 'utterer's meaning' will illuminate what is distinctive about literary interpretation*

Here matters get a bit more controversial because I am inclined to think that the importation of theories of meaning and the philosophy of language into explanations of literary interpretation has had a baleful effect in the philosophy of literature. Naturally if you think that literary interpretation has the aim of giving the meaning of a literary work then it makes sense to reach for familiar and well-developed accounts of meaning elsewhere to explain what's going on. But the reservations in my Thesis 2 should already give pause for thought. Robert Stecker, for example, unequivocally asserts: 'the meaning of a work [...] is identical to its utterance meaning'[5]. He elaborates: 'Utterance meaning specifies what someone has said or done by using language on a particular occasion'[6]. This is really not helpful. There is no problem thinking of writing as a mode of utterance but to suppose a whole work – say, a novel – possesses utterance meaning explained as 'what someone has said or done by using language on a particular occasion' simply strains all credibility. What is the 'particular occasion'? The novel might have taken ten years to write, it might have been published in monthly instalments.

The problem here is that quite the wrong model of meaning is being appealed to: the model in effect of speech as the conveying of thoughts using single sentences or small clusters of sentences in well-defined communicative contexts. It just doesn't fit whole literary works conceived as works of art.

Noël Carroll has had an inkling of what's wrong here when he identifies what he calls 'The Linguistic Fallacy' described, in his Richard Wollheim Memorial Lecture, as 'the presumption that all art interpretation can be modelled on the interpretation of the linguistic meanings of a word or a sentence'[7]. He applies this quite rightly to literary works:

> Thematic interpretation of entire literary works and even parts thereof is radically different than the comprehension and interpretation of word meaning and sentence meaning. [...] Most literary interpretation, like most art interpretation in general, should not be modelled on the comprehension and interpretation of word and sentence meaning.[8]

I entirely concur with this but I think the Linguistic Fallacy should be pursued even more rigorously and include not just word and sentence meaning but utterance and utterer's meaning

---

5   Robert Stecker, *Interpretation and Construction: Art, Speech and the Law* (Oxford: Wiley-Blackwell, 2003), p. 59.
6   *Ibid.*
7   Noël Carroll, 'Art Interpretation: The 2010 Richard Wollheim Memorial Lecture', *British Journal of Aesthetics*, 51, no. 2 (2011), pp. 117-135 (p. 121).
8   Carroll, pp. 124-125.

as well. I fear that Carroll himself sometimes gets snared in the web of the Fallacy, notably through what might be called his continuum thesis, the emphasis, in his words, on a 'continuum between how we understand the words and deeds of others on a daily basis and the interpretation of art and literature'[9]. Stressing such a continuum, particularly in his appeal to a conversational or communicative model of literary works, conflicts with my Thesis 1, which insists on the distinctiveness of interpretation in its different domains.

The Linguistic Fallacy has proved awfully seductive in literary theory. Structuralists used sentential grammar, appealing to transformations, deep and surface structures, etc. as a model for literary works; New Critics saw metaphorical utterance, with its tensions, interactions and connotations, as paradigmatic in criticism; philosophers of literature have appealed to speech act theory and Gricean theory to explain, well, the meaning of a literary work. The problem with all this is the Linguistic Fallacy. All that has resulted is the obfuscation of the true aims and procedures of literary interpretation.

Note, however, that the Linguistic Fallacy does not apply to *explication*. Here it seems perfectly appropriate to appeal to philosophy of language in explaining aspects of textual meaning, which does precisely lie at a verbal and sentential level. Also the kinds of pragmatic inferences explored by relevance theorists do gain purchase in textual explication as well as narrative reconstruction. They do not gain purchase, though, in literary interpretation.

4. *What matters in literary interpretation is not meaning but appreciation*

What is needed in philosophy of literature is a radical reorientation. Rather than thinking of a literary work as a text communicating an utterance meaning that invites understanding, it is more fruitful to think of it as a work, indeed a work of art, engaging a practice, and inviting a distinctive mode of

---

9   Ibid., p. 127.

appreciation. The kinds of commentary in our sample passages do not aim at recovering the meaning of the work or even at advancing understanding of the work in any literal sense, they aim rather at providing a perspective on the particulars of the work which enhances its interest and offers a further web of concepts through which to reflect on the work.

Eagleton's comments on *Wuthering Heights* deploy concepts like 'economically progressive', 'capitalist aggression', and 'old yeoman class' to characterise the relation between Heathcliff and Hareton; Marilyn French in turn offers us concepts like '"masculine" definitions of the human', '"feminine" suffering' and 'thwarted wholeness' to capture the psychological state of King Lear. Such concepts offer us a lens through which to appreciate aspects of the characters that perhaps had not been initially evident but which might enrich our experience of them. Attridge finds significance in the poem through reference to 'reassurance', 'something disturbing about the notion of faces [...] meeting'.

Literary interpretation of this kind must presuppose and build on prior activities of grasping textual meaning and reconstructing narrative content. For example, the narrative world of *Wuthering Heights* is fairly complex. The story is presented through two narrators, Lockwood and Nelly Dean, both with strong points of view on what they report – these points of view need to be identified and carefully weighed; the subtle social differences between the two households of Wuthering Heights and Thrushcross Grange must be understood; Heathcliff's humiliation and abuse of Hareton must be recognised as revenge for the way that Hareton's father Hindley Earnshaw had humiliated him, and so forth. These are indeed species of understanding, they involve close attention to verbal meaning and story content. To reach that understanding we might need to deploy familiar mechanisms from pragmatics or textual analysis.

Interpretation, however, moves beyond this not in a search for further meaning but to explore aspects of the literary achievement which are not just meaning-based or story-based but which provide further reasons for valuing and reflecting on the particulars. This is what I call appreciation. To judge something as a literary work is to find it especially suitable for or encouraging of responses of this kind.

5. *The perennial debate about authorial intention – notably between 'actual intentionalism' and 'hypothetical intentionalism' – is of only marginal relevance to literary interpretation*

The debate about intention has so dominated discussion about interpretation in the philosophy of literature that this Thesis might seem surprising, even perverse. The claim in the Thesis, though, needs to be understood carefully. It is a thesis about literary interpretation not about other stages or aspects of critical practice. The intention debate might well gain purchase at the level of textual explication or even concerning the reconstruction of narrative content (the world or story presented in a work). It is only interpretation of the kind illustrated that seems not to be illuminated by the terms of the debate.

Also the Thesis is a claim about the relevance of a *debate*, not about the relevance of authorial intention. It is not then a statement of anti-intentionalism. Indeed if anti-intentionalism states that authorial intention can be, or must be, entirely ignored in critical commentary then it is virtually unintelligible. Literary works are products of intentional acts so to reflect on a work is to reflect, ipso facto, on the intentions the work embodies.

What the thesis rejects is the thought that philosophers must choose between certain candidate theories – anti-intentionalism, 'actual intentionalism', 'hypothetical intentionalism', or something called the 'value-maximizing theory'[10] – if they are to make progress in understanding literary interpretation; it is that that strikes me as perverse and quite out of accord with standard critical practice.

Look again at the examples where we started. Where is authorial intention supposed to surface here? Eagleton states that Heathcliff 'represents a turbulent form of capitalist aggression which must historically be civilised'. Must we refer to Emily Brontë's intentions to assess that claim: to judge whether it is true, whether it is insightful, whether it offers a plausible way of thinking of the character? But it's highly unlikely that Emily Brontë would have any conception of what capitalist aggression means. Does that matter? Similarly with Marilyn French's comments about Lear.

---

10 Stephen Davies, 'Authors' Intentions, Literary Interpretation, and Literary Value', *British Journal of Aesthetics*, 46, no. 3 (2006), pp. 223-247.

She says, for example, that Lear's '"madness" in the field outside Dover is not really madness at all: it is thwarted wholeness'. Is that what Shakespeare had in mind? Must we ask that – must we try to establish that? – before we can pass judgement on French's observation? The very suggestion strikes me as absurd. Did Shakespeare ever entertain the concept of thwarted wholeness? Who knows? Who cares?

None of the candidate theories has anything to offer here that will help us assess the interpretations proposed. Stephen Davies's value-maximizing theory might sound the most promising because it mentions literary value but Davies bases his whole discussion on the discredited idiom of the meaning of a work and in any case the idea of maximizing value seems inappropriate. Eagleton finds something of interest to say about *Wuthering Heights*, as does French with *King Lear*, and Attridge with the Serote poem. Their interpretations could be illuminating without identifying any maximum degree of value. Hypothetical intentionalism in turn looks like a non-starter. It allows that a reader could form a hypothesis about the author's intentions, on the best available evidence, but then *even if the hypothesis turns out to be false* insist that we stick with it. That makes nonsense of the very idea of a hypothesis. And the trouble with actual intentionalism is that it over-emphasises intention. To be obsessively concerned with what was in the author's mind badly distorts the reading process by imposing a gratuitously disabling constraint. It also gets the direction of explanation the wrong way round in the majority of cases. Rather than deriving an interpretation from premises about what the author intended more often than not we infer what the author intended from a careful reading of the work.

6. *Interpretations proposed for works of literature can draw on many sources, internal or external, but their validity is ultimately answerable to the works themselves*

For an interpretation to be credible it must be supported by evidence; that evidence could be drawn from different sources but is ultimately answerable to the works and their immediate contexts. Eagleton's commentary on *Wuthering Heights* in terms of social and class conflicts conforms to and is supported by many overt references in the novel itself to the different social positions of, say, the Lintons at the Grange and the Earnshaws at the Heights. Catherine marries Linton rather than Heathcliff at least partly because of her social ambitions. The narrator Lockwood thinks of Heathcliff as a gentleman although others, including Nelly Dean, disabuse him of that. As for French's remark that Lear 'renounces power-in-the-world, and desires only felicity, love, harmony' that seems well-enough supported by scenes in the play after Lear's reconciliation with Cordelia. Whether, as French states, this amounts to him achieving 'full humanness', given his state of decrepitude, is a moot point. However, Cordelia's involvement in this achievement is beyond doubt. Finally whether we accept that Lear 'has seen through the self-delusion of "masculine" definitions of the human' will depend not on unearthing Shakespeare's intentions but partially at least on our attitude to the presuppositions about gender differences.

So what counts as support for an interpretation? Most obviously the text itself must be cited. But a text is a pliable entity[11] that can be stretched and manipulated. Andre Green in his psychoanalytic reading of *Othello* cites Iago's lines: 'Were I the Moor, I would not be Iago. / In following him, I follow but myself' as pointing to a kind of identity between Iago and Othello leading to the thought that Cassio becomes a shared 'love-object' between them. 'If we recall,' Green writes, 'that Freud sees in the process of paranoia a regressive path from homosexuality to narcissism, Iago stands before Othello like a mirror that makes his desire all the more unbearable the closer it gets to him'[12]. Note that the evidence doing the work here leans far more towards Freud's psychoanalytic theory than to Shakespeare's own text. As such the validity of the interpretation rests substantially on the validity of the theory. For those sceptical of psychoanalysis this weakens the interpretation. Arguably, though, and in contrast, the validity of Eagleton's reading of *Wuthering Heights* is sufficiently in line with

---

11 The phrase comes from Torsten Pettersson, 'The Literary Work as Pliable Entity: Combining Realism and Pluralism,' in *Is There a Single Right Interpretation?*, ed. by Michael Krausz (Philadelphia: Penn State Press, 2002).
12 Andre Green, quoted in Drakakis, *Shakespearian Tragedy*, p. 348.

both textual evidence and a contemporary background of social attitudes that its validity does not stand or fall with the validity of Marxism, in spite of that being its overriding framework.

For those interested in the role of intentions, what about cases where an author states explicitly what he had in mind and what he had in mind is far from evident in the work itself? An example might be some difficult lines in a poem by Louis MacNeice:

> One was found like Judas kissing flowers
> And one who sat between the clock and the sun
> Lies like a Saint Sebastian full of arrows...[13]

A reader's perplexity might be eased by an explanation from MacNeice himself:

> MacNeice tells us that his poem is in praise of those who live by routine. [...] The image of the man kissing flowers is meant to depict a person who has neglected his routine duties for an alien preoccupation which may prove as fatal to him as kissing Christ proved to Judas. The clock and the sun are symbols of time and routine [...]; the ticking of the clock has its equivalent in the dust-motes illuminated by the sun.[14]

Is this legitimate evidence for an interpretation? Yes, indeed. What we should note, though, is the proviso in Noël Carroll's 'modest actual intentionalism' that citing a statement of this kind is only legitimate if the intention is, as he puts it, 'consistent with the way the work is'[15]. Arguably that is the case here. Does that validate actual intentionalism after all? No, it doesn't. The single-minded pursuit of what was in the author's mind remains, as I put it earlier, a gratuitously disabling constraint.

---

13 Louis MacNiece, 'Hidden Ice', from *Modern Poetry: A Personal Essay* (1938): quoted in John Press, *The Chequer'd Shade: Reflections on Obscurity in Poetry* (Oxford: Oxford University Press, 1963), p. 158.
14 Press, p. 158.
15 Carroll, p. 119.

7. *Any final judgment about an interpretation of a work of literature, however well-supported, must be in terms of how far it furthers appreciative experience of the work*

To answer the question of how good an interpretation is we need to ask why readers attempt interpretations in the first place, interpretations of the kind illustrated. What is the aim? What is the point? The standard answer is that interpretation helps us understand the meaning of a work. A good interpretation is one, presumably, that makes the meaning as clear as possible. That picture is one I have questioned, indeed rejected. I find it hard to see what value there might be simply in aiming to recover a work's meaning as if it were a puzzle to be solved. Nor am I persuaded that seeing literary works as kinds of communication is particularly apt or helpful. Instead I have proposed that we think of interpretation not in terms of understanding, not even in terms of meaning, but in terms of providing a perspective through which the particulars of the work can be reflected on. This perspective affords a higher-order reflection on the content and world of a work that enhances a reader's experience and partly explains any pleasure the work affords.

Understanding is not the same as interpreting, although the latter might presuppose the former. It is possible to understand a narrative and take pleasure from it without adopting any higher-order perspective offered by interpretation. Such a reader merely grasps the story content. Of course there is no guarantee that an interpretation, however ingenious, will in fact serve to increase an appreciative experience in a reader. Freudian interpretations of *Othello* might even detract from a reader's experience, as might an overemphasis on class distinctions for readers of *Wuthering Heights*. We judge literary interpretations not just on their faithfulness to a work but on the additional interest they impart to the work by characterising broader themes being explored. Criteria, then, for assessing an interpretation are of two kinds, both essential: Is it supported by the work itself? Does it serve to enrich our experience of the work?

8. The aim of finding some single interpretation of a work of literature is ill-conceived

There is a longstanding debate between critical monists, who see it as an aspiration of criticism to find some single overriding reading of a literary work, and critical pluralists, who allow for multiple and diverse readings not necessarily in competition. The issue cuts across intentionalism: there have been intentionalist and anti-intentionalist supporters in both camps. It is too big a debate to enter here in any seriousness. But it should be plain that the view of literary interpretation as offering higher-order reflections on a work through perspectives taken to particulars is especially congenial to pluralism. Indeed one could go further and say that the aspiration to find a single interpretation seems ill-conceived on this picture. Similarly, although the analogy is only partial, it would seem equally ill-conceived to aspire to some single correct and final interpretation of a musical work or a theatrical work in performance. Conductors and theatrical directors seek to offer new and illuminating perspectives on works, just as do interpreters of literature. They do not seek some single ideal.

Charlotte Bronte's *Jane Eyre* has offered more scope for different interpretations than Emily's *Wuthering Heights*. Thus a feminist approach centres on the motif of the madwoman in the attic, whereby Rochester's wife Bertha, trapped in the attic and now mad, is seen to symbolise Victorian marriage as a prison of suffering and isolation. Also there is a postcolonial theme centred on Bertha's Jamaican and Creole ethnicity, now symbolising colonial oppression and exploitation: a symbol forcefully dramatized in Jean Rhys's novel *Wide Sargasso Sea*. There is a Marxist interpretation, again from Terry Eagleton, who reflects on the 'complex structure [in the novel] of convergence and antagonism between the landed and industrial sectors of the contemporary ruling class'[16]. Yet another interpretation sees the novel as a religious allegory. Rochester becomes 'part of the great archetypal pattern of sin, suffering and redemption'[17].

---

16 Eagleton, p. 4.
17 Robert Bernard Martin, 'Religious Discovery in *Jane Eyre*' [from *The Accents of Persuasion: Charlotte Bronte's Novels* (New York: W W Norton

The monist might offer two responses to this diversity: either we must choose between them or we must somehow combine them into a single interpretation. But both moves are flawed. All the interpretations are reasonably well-grounded in the work and fruitful as perspectives to adopt. There is no reason to accept one and reject the others. But a kind of aggregation of all makes nonsense of the idea of a work offering a coherent experience. When we experience the work under any one of these readings the perspective is comprehensive; different elements are assigned significance within it. We can shift perspectives but we cannot adopt them all at the same time.

9. *No empirical study (e.g. in psychology) will reveal what is distinctive and valuable about literary interpretation*

A great deal of empirical work has been done on narrative comprehension and narrative processing. This is of interest in many spheres including revealing how children grasp stories, how people learn facts from stories, how the imagination works, and how emotional responses are triggered by narrative devices. Where I suggest it is not of much value – and perhaps it makes no claim to value here – is in casting light on literary interpretation of the kind at issue. Empirical studies of how readers process and reflect on narrative texts might reveal important facts about mechanisms hitherto unidentified. But literary interpretation as described is not a natural text-processing activity but rather an acquired skill subject to norms within a practice. To understand what is going on one must understand the norms and engage the practice. Interpretation can be taught, it calls on special skills, aptitudes and sensibility, it is normative because it can be done better or worse, and it can be improved with practice. Not all readers will have the aptitude or inclination to engage in interpretation even though they might get pleasure from and show skills at text comprehension and narrative reconstruction. Indeed there are readers – even readers of canonical works – who find the exercise

---

& Co, 1966)], in Charlotte Bronte, *Jane Eyre*, ed. by Richard J. Dunn (New York: W W Norton & Co, 1971), p. 488.

of literary interpretation elitist or superfluous. However, reading for thematic interpretation remains absolutely central to the institution of literature and a mark of what gives value to literary works as works of art.

10. *The perspectives offered in interpretation provide further filters through which literary narratives, already exhibiting deep opacity, are contemplated and valued*

I want to end briefly with some remarks connecting literary interpretation to the idea of the opacity of narrative. It is possible to read any narrative opaquely or transparently[18]. To read opaquely is to afford special salience to the representational modes of the narrative. At its extreme this means that events and characters comprising the content are taken to be *constituted* by the modes of their presentation in the narrative. Their identity is determined by the narrative itself such they are not merely contingently but essentially connected to the descriptions that characterize them. To read transparently is to loosen the connection between identity and mode of presentation. Those who read novels merely to enjoy character and plot such that other ways of representing the content, say, in a film adaptation or even a good plot summary could count as the same characters and plot, are not giving salience to any precise narrative form. To read through opacity is to read from a literary point of view or to read literature as literature. It amounts to fine-grained reading where resonances, nuances, impressions, mood, and connotations emerge from a text as significant and valuable. These colour and define narrative content which is thus experienced through a filter of linguistic expression.

Interpretation also involves reading literature as literature. But the connection is deeper because it too offers a filter through which narrative content is experienced and through which value is identified. Interpretation, as we have seen, provides a web of further concepts or descriptions to connect, to enhance, to expand and to contextualise the content as given. It provides a

---

18   This idea is developed in my book Peter Lamarque, *The Opacity of Narrative* (London: Rowman & Littlefield International, 2014).

higher-order perspective on that content which shows something interesting or unanticipated about the content. So opaque reading and interpretation share in common that both are grounded in an experience and both are perspectival.

This leads me to a brief observation about truth in relation to literature. It is sometimes supposed that one of the core values that interpretation can yield is truth or cognitive value. The implicit suggestion is that through extracting generalisations from a novel, interpretations enhance our understanding of important psychological, philosophical or sociological matters concerning the real world. We learn from novels, it is said, because the novels offer truths that perceptive interpretations uncover. So the novel *Jane Eyre* can teach us about the position of women in oppressive marriages or about colonial attitudes in Victorian England or about how social class and social aspiration can poison both family and sexual relationships.

My own view of literary interpretation, as is evident, is rather different. I do not deny the possibility of cognitive benefits of this kind. But I do not think they are at the heart of literary value. The primary function of interpretation is not to extract generalised truths applicable to the nonfictional world but to heighten our experience of a fictional world, to broaden the perspectives through which the particulars of that world can be envisaged. By contemplating character and incident opaquely and bringing them to mind through fine-grained representation we can, to use a metaphor, *reshape our minds* or *change our inner landscape* in ways that are themselves a kind of cognitive achievement.

The cognitive benefits of literature, such as they are, rest not principally on the acquisition of beliefs or the revelation of truths, but in the way that narrative content lodges in the mind, imagistically or propositionally, under the very perspectives that inform the content itself. Attending to fictional particulars under both first-order, fine-grained narrative perspectives and higher-order interpretative perspectives can shape the mind by inducing and guiding thoughts and thought processes. The building up of such thoughts can reconfigure our minds, usually, although not inevitably, in positive ways. This is what can make the experience of reading a novel valuable and valuable for its own sake.

What we go on to do with the thoughts thus accumulated is another matter altogether. They might affect our subsequent actions and attitudes, they might re-order our conception of ourselves. They might have no practical effect whatsoever. But any effects they do have will be contingent and largely dependent on local psychological dispositions of individual readers. This is why one should be wary of proposing too ambitious a truth-revealing capacity for works of fiction over and above the capacity to present particularities literally in thought-provoking ways.

References

Attridge, Derek and Henry Staten, *The Craft of Poetry: Dialogues on minimal interpretation* (London: Routledge, 2015).
Attridge, Derek, *The Singularity of Literature* (London: Routledge, 2004).
Noël Carroll, 'Art Interpretation: The 2010 Richard Wollheim Memorial Lecture', *British Journal of Aesthetics*, 51, no. 2 (2011), pp. 117-135.
Davies, Stephen, 'Authors' Intentions, Literary Interpretation, and Literary Value', *British Journal of Aesthetics*, 46, no. 3 (2006), pp. 223-247.
Dradakis, John (ed.), *Shakespearian Tragedy*, (London: Longman, 1992).
Eagleton, Terry, *Myths of Power: A Marxist Study of the Brontës* (London: Macmillan, 2nd ed., 1988).
French, Marilyn, 'Shakespeare's Division of Experience' (1982), repr. in Dradakis, *Shakespearian Tragedy*.
Lamarque, Peter, *The Opacity of Narrative* (London: Rowman & Littlefield International, 2014).
Martin, Robert Bernard, 'Religious Discovery in *Jane Eyre*', in *The Accents of Persuasion: Charlotte Bronte's Novels* (New York: W W Norton & Co, 1966], repr. in Charlotte Bronte, *Jane Eyre*, ed. by Richard J. Dunn (New York: W W Norton & Co, 1971).
Pettersson, Torsten, 'The Literary Work as Pliable Entity: Combining Realism and Pluralism,' in *Is There a Single Right Interpretation?*, ed. by Michael Krausz (Philadelphia: Penn State Press, 2002).
Press, John, *The Chequer'd Shade: Reflections on Obscurity in Poetry* (Oxford: Oxford University Press, 1963).
Stecker, Robert, *Interpretation and Construction: Art, Speech and the Law* (Oxford: Wiley-Blackwell, 2003).

Severin Schroeder
SENTIMENTALITY AS AN AESTHETIC FLAW

What is – and what is wrong with – sentimentality in literature? Over the last decades there have been a number of attempts to explain sentimentality in literature as, primarily, a *moral* defect. On this account, if in literary criticism we disparage something as sentimental, a negative aesthetic evaluation (in a broad sense of the term 'aesthetic') is based on a moral judgement. This would be an instance of the relevance of moral considerations for aesthetic criticism.

Current arguments for censuring literary sentimentality on moral grounds proceed in two steps (although the second one is often taken for granted):
- First, sentimentality in a person is analysed as a moral failing.
- Secondly, such moral censure of a person is then transferred to an artefact: a work of fiction.

I shall mainly be concerned with two such moralising accounts of literary sentimentality. The first (I) goes back to a remark by Oscar Wilde that was picked up by Michael Tanner, Roger Scruton, and others. The second (II) was propounded by Anthony Savile, and to some extent by Mary Midgley.

I

The Oscar Wilde view. In his long letter of accusation to his former lover Lord Alfred Douglas, written from Reading Prison and posthumously published under the title *De Profundis*, Oscar Wilde explains that:

a sentimentalist is simply one who desires to have the luxury of an emotion without paying for it. [...] We think we can have our emotions for nothing. We cannot. Even the finest and the most self-sacrificing emotions have to be paid for. Strangely enough, that is what makes them fine. The intellectual and emotional life of ordinary people is a very contemptible affair. [...] they always try to get their emotions on credit, or refuse to pay the bill when it comes in. [...] Remember that the sentimentalist is always a cynic at heart. Indeed sentimentality is merely the bank holiday of cynicism.[1]

The occasion that led Oscar Wilde to this remark was one where an emotion was literally going to cost money: Lord Douglas wanted to be considerate to his mother by not asking her for financial support, but at the same time he was unwilling to do without any of his wonted luxury and extravagance. So he sponged on Wilde instead, which made his gesture towards his mother hollow: 'To propose to spare your mother's pocket was beautiful. To do so at my expense was ugly'[2]. He indulged in feeling beautifully unselfish at the time, but he wasn't really.

Or wasn't he? The fact remains that Lord Douglas spared his mother's money, which might well have been an act of sincere affection, even if in the end it didn't cost him much. It wasn't a heroic self-sacrifice, but, for all we know, it could still have been a sincere act of kindness. But let us assume that Lord Douglas did revel in the feeling of a grand self-effacing deed, which his act did not in fact amount to. Is that, then, a paradigmatic case of sentimentality? In other words, is sentimentality a matter of having, perhaps indulging in, the feelings of an emotion, while shrinking from the behavioural consequences that emotion, if genuine, would require (refusing to pay the bill)?

I am not entirely sure that such ineffectuality of feeling should be called sentimentality. Suppose I feel passionately in love with a girl, but then refuse to do anything for her when she needs help. Obviously, it wasn't love, only a passing fancy, but it seems less

---

1   Oscar Wilde, *De Profundis* (1897), in *Plays, Prose Writings and Poems*, ed. by Terry Eagleton, Everyman's Library (New York: Alfred Knopf, 1991), pp. 543-650, (pp. 636, 640).
2   Wilde, p. 636.

clear whether it should be described as sentimentality. Or think of somebody who listening to another's tales of misfortune, witnessing their dire straits, feels touched and eager to help, promises to do so, as soon as possible – but, somehow, never does. That person's intention to help, though quite sincere and heartfelt at the time, does not prove strong enough to last and to lead to action. Is this a case of sentimentality, or is it not more aptly called shallowness? (which Oscar Wilde calls 'the supreme vice', and of which, incidentally, he also accuses Lord Douglas[3]).

Moreover, there are clear cases of sentimentalists that are not lacking in real action. An elderly lady that gets soppy about cats may spend all her money on trying to improve their lives. And, as Michael Tanner observes, sentimentality may lead to various forms of violent behaviour, even suicide[4].

Nonetheless, Michael Tanner regards those remarks, from *De Profundis*, as Oscar Wilde's most profound observation. As he puts it, 'a dominant element in sentimentality is that the feelings which constitute it are in some important way unearned, being had on the cheap, come by too easily'[5]. Yet this is not exactly the case of Lord Alfred Douglas. Wilde's metaphor was that of not paying the bill *after* the luxury of an emotion; which suggests that the feeling was (or could have been) real enough at the time and only devalued subsequently by one's refusal to face the consequences. Whereas Tanner's words suggest a slightly different picture: there is something wrong with one's even having those feelings in the first place. They are come by too easily, unearned, i.e.: it should have been more difficult to experience them.

The same metaphor is used by Roger Scruton who at one point calls 'sentimentality': 'the desire for the glory of some heroic or transfiguring passion, without the cost of feeling it'[6]. This may be the sentimentality of somebody longing for the ardour of religious belief, but unwilling seriously to engage with it. In another context

---

3 Wilde, p. 580
4 Michael Tanner, 'Sentimentality', *PAS, New Series*, 77 (1976-77), pp. 127-147 (p. 131).
5 Tanner, p. 128
6 Roger Scruton, *Modern Culture* (London: Bloomsbury, 2000), p. 86.

Scruton writes that: 'Kitsch is an attempt to have the life of the spirit on the cheap'[7].

I agree that there is some truth in this metaphor (of having feelings on the cheap), which I shall return to later. For the moment, however, I want to point out that this idea of sentimentality as emotions on the cheap seems extremely inappropriate as a basis for literary criticism. For is it not rather a neat characterisation of all fiction, including good literature, perhaps especially of well-crafted effective literature, that it gives us 'emotions on the cheap'? Novels and plays allow us imaginatively to live through and respond to all types of human passion or suffering, in a well-controlled and risk-free manner: without the inconvenience of being overwhelmed, traumatised, actually ruined or killed by the real thing. That it affords us emotions on the cheap is the very beauty and attraction of fiction, fiction at its best; – not a defect called 'sentimentality'.

Here we encounter the second stage of arguing that sentimentality in literature is a moral flaw: transferring the moral objections to sentimentality in a person to a work of fiction. One natural way of making this move is this: A person is sentimental if he has certain kinds of emotions; a work of fiction is sentimental if it is likely to evoke in you that kind of emotion. But if sentimentality is emotions on the cheap, then on this account *all* emotional fiction comes out as sentimental, which is absurd.

Of course, this is not the only way of making the move from person to artefact. It may be more plausible to say that sentimental fiction expresses sentimentality, rather than arousing it. But even so, the characterisation of sentimentality as emotions on the cheap faces a problem. For it means that, even if we don't regard the literature itself as sentimental, it would still appear that all appreciative readers are. Reading fiction with the appropriate emotional sensitivity is undoubtedly a cheap and convenient way of enriching your emotional life. So on this account, reading fiction or watching it on the stage would be indulging in sentimentality, or shallowness. Leaving the theatre or putting the book aside we leave those borrowed feelings behind; just as Bingo Little (in P.G.

---

7   Roger Scruton, 'Kitsch and the modern predicament', *City Journal*, Winter (1999).

Wodehouse's *Jeeves* novels) is passionately in love one moment and forgets all about it the next.

II

Let us now consider *Anthony Savile's analysis* of sentimentality as a moral failing. According to Savile, sentimentality is always reprehensible because it involves an element of self-deception: A sentimentalist falsifies certain aspects of his experience, idealizing them, 'under the guidance of a desire for gratification and reassurance'[8]. That is, either in order to experience an agreeable emotional response, or in order to experience an emotion that, although perhaps not pleasant in itself, allows one to feel good about oneself, or a combination of both.

A common example is the sentimentalization of children and domestic pets: 'Projecting onto them an exaggerated vulnerability and innocence, I encourage myself to feel a tender compassion for them', which is pleasant, but also supports 'a view of myself as a man of gentleness and fine feeling'[9].

An example exclusively of the second type is this: 'a man who idealizes a distant political cause may be sentimentally angry or indignant when one of its exponents is extradited from the country, even though he does not experience these feelings with pleasure'. The point is rather that they 'enable him to take a gratifying view of his own character'[10].

A first objection to Savile's analysis is that it takes extreme, quasi pathological cases as the paradigm of sentimentality. This is comparable to making violent behaviour a defining feature of alcoholism. It is of course true that many, and perhaps very typical, cases of alcohol addiction involve violent behaviour; but obviously not all. Similarly, Savile's examples of self-deception are undoubtedly telling specimens of sentimentality, but it's easy to come up with more benign instances of sentimentality that do not

---

8   Anthony Savile, *The Test of Time* (Oxford: Oxford University Press, 1982), p. 241.
9   Savile, p. 239.
10   *Ibid.*, pp. 239-40.

involve any self-deception or falsification. Imagine somebody who takes great delight at the sight of cuddly little animals; who is in raptures when seeing a mother cat licking her kitten; and who is inordinately fond of their own cat and extremely concerned about its comforts. Such a person is sentimental about their cat, but need not for that matter be deceived or self-deceiving about cats' nature and limited intelligence. Or again, I may be a lover of romantic comedies and particularly relish the touching moments at the end when all is bliss and happiness. That, no doubt, would betoken a sentimental streak in me, but it doesn't make me guilty of any kind of idealizing self-deception. I may be well aware that things are rarely as neat and tidy as that in real life. Indeed, that may be the very reason why I'm so keen on romantic fiction: that it's more beautiful than real life.

Savile distorts the concept of sentimentality by defining it in terms of its – admittedly typical, but not inevitable – excesses. And what is more, even those excesses may not always deserve Savile's harsh censure. There are many cat or dog lovers whose fondness of their pets makes them entertain a somewhat idealized picture of those animals' feelings and intelligence. You like to believe, for example, that your cat has some personal attachment to you, in the way people do; – which is clearly an illusion. But is such a sentimental idealization morally reprehensible? Think of a lonely old woman who has nobody to talk to but her cat: Is she morally wrong to cultivate this kind of sentimental self-deception of thinking of her cat as listening to her? – It seems to me that such common instances of sentimentality are usually quite harmless, since they remain well localised: you please yourself with entertaining the idea of your cat's perceptiveness, but you never actually make a fool of yourself by expecting your cat to do anything intelligent (fetch the post, or make a telephone call). And in some cases such mildly self-deceiving sentimentality may be of considerable psychological benefit.

Finally, there is the question of how Savile's analysis is to be transferred from a sentimental person to a sentimental piece of fiction. There are, of course, idealizing representations in fiction. But what about the idea of self-deception? Would authors have to deceive themselves in order to produce a sentimental piece of fiction? Surely not. We would criticize a novel as sentimental even if it was obvious that the author knew perfectly well what he was doing; say, as somebody who makes a living out of producing cheap fiction according to familiar patterns. So it would be more plausible to say that sentimental fiction contains falsifying idealizations, while the effect of emotional gratification or reassurance would have to be located in the intended reader, not necessarily the author.

This is a point developed by Mary Midgley, who agrees with Savile that sentimentality consists in 'misrepresenting the world in order to indulge our feelings'. And in fiction such misrepresentation is calculated to indulge the readers' feelings; which is reprehensible because 'it distorts expectation; it can make people unable to deal with the real world'[11].

But is that a plausible complaint? – Don Quichote springs to mind: whose long exposure to romantic literature and seclusion from the world made him mistake windmills for dangerous giants. But then, the conceit of Cervantes's novel is more satirical than realistic. In fact, people are not as naïve as that; they have a fairly good understanding of the institutional concept of fiction as something that is not intended to be taken at face value[12]. Indeed, misrepresentation of the world is understood to be a key device of many literary genres, such as fairy tale, fantasy, or science fiction. Of course there are also genres that aim for thoroughgoing realism. But then, that is understood to be an artistic challenge, which readers are invited to judge as more or less successfully met, by drawing on their knowledge of the real world. Readers admire a realistic novel if they find that it is true to life in all its psychological details; they do not take it for granted that that is always the case. (And if they did, they would not be sentimental in Savile's sense: they would not be self-deceiving, but merely mistaken.)

If we consider an unrealistically sentimental description in literature, for example, some angelically virtuous and well-behaved children in Charles Dickens's novels, it is rather difficult to imagine

---

11   Mary Midgley, 'Brutality and Sentimentality', *Philosophy*, 54, no. 209 (1979), pp. 385-389 (p. 385).
12   Mark Jefferson, 'What is Wrong With Sentimentality?', *Mind*, 92, no. 368 (1983), pp. 519-529; Ira Newman, 'The Alleged Unwholesomness of Sentimentality', ed. by Alex Neill & Aaron Ridley, *Arguing about Art* (London: Routledge, 1995).

how an adult reader might be deceived by such a description so as to expect all children to be like that. You would have to imagine someone who has never seen any real children in his life.

III

In sum, I am not convinced by the view that sentimentality is a moral failing, a reprehensible falsification, as Savile claims, so that sentimentality in literature too would be morally reprehensible. What then is sentimentality, and is there anything wrong with it?

Robert Solomon, in his 'Defense of Sentimentality', asserts that sentimentality is 'nothing more nor less than the "appeal to tender feelings"', and denies boldly that there is anything wrong with it, either in people or in literature[13]. I think that is going too far. It may not be the grave moral defect that Savile, Midgley and others make it out to be, but it isn't all fine either. In many uses of the word 'sentimental' (where it isn't merely used to mean: 'having to do with tender emotions'), it serves as a pejorative term. Sentimentality is a tendency to have and express tender feelings; but the word also carries an implication that those feelings or expressions are a bit over the top: *excessive* relative to the circumstances. A woman's grief over the death of her child, for example, would *not* be called sentimental, as it is clearly not excessive, but fully appropriate, to feel and express such grief, even very loudly and openly.

In short: sentimentality is an *excessive* tendency to have and express tender feelings. That means, the sentimentalist tends to *seek out* occasions for tender feelings; tends to have a *lower threshold* for having tender feelings; and tends to *prolong* the experience, to savour it fully and revel in it. Sentimentality cherry-picks suitable objects at which to direct beautiful feelings, and makes a meal out of it.

If this is correct, it is easy to see how sentimentality, although it is not intrinsically a falsifying attitude (cherry-picking, but not falsifying), can lead to the kind of misperception or

---

[13] Robert Solomon, 'In Defense of Sentimentality', *Philosophy and Literature*, 14, no. 2 (1990), pp. 304-323 (p. 305) [repr. in *Emotion and the Arts*, ed. by Mette Hjort & Sue Laver (Oxford: Oxford University Press, 1997].

misrepresentation described by Savile. If you are on the look out for suitable objects at which to direct your tender feelings, and if you have an excessive desire to find some, it is very likely that you cut some corners: that you eke out things in your imagination, or carefully overlook certain unsuitable details, in order to find what you're looking for.

Sometimes there is a grey area between convenient ignorance and self-deception. When after her fatal accident people got sentimental over Princess Diana, the ready object of their tender feelings was only her public persona: pretty and nice. Better knowledge of the real person might have made it more difficult to mourn her like a saint. Some, in this case, may have manipulated their image of her to suit their feelings, but others would simply not have been aware of more of her than those lovable innocent features. Their intense sympathetic response might still be censured as excessive (after all they had never met her) and naive, but it wouldn't involve any active falsification.

Compare the sentimentalist (who enjoys strong sympathetic feelings) with other types of people with a penchant for certain kinds for experience (as usefully listed by Mark Jefferson), such as: the thrill seeker; the melodramatic man (who enjoys and likes to emphasise the poignant and dramatic aspects of situations); or the wondrous man (who delights in the mysterious).

What they all have in common is a predilection for a certain kind of experience, which they seek out to an extent that others find excessive. And in all these cases there is a danger of self-deception: of pretending to be in a suitable situation for the desired emotion, when in fact that is not so. The thrill seeker may exaggerate to himself the danger of the situation he is in; the melodramatic man overstates and inflates the dramatic aspects of a situation; the wondrous man may project something mysterious into ordinary coincidences; and the sentimentalist may be tempted to deceive himself in order to indulge his tender feelings. But then again, they all may resist the temptation to cheat and find some honest gratification for their temperaments. The world is full of real dangers for thrill seekers; there is occasionally real drama in human relations; real mystery in scientific research; and certainly plenty of appropriate occasions for sympathetic feelings. None of these types is, as such, a self-deceiver; just as a drug addict is not a thief, even though drug addicts may often be likely to become thieves.

Let us now reconsider Oscar Wilde's idea that sentimentality means having emotions on the cheap. If sentimentality is an inclination to cherry-pick and dwell upon suitable objects of tender emotions, it will typically go for *easy options*. That is to say, trying to gratify a sentimentalist temperament you will naturally prefer clear-cut, straightforward simple cases, of thoroughly good, innocent creatures, where you can wholeheartedly sympathise, pity or rejoice. That is the sentimentalist's emotional taste: strong pure feelings, without any distracting admixtures or confusing complications (such as victims that are far from innocent and lovable; or good deeds done from selfish motives). And that, it seems to me, is what may strike us as 'cheap' about a sentimentalist's feelings. It is cheap and easy to sympathise extensively with innocent and lovable victims of evil villains. It is a lot more demanding to sort out one's feelings in less clear-cut cases. There is nothing morally wrong with the sentimentalist's preference for easy options; it may however appear a little immature, lacking in emotional sophistication. Thus, to call it cheap is probably more an aesthetic criticism.

Finally, the charge of sentimentality in literary criticism should certainly be seen as an aesthetic censure and not as a moral, or ethically motivated, one. It is implausible to hold that the aficionado of fairy tales or simple-minded romances fails to notice the unrealistic idealizations. It is rather a taste for simple-minded narratives involving pure good and evil, which neither real life experience nor realistic fiction can satisfy. Such a taste is not morally reprehensible, though we may find it rather crude and primitive. To more sophisticated, adult, literary interests, sentimental fiction is just boring (at least from a psychological point of view). It is more interesting, hence aesthetically more effective, to have psychologically less clear-cut and more complicated cases: where, for example, the suffering is not of an all-noble hero or a blue-eyed innocent girl, but of somebody with a more realistically mixed and warped character.

However, if I am right in thinking that the word 'sentimental' is used in this context as a pejorative term, it should be noted that not every stylized or idealized representation in literature should be called sentimental. Dickens's *A Christmas Carol*, for instance, is not meant to be realistic. It is a fairy tale, and in this genre simplified and idealized characterizations (such as those of the Cratchit family) are aesthetically quite appropriate. The death of little Nell (in *The Old Curiosity Shop*), by contrast, is certainly sentimental by our standards of a realist novel, though was perhaps less so in Victorian times.

It is worth noting that if 'sentimental' means excessive in expressing tender feelings, sentimentality must be relative, first, to the cultural standards of expressing one's feelings in a given society, and secondly, to the standards of literary taste, which may allow for genres that are self-consciously stylised and artificial, both linguistically and psychologically.

References

Jefferson, Mark, 'What is Wrong With Sentimentality?', *Mind*, 92, no. 368 (1983), pp. 519-529.

Midgley, Mary, 'Brutality and Sentimentality', *Philosophy*, 54, no. 209 (1979), pp. 385-389.

Newman, Ira, 'The Alleged Unwholesomness of Sentimentality', in *Arguing about Art*, ed. by Alex Neill & Aaron Ridley (London: Routledge, 1995).

Savile, Anthony, *The Test of Time* (Oxford: OUP, 1982).

Scruton, Roger, *Modern Culture* (London: Bloomsbury, 2000).

—, 'Kitsch and the modern predicament', *City Journal*, Winter 1999, https://www.city-journal.org/html/kitsch-and-modern-predicament-11726.html.

Solomon, Robert, 'In Defense of Sentimentality', *Philosophy and Literature*, 14, no. 2 (1990), 304-323 [repr. in Hjort & Laver (eds), *Emotion and the Arts*, Oxford: Oxford University Press, 1997].

Tanner, Michael, 'Sentimentality', *PAS, New Series*, 77 (1976-77).

Wilde, Oscar, *De Profundis* (1897), in *Plays, Prose Writings and Poems*, ed. by Terry Eagleton, Everyman's Library (New York: Alfred Knopf, 1991), pp. 543-650.

Garry L. Hagberg
THE MELODY AND THE SENTENCE
Wittgenstein's *Philosophical Investigations*, Culturally Interwoven Perception, and the Analogy Between Music and Words[1]

In the collection of remarks brought together as *Culture and Value*[2], we see that Wittgenstein wrote, in 1946, the following entry in his notebook:

> Schubert's tunes can be said to be full of *climaxes*, and this can't be said of Mozart's; Schubert is baroque. You can point to particular places in a tune by Schubert and say: look, that is the point of this tune, this is where the thought comes to a head.
>
> We can apply to the tunes by the various composers the principle: each species of tree is a 'tree' in a difference *sense* of the word. That is, don't be misled by the fact that we say all these are tunes. They are stages along a path which leads from something you would not call a tune to something else that you would equally not call a tune. If you just look at the sequences of notes and changes of key all these entities seem to be on the same level. But if you look at the context in which they exist (and hence at their meaning), you will be inclined to say: In this case melody is something quite different from what it is in that one (amongst other things, here it has a different origin and plays a different role).[3]

There is much compressed within this remark, but before considering that, I want to quote what Wittgenstein wrote

---

1   Special thanks to Jerrold Levinson for an extraordinarily helpful close reading that yielded many improvements to this essay.
2   Ludwig Wittgenstein, *Culture and Value*, trans. Peter Winch (Oxford: Basil Blackwell, 1980).
3   Wittgenstein, *Culture and Value*, p. 47.

immediately following the above, which is in its way remarkable for what we will uncover below as its conceptually reorienting power: 'The thought working its way towards the light'[4].

1. *The sense of a word: 'melody'*

So first: what can be said of one melodic genius cannot be said of another. That this is true is commonplace; why it is true is, as we shall see, a more interesting matter. In Schubert, one can indeed identify the point of a melodic statement, and one can indeed locate the precise place at which the idea comes to a head; that is, we can locate the place at which the melodic idea reaches its culmination and articulates fully what it has been developing. A summation in the form of a conclusion. With Schubert, because of the frequency of what Wittgenstein is identifying as melodic climaxes, one can do this fairly unproblematically, where one senses that periodic conclusions are easy to spot and straightforward. This is one mark of his compositional mastery and melodic gift – these melodic lines frequently combine ready accessibility with deep intelligence. Although Wittgenstein does not make the contrast here (he does mention Mozart), the case of Brahms is very different: the power of the melodic writing (on which Wittgenstein does comment in various places) is nothing short of tremendous, the melodic structure often profound. But the way in which we recognize the point of the melodic line is different: it is not easy to gesture to one single place and feel that one has in a circumscribed way captured, in a full and convincing or settled manner, the point of the melodic composition. One feels that one has to refer to a good deal more of what came before, and what will follow, to so much as identify

---

[4] In every interaction I had with my friend and philosophical compatriot Jean-Pierre Cometti – at various conferences in North America, at conferences in England and Europe, and at an unforgettable symposium he organized in Provence, where after the conference he and I retraced the footsteps of Cézanne while discussing Wittgenstein and the kinds of considerations I discuss here, he exemplified philosophy at its best: patient, always carefully listening and interacting, always looking closer, and – his most distinctive trait – slowing down in pursuit of the telling detail. I am honored to have had him as a friend and dedicate this essay to him as a small gesture of warm remembrance.

a single place where the point is made, where the melodic writing comes to a head. One also has to refer to what one might call the logic of the phrase – what it makes possible, what it closes off or turns away from, and how it seems to reach beyond by melodic implication what it explicitly states. And because of that, one has difficulty identifying such a point – precisely because it is not and cannot really be a *single* point.

Each species of tree is distinctive, and yet we call them all, generically, by the same word. So what is Wittgenstein's point here when the subject is melody and musical understanding? Wittgenstein thought as deeply as anyone about Frege's work on reference, and he thought as deeply as anyone about the issue, as he employs the term here, of *sense*. A moment's research shows that there are over six thousand species of trees, and one will find that they exhibit a vast range of 'behavior' in terms of growth and foliage, that they have been used to represent a vast range of political and religious ideas and events, that they are the sites and the instruments of major historical events. (Anne Frank's tree in Amsterdam; the tree just outside the Forbidden City where a just-escaped captive former emperor hanged himself; the tree under which the Buddha achieved enlightenment; trees as planted colonnades in landscape architecture; the deeply disturbing and morally hideous image of a tree in Billie Holiday's rendition of 'Strange Fruit'; countless others). Yet the word – the *single* word – 'tree', we tend to think, must refer to a single feature that all trees have in common and in virtue of which they are classified as trees; platonic essentialism, as Wittgenstein discussed throughout his work, manifests its conceptual impulses throughout our language, and more to the point, throughout our thinking about language. Without naming a single invariant essence, the word, we fear, would not have meaning, and with that background of thought, we could very easily be 'misled by the fact that we call all these tunes.'

Just as there are differing language-games[5], as Wittgenstein called them, where the word 'tree' will be situated in a highly variegated meaning-determining and reference-specifying

---

5   I discuss Wittgenstein's conception of a language-game and the way he employs it in Garry Hagberg, *Meaning and Interpretation: Wittgenstein,*

contexts, so there are analogues to language games in music – melodic language-games. The reason Wittgenstein brings in the issue of sense is that *actual* sense in the complex world of usage and human interaction is irreducibly complex, in such a way that reversion to the alleged essence at the philosophically imagined bottom of a word's meaning will yield incoherence and incomprehension, and not an immediate recognition of the deep truth of the matter with regard to meaning. Given the set of philosophical assumptions to which Wittgenstein is alluding, which I have just labeled 'platonism', the intertwined elements in a given context that would activate networks of connotations and associations, and that would determine the actual sense of the word as then used, would be regarded as circumstantial accretions layered over the universal 'signal' beneath all the 'noise'. Thus Wittgenstein's admonition, 'Don't be misled', means in this context: what one can feel impelled to call 'noise' *is* the signal, and to reverse them renders one meaning-blind.

Suppose then that I have a generic theory of melody: I assert that I have uncovered, beneath all the differentia, the necessary and sufficient conditions for a musical event to be a melody. The conditions that I list are: (i) a set of pitches that display a traceable contour; (ii) where that set of pitches exhibits an audibly discernible beginning; and (iii) where that set of pitches, at the close of the contour, exhibit an audibly discernible ending that conveys a sense of resolution. Something remotely like this may in effect be true (though not holding for mature Schoenberg, Webern, some Berg, and Gesualdo, among others), which would correspond to the truth of the fact that there are, after all, scientifically determinable conditions that make a given thing a tree. But in the case of melody, the parallel definition would in the end, after exhausting ourselves responding to counterexamples, be so heavily laden with qualifications that it would be unworkable and unusable as a *definition*, which was the idea motivating the attempt to find necessary and sufficient conditions in the first place. Wittgenstein sees all this within the

---

Henry James, and Literary Knowledge (Ithaca: Cornell University Press, 1994), pp. 9-44.

context of the passage above, and it is for this reason that he refers to 'stages along a path.'

Wittgenstein's remarks on the family-resemblance metaphor are very well known. The metaphor is designed not to replace one theory with another, but to break the hold of the platonic picture, to offer a changed way of seeing whereby classes do comprise members, but those members need possess no single property they all share and by virtue of which they are classified. This is put forward not as a contribution to ontology, but rather to the philosophical understanding of meaning. Not all trees are deciduous – some are; not all melodies exhibit my imagined three conditions – but some do. What follows from this – a fairly large matter, rightly understood – is that a grasp of those conditions is not a precondition for our understanding of the word or concept in use. Knowing the meaning of the word does not presuppose a grasp of such conditions.

'Melody', Wittgenstein is suggesting, is like this. There are, at one end of the continuum he is describing, random noises heard as a sequence of pitches that we would not accept as a melody (though such a sequence may suggest one by its interval skips) just as there are, at the other end, complexes of pitches we may recognize as a set but not as a melody (as in the theory of pitch classes). Everything that falls between these polar extremes may be acceptable as a melody, though there will probably also be ambiguous cases, that will be decided, not by appeal to an essential ingredient or set of conditions, but rather, by their connections to related cases, ones nearby along Wittgenstein's 'path'. It will be case-by-case reasoning that decides the case at hand, and that reasoning will proceed on the basis of precedent and analogy, and not by invariant word-meaning.

What Wittgenstein says next in the passage above also reaches out to broad issues, in this case to the powerful and often unwittingly assumed analogy between an analytical program in the philosophy of language and an analytical program in music. If we focus entirely on the sequences of notes and changes of key, 'all these entities seem to be on the same level.' That is to say, the delineation of what will be regarded as critically or interpretively relevant will be narrow, and in a manner perfectly parallel to the false ideal of the word that secures its meaning most by naming an invariant essence, whatever supplemental role the word may play in actual usage. 'Melody', on this misguided model, will be taken, on the linguistic side, to be a word with a unitary referent, and on the musical side, to signify an essence that properly allows only those criteria of evaluation and determinations of sense that apply with equal force and relevance to all other melodies. And this – a formalistic[6] analysis both motivated and justified by a reductive concept of a word – would end up eliminating the 'noise' that is in truth the signal. But then *why*, in the case of melody, can we say, 'in truth the signal'? This is in effect the import of Wittgenstein's next sentence, one that resonates with so much of his mature philosophy.

The sentence begins, 'But if you look at the context in which they exist'. Yet immediately against this thought, one might not unreasonably ask, how could a given entity, circumscribed by unambiguous entity-defining 'lines', requiring no boundary-imposing mental act on the part of the listener, be either changed or constitutively determined by anything outside of itself? That entity, as Bishop Butler famously averred, is already itself and not another thing. A sentence, the thought in immediate reaction to Wittgenstein's remark would continue, is a bounded linguistic entity contained unto itself, and a melody a musical entity parallel to that. That a sentence has its coherence, its meaning, and so its repeatable use across cases is, in a sense, accidental, for its meaning is *its* meaning. Thus a melody – a 'sentence' in music – should prove autonomous in the same way.

Wittgenstein had moved to a place in the philosophy of language and a degree of sophistication far beyond these simple pictures and reductive analogies, and his passage here depends on all that work on linguistic meaning. If each word in a sentence carried and contributed its invariant meaning, and if those words were assembled in accordance with syntactic rules, then coherence

---

6   'Formalism' can mean a number of different things; here I am referring to the most reductive version that would exclude all matters outside of the kind of structural analysis that remains wholly internal to the work so that from the analytical approach it appears that it could have arisen in or emerged from any cultural context whatsoever, or where the sense that the work exhibits is viewed as being exclusively 'inside out' and never, culturally speaking, 'outside in'.

would be achieved and meaning internally contained. And so a melody, with notes as word-analogues and if structured according to musical-syntactic regularities or norms, would also be coherent, with meaning internally contained. But neither is true to the facts of usage, in either linguistic or musical life. The heart of Wittgenstein's passage, and the line most resonant with his work in the philosophy of language in *Philosophical Investigations*, is given in parentheses: '(and hence at their meaning)'. And *hence*? That one word places him far from the line of thought above concerning sentential autonomy and its aesthetic analogue.

The point that the phrase 'and hence at their meaning' conveys is: a melody, like a phrase in speech, does not display within its own boundaries what we might on a two-part model picture as its fundamental content, which on that model we believe we see first, and then only subsequently, situate in the broader musical context surrounding it. Rather, on Wittgenstein's more radical and thoroughly anti-atomistic view, we do not see the melody for what it is either prior to or independently from the extensive compositional context within which it has a life, and only within which it has meaning. To truly perceive a melody is to grasp it as it occupies musical space within a larger sense-determining web of relations. And in a compositional context such relations are constitutive, not external – so 'hence' is precisely the right word. It is only on a misconstrual of what the word 'melody' means – in this case a mistaken belief in the ontological kind of thing to which the word 'melody' refers, along with the belief that it must refer to a single kind of entity, that would lead us to see the 'hence' clause as odd or surprising. The two-part model of melodic perception, and the directly corresponding two-part model of melodic understanding, is a simplifying myth born of the parallel misconception in linguistic perception and understanding. Freed of this model, we are able to see in music what Wittgenstein describes in his next line: that in one case the melody is something quite different from what it is in that one. But here again, he condenses substantial content in a subsequent parenthetical remark.

When Wittgenstein writes '(amongst other things, here it has a different origin and plays a different role)', he is acknowledging difference and its importance: philosophers have often looked for sameness, for fixity, for neatness of categories, underwritten by hidden essences. Wittgenstein, here thinking about musical understanding on analogy to linguistic understanding, sees philosophical progress as the reverse of this – as conceptual liberation from those narrowing presuppositions so that we can see what lies before us in a way true to its complexity, to lived experience, and to our established and evolving practices[7].

Seeing that one melody has a different origin from another can be a complex matter that involves fairly subtle relational comparisons. For example, a melody can emerge in a composer's work as itself the originary germ, where much that follows it unfolds as does the articulation of a range of implications in language. The structure of theme and variations constitutes a clear example of this. Or a melody can emerge as the top line of a given chordal or harmonic sequence voiced one way and not another way – that is, rather than harmonizing a melody, one in a sense 'melodizes' a harmony. Or a melody can emerge as an adjusted or imperfect transposition of an earlier melody; it is both like the original and different from the original. Or in serial or twelve-tone composition or baroque counterpoint, a melody can be inverted, or reversed, or both. These three melodic gestures have the same 'parent', and yet, while deeply structurally related, exhibit very different surface appearances.

Or a melody can from within itself draw from its own content and bifurcate into two planes, so that it both retains its integrity and yet still divides it (Johnny Mandel's classic song 'The Shadow of Your Smile' does precisely this[8]). Or a melody can in a sense compress the theme and variations structure into a single melodic line (the song 'Strangers in the Night' does this well). Or it can invert the usual relations between melody and harmony, so that the melodic movement is minimized to almost nothing, and yet that non-

---

7   On this point, see Wittgenstein *and the Creativity of Language*, ed. by Sebastian Sunday Grève and Jakub Mácha (London: Palgrave, 2015).
8   I mention this and the next few examples in memory of Jean-Pierre. At his beautiful home in the south of France his Gibson jazz guitar – for the cognoscenti, a nice sunburst 175 with low and smooth action, an instrument set up, like Jean-Pierre himself, for subtlety, not bombast – was always nearby, and he loved playing jazz standards from the American Songbook, which he did very well.

movement becomes interesting because each few repeated notes are harmonized differently – the negation of melody becomes, through reversal of roles, strong melody. (Antonio Carlos Jobim's "One Note Samba" is a study in this approach, and bossa nova not infrequently employs versions of this largely because the chromatic voice-leading in the harmony is usually written idiomatically on the guitar – which is still another kind of melodic origin.) And Wittgenstein concluded this passage with 'and plays a different role'. This too fans out into great and compositionally intricate complexity, but at one point in *Philosophical Investigations* Wittgenstein provides a list of some of the many things we can do in language other than describe[9], thus shaking his readers free of the grip of the definitional presupposition that description is both the essence and primary function of language. Melodies can assert, proclaim, question, answer, reinforce, look back, promise much, represent, motivate, show a way, develop an idea, establish a mood, inflect a mood, change a mood, redirect attention, summarize, expand upon, quietly close, and countless other things. And they will do so in such a way that the role they play is perceivable only in the expanded field or enlarged frame of the context, the sense-determining material that Wittgenstein's 'hence' accommodates. But as mentioned at the outset, the brief fragment following the passage we have considered thus far is remarkable in capturing yet still a different aspect of a melody and its life.

In the phrase 'The thought working its way towards the light', although this immediately follows the above passage, it is not specified whether the thought is verbal or musical. Tellingly, it does not matter for the truth of the remark. The parallel between language and music on which Wittgenstein is relying is implicit within the doubly directed word 'thought' as used here. A musical thought, especially in the hands of a genius, can in its way strive, can work its way through, can discover its various articulations, can endure change and transformation, can find its own reinvention, can accommodate change or experience transfiguration, can struggle to reassert itself against that change, can find itself in

---

[9] See Ludwig Wittgenstein, *Philosophical Investigations*, Revised 4th ed., ed. P. M. S. Hacker and Joachim Schulte, trans. G. E. M. Anscombe, P. M. S. Hacker, and Joachim Schulte (Malden: Wiley-Blackwell, 2009), §§ 23 & 27.

unfamiliar territory, can prove resourceful in that territory, can adapt, can reform, can suddenly retreat, can turn darker in mood – and a thousand other things. Think of the transformations within the musical argument or the musical logic of only the first movement of Beethoven's *Fifth Symphony*. All of this taken together is what any reference to the 'life' of a melody means: it is a melody working its way towards the light. Consider the finale of the *Ninth Symphony*. And by *its* way we refer to the unfolding musical logic of *its* implications, working toward full realization[10].

All of the foregoing, properly understand in the context of examples it would take a book to work through, is what 'melody' means. To reduce this to the imagined conditions listed above as a minimal definition would be to exclude content-contributing relations, roles, functions, and the contextual differentia that woven together make a given melody precisely what *it* is. Wittgenstein would insist that if someone then said, 'Well, I see all that, but I am after a unitary definition that truly defines the term and thus extracts the true essence, the signal from the noise', that person, under the influence of misleading governing analogies, is, as Wordsworth said of a particular approach to conceptual analysis, murdering to dissect[11]. As with 'tree', there are indeed importantly 'different *senses* of the word'.

2. Musical Thinking

In *Philosophical Investigations*, Wittgenstein writes:

> We do not analyze a phenomenon (for example, thinking) but a concept (for example, that of thinking), and hence the application of a word. So it may look as if what we were doing were nominalism. Nominalists make the mistake of interpreting all words as names,

---

10   For an incisive examination of issues directly related to those discussed here, see Jerrold Levinson, 'Musical Thinking', *Midwest Studies in Philosophy*, 27, no. 1 (2003), pp. 59-68 [repr. in Jerrold Levinson, *Contemplating Music* (Oxford: Oxford University Press, 2006).]
11   William Wordsworth, in his poem *The Tables Turned*.

and so of not really describing their use, but only, so to speak, giving a paper draft on such a description.[12]

If indeed we think of, or picture, all words (at an essential foundational level, despite what we then think of as surface-level variations) as names, we will naturally be led to picture meaning as a matter of ostensive definition. Wittgenstein's critique of this picture in *Philosophical Investigations* is widely familiar and well known, but it is worth pausing to consider the analogy to music. Under the influence of this analogy we will turn to the project of analyzing not the phenomena, but the concept, of melody, or harmony, or rhythm, or silence, or any other terminology embedded within a world of musical practices. The nominalists begin from the underlying presupposition that all words are at bottom names, and so they fail, as Wittgenstein says, to correctly describe their use. So what is at issue here for us? Wittgenstein writes in the next section a single sentence of enormous philosophico-linguistic power: 'You learned the *concept* "pain" in learning language'[13].

That is, we too easily tend to think of language as a system of words that grows one-by-one, and that we start our life in language by learning a single name-object relation. We then imagine that we add some more, learning each new word as a new connection between a sound and a thing[14]. On this view our first word may have been 'pain', as we make the association between that sound and the feeling of a bee-sting. But Wittgenstein's point is that it could not have proceeded in this simplified manner, precisely because the idea or pre-understanding (a thoroughly difficult matter itself) of a relation (an advanced concept itself) between (another advanced concept now involving a spatial metaphor) the inner sensation (and thus the concept 'sensation' would have to be in place, thus removing 'pain' as the first word) on which we focus (not an easy concept drawn from optics) our attention (part of a mental vocabulary) in order to identify (not a pre-given concept) the entity relying on an analogy between outward things

---

12 §383.
13 §384.
14 This is, of course, the Augustinian picture, with which *Philosophical Investigations* begins.

(also requiring prior basic-ontological understanding) and inward (now requiring that a kind of dualism be pre-understood) 'things' (depending on a knowledge of the extension of the material sense of the term to an immaterial sense).

In short, this approach is interestingly hopeless. We learned the concept 'pain' in learning language, or from a position already inside language, already equipped with a grasp of all the foregoing conceptual elements or tools. It is for this reason that the term 'holism' has been used in very general descriptions of Wittgenstein's larger conception of language. But be that as it may on that general level, what Wittgenstein is underlining here is the enormous complexity beneath and surrounding what we can falsely take to be the most simple and originating linguistic act imaginable. Or to summarize the point of *Philosophical Investigations*, § 384: no such *simple* act is truly imaginable.

Wittgenstein's example – one carefully chosen – in § 383 is that of thinking. If we took the word 'thinking' in the direct-referent terms discussed above in connection with the word 'melody', we would expect it to possess meaning by referring to a given state or mental process that all cases of thinking have in common and by virtue of which they are rightly categorized as thinking. But by analogy to the word 'tree' and to the word 'melody' above, were we to investigate at length many cases of what we would unproblematically and naturally call thinking in particular cases we would find a parallel range of diversity. But at present, it is the significance of the nominalist picture for music and its often-undetected influence that is important to bring out.

Wittgenstein referred above to the issue of the origin of a melody and to the importance of seeing differences under this heading. The simplest model of the origin of any melody that presents itself immediately to reflection is the nominalist picture of compositional thinking. That is, the origin of the melody would be a hermetic mental event private or internal to the mind of the composer. 'Thinking the melody' would thus be the name of a uniform psychic event that all melodies have in common as an internally contained cognitive origin. This picture is clarifying in its reductionism, simple, intellectually clean, internally bounded, universal in application – and profoundly false.

It is certainly true that composers think: as mentioned above, Wittgenstein mentioned with special emphasis the strength of the thoughts in Brahms. But 'thinking' does not reduce to any single event any more than does 'melody'. The situated phenomena of thinking *in situ* are, one might say, centrifugal rather than centripetal; the content of the cognition involved is at once relationally nested and culturally interwoven. Compositional thinking and the creation of melodies could itself be usefully seen as a Wittgensteinian language-game rather than an inward act of pure Cartesian cognition. David Pears captures the difference of approach very well:

> The shift from atomism to holism is just as important as the associated shift from depth analysis to description and experimental variation of our language-games. It does not stop us speaking of the structure of a concept like that of the ownership of sensations, but we do have to admit that this is a different notion of structure. There is no longer any implication that a complex concept is one that we must take to pieces and then subdivide the pieces, thus zeroing in on its final atomistic analysis. On the contrary, we mean that the concept has lateral connections radiating outwards in different directions, and it is the exploration of these lateral connections that will yield philosophical understanding.[15]

We can still speak of the 'ownership' of the musical idea, but this kind of ownership does not follow from a deeper truth concerning metaphysical psychological privacy. And as Wittgenstein suggests in many ways throughout his remarks on music, what is crucial is not atomistic analysis, but rather the seeing of a musical thought, a musical idea, a melodic invention, as an idea that radiates outward with lateral connections extending in different directions simultaneously. It is for this reason that a musical thought is relationally nested: first, it can be a melody that is the end result of a number of possible melodies and melodic fragments that were rejected in sequence, ultimately resulting in the melody that, for instance, Brahms retained to open his *Fourth Symphony*. That final melody is thus nested into, and in an important sense

---

15 David Pears, *The False Prison: A Study of the Development of Wittgenstein's Philosophy*, vol. 2 (Oxford: Oxford University Press, 1988), p. 256.

defined by and evolved from, what it is not or is not any longer. (Sketches, drafts, and preliminary scores and notebooks are interesting for this reason.) Second, the final melody before us can be informatively compared with other related but different melodies within the same composition or within a set of works or within the entire oeuvre of the composer. Third, the melody can be of its time, ahead of its time, or behind its time, and our ability to perceive these aesthetic aspects always depends on our ability to compare across cases – a melody's aesthetic aspects are not contained hermetically within what we think of as the melody itself. Fourth, a melody can assume its identity by comparison to others within a theme and variations structure, where the musical content of the melody, as created by the composer, requires cross-melody relations to be perceived in order to see it for what it is.

This list could easily continue, but consider just one more feature for now: a melody can be embodied in a manner belying the nominalist's pure-cognition model. Wittgenstein contrasts the experience of (a) imagining a melody purely quietly with (b) the common experience of imagining a melody by slightly clicking one's teeth together to define the melody's rhythm. And then one might recall: a composer can work by tapping out rhythms on a table, by humming it, by singing it, by starting it from a single pitch on an instrument, by playing part of it on that instrument, or by playing all of it. These are all stations on the way from what we might think of as pure or interior musical cognition to the sounding out of a full melodic idea on an instrument. I would expect that the great majority of cases of creative melodic thinking take place at many of the countless stops between the extremes.

And so melodic thinking is itself culturally enmeshed. The very idea of musical thinking in a psychic or cultural vacuum is disorienting, and here we return to a direct connection to the 'first-word' problem above. We learn the concept 'pain' in learning language; this is not explicable in terms of private word-referent associations that allegedly take place, because in every attempt to explain the first simple or atomistic associative act we quickly see that we have to know far too much too soon in order to so much as initiate the alleged mental act of naming. Relying on this unearthing of a falsely-modeled misunderstanding of language and the more realistic vision that supplants it, we can see that the same is true of melodic thought: we cannot genuinely imagine the case of a composer who thinks, within a private compositional interior, of a set of pitches that she has assembled as a melodic statement in any way isolated from a rich background and personal history of musical engagement. And that personal history will also necessarily take place within a culture, with the musical analogues to the word 'pain' learned within a holistic network or web. Simply stated: The idea of private musical thought is unintelligible. It is true that one could declare independence from a culture, a prevalent style, a set of cultural norms, or any form of prescriptive regulation. But that proclamation, like the word 'pain', is itself already within a culture, already within a larger network of relations that is required for its rejection.

Of thinking, Wittgenstein writes,

> I can know what someone else is thinking, not what I am thinking. It is correct to say 'I know what you are thinking', and wrong to say 'I know what I am thinking'.[16]

And it is here that he adds his famous parenthetical remark: '(A whole cloud of philosophy condenses into a drop of grammar.)'[17]

By insisting on what it is wrong to say, in reminding us of what we do and do not say, Wittgenstein is here shaking his readers free of the grip of the dualistic picture of interiority as a metaphysically kept secret. Although it would take a separate paper to examine the issue in even a preliminary way, what is especially important for present purposes – for rightly understanding compositional-melodic thinking – is that the melodic thoughts a composer has will occur within a public – or in Pears's sense, lateral – context. And that context will be the cultural-historical web within which those thoughts emerge and within which they have a life.

A moment later Wittgenstein writes: 'If I were to talk to myself out loud in a language not understood by those present, my

---

16 Wittgenstein, *Philosophical Investigations*, Philosophy of Psychology – a Fragment (Formerly Part II), §315.
17 *Ibid.*

thoughts would be hidden from them'[18]. What this remark does is to 'publicize' the private: we can use the concept of the hidden, but this is *in*, and not *prior to*, language, just as a composer may hide musical ideas and keep them hidden, but within a cultural and social setting that allows that use of 'hidden' to have meaning. That composer's melodic thinking – for Wittgenstein, primary examples of this are found in Haydn, Mozart, Beethoven, and Brahms – will be in what we can call, with due caution, the 'language' of music, and which, like language proper, will not be explicable in terms of originary ideas private to a single mind and metaphysically isolated from the world of musical practice. On the contrary, it is there that we can understand them as having, as Wittgenstein said in his remark, one origin or another, playing one role or another[19].

3. An Earned Freedom from the Reductionist Picture

Rush Rhees remarked at one point: 'Unless you do see what the connexion is between language and life, you will never see what understanding language is'[20]. Understanding language is not clairvoyance, not mind reading. If it were, it would be impossible, because those things are impossible. Yet we do occupy countless stations along the way from deep and profound understanding to complete non-understanding with misunderstanding lying somewhere in the middle of the continuum. This is true of our understanding of people, of their language, and of their music. As is clear from the remarks on these issues woven throughout his life's work, Wittgenstein saw these connections and parallels acutely, and as we have seen in the foregoing he saw the misleading power of the essentialistic picture of word meaning, the narrowing and blinding effect of a generalizing reductionism, and the false

---

18   Ibid., §317.
19   It is worth noting that Wittgenstein's musical diet was not entirely confined to the classical repertoire. On Ray Monk's list of Wittgenstein's favorite music, in addition to the composers mentioned here, we also find the cabaret singer Yvette Guilbert, a favored subject of Henri Toulouse-Lautrec and star of the Moulin Rouge.
20   Rush Rhees, *Wittgenstein and the Possibility of Discourse*, 2nd ed., ed. by D. Z. Phillips (Oxford: Blackwell, 2006), p. 130.

presuppositions of the nominalist model. These misbegotten models of the complex phenomena before us distort our view, and his conceptually clarifying work on language laterally reaches across to human understanding and musical understanding. So we might adapt Rhees's phrase: unless we see what the connection is between music and life, we will never understand what understanding music is. That connection is, of course, vast and intricate and could not be captured briefly; what a consideration of Wittgenstein's remarks on music and related work in *Philosophical Investigations* does is to bring to light the intellectual influences on thought that would obscure our view of, and openness to, that multifarious connection. A consideration of Wittgenstein's remarks exposes the etiology of misconception, where therapeutic philosophical work constitutes conceptual progress of a distinctive kind – a kind very different from that of essence-analysis.

In a book of Jean-Pierre Cometti's on Wittgenstein's philosophy of psychology, there is a chapter entitled 'The Invention of Interiority'[21]. The title itself performs this kind of therapeutic work: one may initially picture hermetic, metaphysically closed interiority as the first fact of human life. But referring to this picture of selfhood as *invention* immediately calls this presumption into question, and with it a number of parallel presumptions that fan out from it – including models or pictures of compositional or melodic thinking. We must *start* from relations, not from privacy.

So words, as we have seen in connection with the word 'melody' and the word 'pain', do not function or have their origin in the way the simplifying model suggests. Free of what Wittgenstein calls the nominalist's mistake, wherein all words are seen at bottom as names, one can then see the range of variation across the full span of usage. And for reasons Wittgenstein has uncovered, word meaning is not reducible either to private cognitive content on one model or to a specific invariant referent on the other. The 'cloud of philosophy' is made up of these models, often starting from a picture of metaphysical hiddenness[22]. Music as well as language,

---

21   Jean-Pierre Cometti, *Ludwig Wittgenstein et la philosophie de la psychologie* (Paris: Presses Universitaires de France, 2004).
22   See in this connection Norman Malcolm, *Nothing is Hidden* (Oxford: Blackwell, 1986).

freed of these pictures, allows us to see things as they are and to find leading, rather than misleading, analogies.

In *Philosophical Investigations*, § 527, Wittgenstein writes:

> Understanding a sentence in language is much more akin to understanding a theme in music than one may think. What I mean is that understanding a spoken sentence is closer than one thinks to what is ordinarily called understanding a music theme.

A subtle listener with a life's engagement with music, Wittgenstein does not ask generic questions of disorienting generality. His heart is in the details, where he finds both light and clarity. But then, how do we grasp what it is to understand a musical theme? He continues:

> Why is just *this* the pattern of variation in intensity in tempo? One would like to say: 'Because I know what it all means.' But what does it mean? I'd not be able to say. As an 'explanation', I could compare it with something else which has the same rhythm (I mean the same pattern). (One says, 'Don't you see, this is as if a conclusion were being drawn' or 'This is, as it were, a parenthesis', and so on. How does one justify such comparisons? – There are very different kinds of justification here.)

Knowing what it all means, and not being able to say, suggests two different things. First, it suggests that the 'language' of music is a language of its own, so that one cannot capture the content of the one in the vocabulary of the other. That is partly, or in particular cases, true – the 'language' one uses to explain interpretations, phrasing, long-form shaping, the timing of the arpeggiation of a chord, the breathing points, the fortissimo attack, the staccato phrasing, and countless other things, is *in* music itself. A teacher normally shows the pupil the phrasing by playing it, and perhaps by exaggerating it in order to better reveal the arc of the dynamics of a melodic passage. But there are countless cases as well where we do use language, as Wittgenstein does here in his imagined example, to explain or to show: 'this is as it were a parenthesis', 'this is an exclamation point', 'this ends with a question mark', and so on. Plus there are *gestural* explanations of this kind as well – they are embodied but not fully linguistic.

But second, knowing but not being able to say suggests that one's inability to say is in truth only the inability to say, to answer, *very succinctly* or in a reduced way – as if one is answering the question 'How high is Mont Blanc?' The true answer to such a question of musical meaning will be lateral in Pears's sense; it will reach out, and it will be full of connections of the kind mentioned above. It will not be an answer that refers to one isolated entity – it will be like the meaning of the word 'melody' and not the false picture of the meaning of the word 'melody'. That is why Wittgenstein turns immediately to the making of a comparison as the beginning of an answer. And the justifications for such comparisons, for instance, 'you will understand this passage better if you see it against the background of that', if the need for a justification arises, will be of very different kinds and as varied as is the concept of justification itself. 'Knowing what it all means', and 'Not being able to say', against how we might initially see the matter on first coming to it, are not in conflict. On the contrary, on Wittgenstein's capacious view of such matters, being able to say what it all means with a tightly circumscribed answer would only arouse suspicion concerning our claim to such knowledge. To actually answer such questions we would need to look comprehensively at the context, the network of relations, in which melodies (and harmonies and rhythms and the rest of musical life) exist. Or one could say: We would need to understand the significance of the 'hence' clause and employ it as an interpretive desideratum in the pursuit of meaning.

Following the above remarks, Wittgenstein writes:

> There might also be a language in whose use the 'soul' of the words played no part. In which, for example, we had no objection to replacing one word by a new, arbitrarily invented one.[23]

This is easy to understand and hard to explain, but it captures much of what is at issue here. We might think of the case of being told that we had to suddenly and permanently substitute the name of a person very dear and now lost to us with another arbitrarily imposed name in our thoughts, our memories, and our

---

23 Wittgenstein, *Philosophical Investigations*, §530.

speech. *That* we would find this to be an outrage, that we would strongly resist or refuse it, is clear; *why* we would do so is intricate and difficult to encapsulate, but it surely has to do with the 'soul' of that name. Wittgenstein continues in the next section:

> We speak of understanding a sentence in the sense in which it can be replaced by another which says the same; but also in the sense in which it cannot be replaced by any other. (Any more than one musical theme can be replaced by another.)
> In the one case, the thought in the sentence is what is common to different sentences; in the other, something that is expressed only by these words in these positions. (Understanding a poem.)[24]

Paraphrase in poetry, generic substitution, is heresy; defining melody generically, or suggesting that melodies in antecedent-consequent phrase structure function in the same way or play the same role or mean generally the same thing, is the same heresy in a different art. Poetry, works of art, music, are always 'only by these words'. So in the end, what should we say of understanding? Wittgenstein continues: 'Then has "understanding" two different meanings here? – I would rather say that these kinds of "understanding" make up its meaning, make up my *concept* of understanding'[25].

The concept 'understanding', it is emerging, is no more reducible, no more simple, than the concept 'melody'. And like the concept 'pain', we learned the concept 'understanding' in learning language, rather than as the name of an invariant mental process or event that is its trans-contextual or semantically fixed essence. The 'soul' of a work of art, or poetry, or music – like the soul of a word – is never discoverable in isolation.

References

Cometti, Jean-Pierre, *Ludwig Wittgenstein et la philosophie de la psychologie* (Paris: Presses Universitaires de France, 2004).

---

24 Ibid.., §531.
25 Ibid.., §532.

Hagberg, Garry, *Meaning and Interpretation: Wittgenstein, Henry James, and Literary Knowledge* (Ithaca: Cornell University Press, 1994).

Levinson, Jerrold, 'Musical Thinking', *Midwest Studies in Philosophy*, 27, no. 1 (2003), pp. 59-68 (repr. in Jerrold Levinson, *Contemplating Music* (Oxford: Oxford University Press, 2006).)

Malcolm, Norman, *Nothing is Hidden* (Oxford: Blackwell, 1986).

Pears, David, *The False Prison: A Study of the Development of Wittgenstein's Philosophy*, vol. 2 (Oxford: Oxford University Press, 1988).

Rhees, Rush, *Wittgenstein and the Possibility of Discourse*, 2nd ed., ed. by D. Z. Phillips (Oxford: Blackwell, 2006).

Sunday Grève, Sebastian and Jakub Mácha (eds), *Wittgenstein and the Creativity of Language* (London: Palgrave, 2015).

Wittgenstein, Ludwig, *Culture and Value*, trans. Peter Winch (Oxford: Basil Blackwell, 1980).

—, *Philosophical Investigations*, Revised 4th ed., ed. by P. M. S. Hacker and Joachim Schulte, trans. by G. E. M. Anscombe, P. M. S. Hacker, and Joachim Schulte (Malden: Wiley-Blackwell, 2009).

LITERATURE AS A KEY TO UNDERSTANDING WITTGENSTEIN

Tore Nordenstam
CLARIFICATION: WITTGENSTEIN'S *GEDICHTETE PHILOSOPHIE*

Wittgenstein's first book, a bilingual publication in 1922 entitled *Tractatus logico-philosophicus*[1], was an attempt to achieve maximal clarity in the notoriously unclear field of competing world views.

He characterized his method as clarification. The traditional fining agent in wine clarification is egg white. In Wittgenstein's first work, it is a combination of logic and literary form that serves as the egg.

In this work of Wittgenstein form and content are two sides of the same thing. In that respect it is more like poetry and other forms of literature and art than standard academic contributions to the field of philosophy. Some years later, he summed it up in the sentence, 'Philosophie dürfte man eigentlich nur dichten'[2]. *Philosophy should really only be done as poetry and fiction.*

Logical clarification and philosophy as poetry and fiction.

What is the place and rank of a work like that in the world of art and literature?

*

Wittgenstein's logical-philosophical treatise was published in a German scientific journal in 1921, and one year later it came

---

1   Ludwig Wittgenstein, *Tractatus Logico-Philosophicus* (London: Routledge & Kegan Paul, 1922).
2   *Wittgenstein's Nachlass: The Bergen Electronic Edition* (Oxford: Oxford University Press, 2000), Ms. 115, p. 30.

out as a book with the original German text on the left and an English translation on the right. The German text begins with the author's own matter-of-fact title, *Logisch-philosophische Abhandlung*, Logical-philosophical treatise (dissertation, article, essay). The English version begins with the title proposed by Cambridge philosopher George Edward Moore, *Tractatus logico-philosophicus*. The Latin title is reminiscent of Spinoza's *Tractatus theologico-politicus*, but similarities with philosophical works from the 17th century was not what Wittgenstein had in mind when composing the logical-philosophical treatise. As he emphasized in the preface to the book, he was totally uninterested in possible similarities with other works. When he referred to this work later in life, he always preferred the German title, which undoubtedly is more in harmony with the style which he considered essential for reaching his aims: short sentences with the right kind of rhythm and tone, with simple and striking expressions, as far as possible with everyday German words, with many analogies and metaphors – picture, limit, space, chain, building stones, network, hit the nail on the head, blurred, clarification, throw the ladder away after having climbed up on it, and so on.

Logisch-philosophische Abhandlung is an apposite title of a logical philosophical work which is similar to many other titles of articles and books in philosophy and logic. As the title of a literary work of art it is remarkably original.

*

That philosophy should only be done as poetry and fiction is a thought which occurs more than once in Wittgenstein's manuscripts from the 1930s. The first instances are to be found in a text from 1933: 'Die Darstellung der Philosophie kann nur gedichtet werden. Philosophie dürfte man eigentlich nur <u>dichten</u>'[3]. Since there is no direct equivalent in English to the poetically loaded word *dichten*, one has to resort to translations like 'The presentation of philosophy can only be done as poetry and fiction'

---

3   *Ibid.*

and 'Philosophy should really only be done as poetry and fiction'. I shall come back to this in a moment.

Wittgenstein returned to the poetry and fiction theme in another handwritten manuscript from 1933-34: 'Ich glaube meine Stellung zur Philosophie dadurch zusammengefaßt zu haben indem ich sagte: Philosophie dürfte man eigentlich nur <u>dichten</u>'[4]. *I think I have summed up my view of philosophy when I said: Philosophy should really only be done as poetry and fiction*[5]. In that passage, one also gets a couple of examples of Wittgenstein's search for the formulation which hits the nail on the head. He first wrote *müßte* (must), then replaced it with *dürfte* (should), and added the word *nur*.

Yet another variation on the theme of philosophy as poetry and fiction occurs in a manuscript from 1938 where Wittgenstein wrote that the philosopher ought to be a *Dichter*, a poet in a wide sense of that word. Here he used the word *sollte* (ought) instead of *müßte* or *dürfte*[6].

I think those statements are not just idle wishes but expressions of an aim that permeates Wittgenstein's philosophical writings from the logical-philosophical treatise in the 1910s to the philosophical investigations in the 1930s and the other manuscripts which together make up his *Nachlass*. It is the *Logisch-philosophische Abhandlung* considered as a literary work of art which is the object of the reflections in the following pages.

Before turning to Wittgenstein's *Abhandlung*, I want to draw attention to the words *dichten, Dichter, Dichtung* and their cognates. The sentence 'Philosophie dürfte man eigentlich nur dichten' exploits peculiarities of the German language which makes it difficult to find good equivalents in most other languages. (Swedish, Norwegian and Danish are exceptions to the rule.) *Dichter* (and the corresponding words in the mentioned Scandinavian languages) has a more solemn aura than the word 'author'.

---

4   *Wittgenstein's Nachlass*, Ms. 146, p. 50.
5   My translations of the German will appear in italics.
6   *Wittgenstein's Nachlass*, Ms. 120, p. 145.

Not all authors are referred to as *Dichter*, a designation which applies most of all to classics like Shakespeare, Goethe and Schiller. And it is not only a question of poetry. Also literary works in other genres can be referred to as *Dichtwerke*, literary works produced by authors who have the status of *Dichter*. Goethe's autobiographical *Aus meinem Leben. Dichtung und Wahrheit*[7] has been translated into English both as *Autobiography of Goethe: Truth and Fiction Relating to My Life*[8] and as *Poetry and Truth From My Own Life*[9]. *Dichtung* is poetry and fiction which presents that which cannot be expressed in the language of facts.

The words *dichten, Dichter, Gedicht* (poem) are related to words like *dicht, abdichten, verdichten, Dichte* and *Dichtigkeit* – tight, dense, compact; caulk, seal; solidify, consolidate; density; impenetrability. Translations of the sentence 'Philosophie dürfte man eigentlich nur dichten' into other languages are bound to be impoverished versions because of the peculiar semantical cluster *dicht, dichten, abdichten, verdichten, Dichte, Dichter, Gedicht, Dichtwerk, Dichtung* and so on. In addition, 'Philosophie dürfte man eigentlich nur dichten' has a special rhythm which contributes to the translation difficulties. If following Roman Jakobson one sees recalcitrance to translation as a sign of poeticness, then 'Philosophie dürfte man eigentlich nur dichten' is a very poetical statement.

Wittgenstein's poetical philosophy, his *gedichtete Philosophie*, is related to calmness, peace, serenity, tranquility. 'Die Beruhigung in der Philosophie tritt ein, wenn das erlösende Wort gefunden ist'[10]. *Calmness in philosophy arises when the redeeming word has been found*. And, in a later manuscript, 'Friede in den Gedanken. Das ist das ersehnte Ziel dessen, der philosophiert'[11]. *Thoughts at peace. That is what one longs for when philosophizing.*

*

---

7   Johann Wolfgang von Goethe, *Aus meinem Leben. Dichtung und Wahrheit* (Tübingen: in der J.G. Cottaischen Buchhandlung, 1811-1814).
8   Johann Wolfgang von Goethe, *Autobiography of Goethe: Truth and Fiction Relating to My Life* (Waiheke Island: Floating Press, 1848).
9   Johann Wolfgang von Goethe, *Poetry and Truth From My Own Life* (London: G. Bell's & Sons, 1913).
10 *Wittgenstein's Nachlass*, Ms. 115, p. 30.
11 Ibid., Ms. 127, p. 41.

In section 4.112 of the *Abhandlung* Wittgenstein described his aim with the help of a suggestive metaphor: 'Der Zweck der Philosophie ist die logische Klärung der Gedanken.' *The aim of philosophy is the logical clarification of thoughts.* Much like the English word 'clarification', *Klärung* is used in many contexts. Legal issues might stand in need of clarification; the technical aspects of building projects should always be clarified in due time; wastewater ought to be purified, hence the need for *Kläranlagen*, wastewater treatment plants; in winemaking clarification is one of the standard steps towards the finished product; and so on. The analogy with purification of fluids is emphasized by the last statement in 4.112: 'Die Philosophie soll die Gedanken, die sonst, gleichsam, trübe und verschwommen sind, klar machen und scharf abgrenzen.' Like wines which are more or less cloudy and dull before being clarified with the help of some fining agent, thoughts may stand in need of clarification: *Philosophy should make clear and delimit sharply the thoughts which otherwise are, as it were, opaque and blurred.* As already noted, the fining agent Wittgenstein used in the *Abhandlung* was formal logic combined with various literary means. In the 1930s and 40s he experimented with a battery of other such agents, but the goal remained the same – making unclear thoughts more clear.

One could also use one of the Greek words for cleansing and purification, catharsis, which might refer to the cleansing of another fluid, menstrual blood. Aristotle used it as a name for the clarification of feelings, which he regarded as the end goal of tragedy.

The logical-philosophical *Abhandlung* tries to do the same in the field of thoughts. The aim is cognitive catharsis.

*

When the theatre performance begins, one is met with a *Bühnenbild*, a stage view.

When one has passed the short preface and the main text of the treatise begins, one is met in section 1 with a *Weltbild*, a worldview: 'Die Welt ist alles was der Fall ist.' *The world is all that is the case.* The rest of the text is a commentary on that statement.

The commentary consists of a series of transformations of the first statement with subsequent elucidations. The basic pattern is *A is B, B is C* and so on. At the end, there is a short conclusion. The most important stations on the road to clarity are numbered 1, 2, 3 and so on. The key statements are followed by elucidations which are numbered on the basis of their 'logical weight', as Wittgenstein put it. The fewer the decimals, the greater the weight. Statements with decimals are like whisperings in the text. The decimal system of the logical-philosophical treatise can be compared to the way dynamical levels are indicated in music: *mp* (mezzopiano), *p* (piano), *pp* (pianissimo), *ppp* (piano pianissimo), and so on; and similarly on the forte side. If one lets the treatise begin moderately soft (*mp*), the passages with five decimals will be like *ppppp*. Tchaikovsky went even further in a passage in his sixth symphony, where he indicated *pppppp*. Wittgenstein regarded the numbers as an essential part of the work and firmly rejected a proposal to leave them out. 'Only the numbers make the book perspicuous and clear', as he put it in a letter to the publisher Ludwig von Ficker in 1919[12]. Without them, it would become 'an incomprehensible jumble'.

Übersichtlichkeit and *Klarheit* was what Wittgenstein strived for both in the logical-philosophical treatise and in the philosophical investigations in the 1930s.

The logical-philosophical treatise is an invitation to take part in a reflective walk that begins at station 1, the statement that the world is all that is the case. Station 2 is the statement 'Was der Fall ist, die Tatsache, ist das Bestehen von Sachverhalten' (*What is the case, the fact, is the existence of states of affairs*), and proceeds to 'Das logische Bild der Tatsachen ist der Gedanke' (*The logical picture of the facts is the thought*), 'Der Gedanke ist der sinnvolle Satz' (*The thought is the meaningful sentence*), and 'Der Satz ist eine Wahrheitsfunktion der Elementarsätze' (*The sentence is a truth-function of the elementary sentences*). After that one comes to a statement about the general form of truth-functions and sentences, and the walk ends at station 7, 'Wovon man nicht sprechen kann, darüber muß man schweigen' (*What one cannot speak about, of that one must be silent*).

---

12 Ludwig Wittgenstein et. al., *Briefe an Ludwig von Ficker* (Salzburg: Brenner-Studien Bd. 1, O. Müller, 1969), p. 103.

Wittgenstein's contributions to logic and the metaphysics he constructed on the basis of formal logic have provoked a huge amount of secondary literature. But that is not my concern in this essay. What I am interested in here is the question of what it might mean to say that the logical-philosophical treatise is a *Dichtwerk*, a piece of poetical philosophy. *Gedichtete Philosophie* – what is that? Are there any other works which it can be compared with? Where on the palette of literary genres should one place a work like that? In the preface to the treatise Wittgenstein explains that it is not a *Lehrbuch*. It is not a textbook. A philosophical *Dichtwerk* which is not a *Lehrbuch*, what is that? Reflection on rhythm and tempo will pave the way for an answer.

*

The difference between Wittgenstein's handling of the question about the nature of the world and other *Weltanschaung* texts is the limitation to that which is logically necessary. 'In der Logik ist nichts zufällig' (2.012). 'Etwas Logisches kann nicht nur-möglich sein' (2.0121). *In logic nothing is accidental. Something logical cannot be only-possible*, which is another way of saying that it is necessary.

According to the *Abhandlung* we must accept that the world is all that is the case and that one must be silent of what one cannot speak about, since that is necessarily so. But in addition to saying something about necessities, those sentences are ambiguous in a way which gives them a floating character. One could call them oscillating sentences.

The conclusion of the treatise can be taken as a tautology, a trivially true statement: we can't speak about what we can't speak about. But the formulation can also be used to express something that is far from necessary, for instance, that something is so bad that it had better be swept under the carpet. M.A. Numminen's musical rendering of some of the sentences of the logical-philosophical treatise is a good example. 'Wovon man nicht sprechen kann, darüber muß man schweigen' can be read like a military march: '<u>Wo</u>von <u>man</u> nicht <u>sprechen</u> <u>kann</u>, darüber <u>muß</u> man <u>schweigen</u>'. One of my friends who once attended a

Numminen performance in Innsbruck reports that many in the audience walked away when the final sentence of the treatise was performed in a parodic fashion accompanied by the sound of tramping boots. In Austria much was swept under the carpet when the Greater Germanic Reich of the German Nation came to an end after its time on earth.

What the last sentence of the treatise suggests without saying so in so many words is that the most important things in life, including ethics, belong to the realm we cannot speak about. The persuasiveness of 'Wovon man nicht sprechen kann, darüber muß man schweigen' depends both on the oscillation between necessity and contextual dependence and on the fact that it comes as no surprise at all. There is an almost identical formulation in the preface.

The message of a truism like *'What one cannot speak about, of that one must be silent'* depends upon the context in which it is used and on how it is performed. Variations of rhythm and tempo might lead to very different meanings. As Wittgenstein put it in a manuscript from 1947: 'Sometimes a sentence can only be understood when one reads it in the <u>right tempo</u>. All my sentences are to be read <u>slowly</u>'[13]. In music one uses tempo designations like *lento, adagio, allegro* and so on. A suitable tempo for the logical-philosophical treatise as a whole would be *Nachdenklich*, thoughtfully.

But there are many ways of reading 'Wovon man nicht sprechen kann [...]' slowly and thoughtfully. One can e.g. read it slowly and thoughtfully, moderately soft with diminishing loudness (diminuendo), and with small variations between stressed and unstressed syllables: '<u>Wo</u>von man <u>nicht</u> sprechen <u>kann</u>, darüber <u>muß</u> man <u>schweigen</u>'. The necessity of being silent regarding that which one cannot speak about is emphasized by stressing the words '*nicht kann*' and '*muß*'.

With that rhythm the sentence comes close to a classical hexameter line, a verse with six feet which one finds in works from Homer to Klopstock and Goethe and Mörike and many others, especially in German literature in the 18th and 19th centuries. It is almost a classical hexameter line, but it fails to fulfill the traditional

---

13   *Wittgenstein's Nachlass*, Ms. 134, p. 76.

demand that the penultimate foot must be dactylic. The virtue of my translation of the conclusion of the logical-philosophical treatise is that it preserves the rhythm of the original if read in the right way.

Works like Lucretius's *De rerum natura*[14] and Manilius's *Astronomica*[15] are classical examples of hexameter texts. We have arrived at the corner of literature called 'Didactic Poems'.

*

The *Lehrgedicht* tradition led a dwindling existence in the 19th century, but it did not disappear completely. There are examples also from the 20th century, e.g. Ezra Pound's *ABC of Reading* (1934)[16]. Pound's magnum opus, *Cantos* (1915-1962) is perhaps the best example of a modern didactic poem, in which reflections on economy, government and culture play an important role[17]. See the informative article *Didactic poetry* in *The Princeton Encyclopedia of Poetry and Poetics*[18], which also mentions Kafka's parables in this context. One of Bertolt Brecht's projects was a didactic poem on the nature of man, in which he intended to treat of the unnatural nature of bourgeois circumstances in the same respectable verse form as Lucretius's *On the nature of things*. The work was not completed, but he wrote some drafts, including several versions of the text which was to be the core of the whole, *Manifest der Kommunistischen Partei*[19].

It is, I suggest, against the background of that venerable literary tradition that Wittgenstein's first literary work of art, the logical-philosophical treatise, should be seen.

---

14 Titus Lucretius Carus, *De rerum natura* (Oxford: Oxford University Press, 1947).
15 Manilius, *Astronomica* (Cambridge, MA: Harvard University Press, 1977).
16 Ezra Pound, *ABC of Reading* (New Haven, CT: Yale University Press, 1934).
17 Ezra Pound, *Cantos* (New York, NY: New Directions, 1996).
18 *The Princeton Encyclopedia of Poetry and Poetics: Fourth Edition*, ed. by Roland Greene (Princeton, NJ: Princeton University Press, 2012), pp. 361-364.
19 Bertolt Brecht, *Werke: Grosse kommentierte Berliner und Frankfurter Ausgabe*, vol. 15 (Frankfurt am Main: Suhrkamp Verlag 1993), pp. 120-157.

At this juncture, I take the liberty of quoting from the lucid entry entitled 'Didactic Poem' in the first edition of the classical Swedish encyclopedia, *Nordisk familjebok* (1886):

> Lärodikt or didactic poem, a versified account of some topic from the fields of morals, spiritual life, the professions, science or art. [...] In the 18th century, when the pseudo-classical taste along with considerations of utility reigned in literature, the didactic poem was cultivated as one of the highest forms of poetry. Thus one sang of e.g. beekeeping and sericulture, the dressage of hunting dogs, navigation, the art of translation, the game of chess, syphilis, wool, health fountains, diatetics, astronomy, the immortality of the soul, education, and so on. For the aesthetic culture of the 19th century that kind of didactic poem has only got the value of historical curiosity.[20]

The anonymous author of the dictionary article contrasts the didactic utility literature with the truly poetic contributions to the genre:

> A genuinely didactic poem is one in which thoughts flow from a turbulent poetic soul that strives for clarity and deliverance through pronouncing them.

As examples the dictionary article mentions a number of works by authors like Hesiod, Parmenides, Lucretius, Vergil, Horace, Ovid and others. Lucretius, in particular, seems to be what the author of the article had in mind when referring to the turbulent poetic soul that strives for clarity and deliverance. *De rerum natura* is said to be 'genuinely poetic in virtue of its enthusiasm'. The list of didactic poets in more recent times includes names like Boileau, Pope, Young, Stiernhielm and Leopold. In spite of his enormous prestige in the literary world of the 19th century Johann Wolfgang Goethe is not referred to in the dictionary article, maybe because of his rejection of the view that the didactic poem is a genre in its own right. Like Wordsworth, he believed that all poetry has

---

20 *Nordisk familjebok. Konversationslexikon och realencyklopedi*, Tionde bandet. Lloyd - Militärkoloni (Stockholm: Gernandts boktryckeri-aktiebolag, 1886), pp. 443-444.

something to teach us[21]. But as we shall see in a moment, there are good reasons to take Goethe into account when searching for the literary and philosophical background of Wittgenstein's *Abhandlung*.

It was the rhythm of the statements 'Wovon man nicht sprechen kann, darüber muß man schweigen' and 'Philosophie dürfte man eigentlich nur dichten' which led me to the didactic poetry tradition. And it was the rhythm of 'Die Welt ist alles was der Fall ist' which led me to the short poem which begins with the words 'Über allen Gipfeln ist Ruh'. As it turned out, both leads went in the same direction.

*

It was on an evening in September 1780 that Goethe wrote the first version of the poem, with a lead pencil on a wooden wall in a cottage at the top of the mountain Kickelhahn some forty miles or so from Weimar. There one could read his graffito until the cottage burned down in 1870. The original had no title. When he published a revised version of it in his collected works 35 years later, Goethe placed it after a poem entitled *Wandrers Nachtlied* (Wanderer's Night Song), and gave it the title *Ein gleiches* (One more). For that reason it is often called *Wandrers Nachtlied II* (e.g. in Schubert's version of it).

> Ueber allen Gipfeln / ist Ruh',
> In allen Wipfeln / Spürest Du

---

[21] In the article 'Über das Lehrgedicht' Goethe defended the view that all poetry is didactic: 'Alle Poesie soll belehrend sein, aber unmerklich; sie soll den Menschen aufmerksam machen, wovon sich zu belehren wert wäre; er muß die Lehre selbst daraus ziehen, wie aus dem Leben.' *All poetry should be didactic, but inconspicuously so; the reader himself must extract the teaching from it, as from life* (Johann Wolfgang von Goethe, *Schriften zur Literatur* (Berlin: Akademie-Verlag, 1970), p. 69). Goethe expressed an attitude which led to the virtual disappearance of the didactic poem as a genre of its own in the course of the 19th century. William Wordsworth had proposed a similar view already in the beginning of the 19th century in the preface to *Lyrical Ballads with Pastoral and other Poems* (London: T.N. Longman and O. Rees, 1802).

Kaum einen Hauch; / Die Vögelein schweigen im Walde.
Warte nur! Balde / Ruhest du auch.[22]

It is not possible to preserve all the relevant features of this dense poem in translations into other languages. Here is Henry Wadsworth Longfellow's compromise from 1845:

O'er all the hill-tops / Is quiet now,
In all the tree-tops / Hearest thou
Hardly a breath; / The birds are asleep in the trees:
Wait; soon like these / Thou too shalt rest.[23]

At the same time, in 1780, Goethe started thinking of a great project which was intended as a synthesis of his scientific research and his work as a *Dichter*. The working title was *Roman über das Weltall*, a novel about the cosmos. The aim was to present the whole universe in literary form, going from inorganic nature through the plants and animals up to the level of man. Like Brecht's project about the unnaturalness of bourgeois life, Goethe's great project did not lead to the envisaged product. He wrote a couple of poems on the metamorphosis of plants and animals, and in his capacity as a natural scientist he spent years and decades amassing a large collection of minerals which was to be the solid scientific basis for the planned grand work. If one allows oneself to be anachronistic for a moment, one could regard the formulation 'Roman über das Weltall' as an early contribution to conceptual art, and the unremitting scientific fieldwork could be viewed as a performance where the activity itself was the work of art.

Über allen Gipfeln can be read in several ways: as a contemplation on nature, a poem about eternal rest, a text on the place of man in the cosmos, or the consummate version of the novel about the universe which Goethe dreamed of[24]. The passage from the

---

22   Johann Wolfgang von Goethe, 'Ein gleiches', *Goethe's Werke*, vol. 1 (Tübingen: in der J.G. Cotta'schen Buchhandlung, 1815), p. 99.
23   Henry Wadsworth Longfellow, *The Complete Poetical Works of Longfellow* (Cambridge, MA: The Riverside Press, 1893), p. 617.
24   Sigrid Damm, *Goethes letzte Reise* (Frankfurt am Main und Leipzig: Insel Verlag, 3. Auflage, 2014), p. 130.

inorganic world to the plants and animals and man is presented with unbeatable brevity, leading to a state which can be described with words like repose, serenity and peace of mind.

Lucretius's didactic poem *On the nature of things* was intended to lead to precisely that kind of mental state – peace of mind, tranquility, ataraxia – based on Epicurus's atomistic philosophy. Goethe's novel about the cosmos can be seen as a modern version of the classical didactic poem, based on recent scientific research, including the author's own mineralogical investigations. And Wittgenstein's logical-philosophical treatise can be seen as a modernist version of the classical didactic poem, based on recent advances in the field of logic, including the logical investigations carried out by the author himself, like the works of Lucretius and Goethe intended to lead to clarity and thoughts at peace.

In literary works of art one does not usually find such things as notes, bibliographies and lists of sources. The logical-philosophical treatise is no exception to the rule. But the first few sentences indicate what it is all about. Metrically the first sentence is like the beginning of *Über allen Gipfeln*, except for the fact that the rhythm is rising in the first case and falling in the second case. *Über allen Gipfeln* begins with a landscape view which opens on what one might describe as cosmic contemplation. The *Abhandlung* begins with a worldview which looks toward philosophical reflection on the nature and meaning of the world. Goethe does not argue in *Über allen Gipfeln*, and Wittgenstein does not argue in the logical-philosophical treatise. He presents suggestively formulated proposals and hopes that the benign reader will accept the suggestions and continue to the next station. He rarely considers the views of other thinkers. But in the second sentence, 1.1, there is a clear rejection of an alternative view of the world: the world is the totality of facts, not of things. The view he rejects is obviously the picture of the world which Lucretius presented in *De rerum natura*. That that is so is supported by sentence 1.13: *The facts in logical space are the world*. According to Epicurus and Lucretius the world consists of things which are made up of atoms moving around in empty space. The metaphorical expression 'logical space' becomes more understandable when one sees it as an alternative to the physical space which Lucretius operated with and looks toward constructing a worldview on the basis of recent logic, which is precisely what Wittgenstein does in the logical-philosophical treatise.

That Wittgenstein treated of metaphysical, logical and ethical themes in the same work has confounded some philosophers. A logician who presents an alternative to Epicureanism could hardly have done it in another way. Lucretius's presence is very clear in the concluding whisperings from 6.41 to 6.54, which deal with the meaning of the world and the nature of life and death. That death is not an event in the world (6.4311) is precisely what Lucretius found in his exposition of the Epicurean worldview. And in both Lucretius and Wittgenstein understanding the nature of the world issues in calm and peace. It is a calmness beyond words and music. This kind of contemplative tranquility does not lead to passivity and retreat from the world. In both Lucretius and Wittgenstein understanding the nature of the world leads to an active life in a spirit of simplicity.

*

The beginning of the 20th century was the time of the great modernistic experiments in painting, music, literature, dance and theatre. To clarify where in this chaotic landscape the logical-philosophical *Abhandlung* might belong comparisons with the visual arts is a good starting-point. At the same time as Wittgenstein completed the treatise during his years as a volunteer in the First World War Piet Mondrian worked incessantly on his great project – to liberate art, architecture, music, city planning and human life from all hindering traditions, by developing new forms of expression heralding a new life in a new world[25]. Mondrian was first of all a painter. In his production from the 1910s to the beginning of the 1920s one can follow the dismantling process which led to his mature style, neoplasticism, in which the means of expression are limited to horizontal and vertical stripes in black and quadrangles of different sizes in a colour scale which

---

25   Harry Holtzmann, ed., *The New Art – The New Life. The Collected Writings of Piet Mondrian* (London: Thames and Hudson, 1986).

consists of the basic colours red, blue and yellow plus shades of white. Mondrian regarded the horizontal and vertical stripes and the selected colors as visualizations of the fundamental forces and elements in the world. All that which Wittgenstein referred to as accidental and only-possible was to be eliminated. The result is usually called abstract art.

Wittgenstein's logical-philosophical work of art is the result of a similar dismantling process in the field of worldviews which led to the elimination of all representative components in the form of narratives, myths and descriptions of landscapes, persons and things in physical space. The result could be called *abstrakte Dichtung*, abstract poetry, in a wide sense of that word.

A hundred years after the creation of this work it continues to fascinate new readers not least because of its double citizenship – it is both an essay treating of logical and philosophical themes and a literary work of art. To understand it as a literary work of art means to place it in an acoustic chamber with special resonances. To understand it as a contribution to logic and philosophy means to place it in other contexts with other resonances. That the work belongs to both contexts at the same time gives rise to shimmering effects of a very special kind.

To construct a worldview on the basis of the propositional and predicate calculi in the form of a prose work which lies in the prolongation of the didactic poetic tradition and to combine clarification in the field of *Weltanschauungen* with original work in the field of mathematical logic is a rather breathtaking enterprise. But the author succeeds in holding it all together through the structure of the work (the passage from 1 to 7), the style (lapidary sentences, metaphors, simplicity of expression, skillful use of classical rhetorical devices), and the dynamics of the work (the different levels of whisperings). My conclusion is that it is high time to include the logical-philosophical treatise in the modernist literary canon.

*

The import of the statement that the world is the totality of the facts depends upon how one regards *facts*. It turns out that the author of the logical-philosophical treatise presupposes a sharp distinction between facts and values. For those who consciously or unreflectively make a distinction of that kind it cannot come as a surprise that all values worth their name must lie outside the world (6.41). In the 1930s Wittgenstein suggested that the philosophical uses of words like 'knowledge', 'being', 'object', 'I', 'proposition', 'name' are based on confusions which can be clarified by bringing the words back to their everyday usage[26]. He could have added such notoriously troublesome words as 'body', 'mind', 'fact' and 'value'. Clarification of wine cannot be done once and for all, it has to be done every year. Purification of wastewater must be done all the time. Philosophical clarification is a never-ending story.

References

Brecht, Bertolt, *Werke: Grosse kommentierte Berliner und Frankfurter Ausgabe*, vol. 15 (Frankfurt am Main: Suhrkamp Verlag 1993).
Damm, Sigrid, *Goethes letzte Reise* (Frankfurt am Main und Leipzig: Insel Verlag, 3. Auflage, 2014).
Greene, Roland (ed.), *The Princeton Encyclopedia of Poetry and Poetics: Fourth Edition* (Princeton, NJ: Princeton University Press, 2012).
Goethe, Johann Wolfgang von, *Aus meinem Leben. Dichtung und Wahrheit* (Tübingen: in der J.G. Cottaischen Buchhandlung, 1811-1814).
—, *Autobiography of Goethe: Truth and Fiction Relating to My Life* (Waiheke Island: Floating Press, 1848).
—, 'Ein gleiches', *Goethe's Werke*, vol. 1 (Tübingen: in der J.G. Cotta'schen Buchhandlung, 1815).
—, *Poetry and Truth From My Own Life* (London: G. Bell's & Sons, 1913).
—, *Schriften zur Literatur* (Berlin: Akademie-Verlag, 1970).
Holtzmann, Harry (ed.), *The New Art – The New Life. The Collected Writings of Piet Mondrian* (London: Thames and Hudson, 1986).
Longfellow, Henry Wadsworth, *The Complete Poetical Works of Longfellow* (Cambridge, MA: The Riverside Press, 1893).
Lucretius Carus, Titus, *De rerum natura* (Oxford: Oxford University Press, 1947).
Manilius, *Astronomica* (Cambridge, MA: Harvard University Press, 1977).

---

26 Ludwig Wittgenstein, *Philosophische Untersuchungen/Philosophical Investigations* (Oxford: Basil Blackwell, 1953), p. 48.

Nordisk familjebok. Konversationslexikon och realencyklopedi, Tionde bandet. Lloyd - Militärkoloni (Stockholm: Gernandts boktryckeriaktiebolag, 1886).

Pound, Ezra, *ABC of Reading* (New Haven, CT: Yale University Press, 1934).

—, *Cantos* (New York, NY: New Directions, 1996).

Wittgenstein, Ludwig, *Tractatus Logico-Philosophicus* (London: Routledge & Kegan Paul, 1922).

—, *Philosophische Untersuchungen/Philosophical Investigations* (Oxford: Basil Blackwell, 1953).

—, *Wittgenstein's Nachlass: The Bergen Electronic Edition* (Oxford: Oxford University Press, 2000).

Wittgenstein, Ludwig et. al., *Briefe an Ludwig von Ficker* (Salzburg: Brenner-Studien Bd. 1, O. Müller, 1969).

Wordsworth, William, *Lyrical Ballads with Pastoral and other Poems* (London: T.N. Longman and O. Rees, 1802).

Allan Janik

ART, CRAFTSMANSHIP AND PHILOSOPHICAL METHOD ACCORDING TO WITTGENSTEIN

> [Philosophy for Wittgenstein] was a craft, a discipline [...] and its value consisted in its being well done. So one should do it well and not preach about it: [...] showing not saying was important. Like all crafts, its exercise at its highest produces beauty, a beauty which requires an intellectual effort to grasp...
>
> Brian McGuinness[1]

1. *Style and Idea in Wittgenstein's Works*

A philosophical style like Wittgenstein's, eschewing conventional arguments, employing in their place aphorisms, thought experiments, unanswered questions etc., with its own peculiar kind of beauty, is rare among philosophers generally and unique to him among analytic philosophers. Moreover, that style is intimately linked to his goal in philosophy, eliminating our tendency to pose questions about the nature of meaning, intention, knowledge, etc. in the manner of traditional metaphysics and epistemology. Further, the very requirement of dissolving our need to pose such questions once and for all confers its uniqueness on Wittgenstein's style of philosophizing.

Yet that uniqueness is a puzzling uniqueness, so puzzling that in the course of the last half of the 20th century Wittgenstein has gone from being the very epitome of a hard-nosed logical positivist to a subversive post-modern pseudo-philosopher in

---

[1] Brian McGuinness *Wittgenstein, A life: Young Ludwig* (London: Duckworth, 1989), p. 77.

the eyes of many analytic philosophers. The latter have come to realize, thanks to philosophers like Richard Rorty[2], that the similarities between, say Wittgenstein and Heidegger, which have long been noted in the literature, are, indeed, not accidental, but a sign that Wittgenstein was never really part of analytical philosophy at all.

At the same time Wittgenstein's intense interest in aesthetic matters as well as his assertion that ethics and aesthetics are one have been taken, together with the striking house he built for his sister, along with that peculiar style, to imply that his deepest intellectual commitments lay outside philosophy in a religiously-inspired concept of art that would replace traditional philosophy. While there is a great deal of truth in this view, it is by no means the whole truth.

Brian McGuinness has given us the reason: Wittgenstein approached philosophy as neither a classical modern theorist nor a post-modern artist-ironist anti-theorist but as a craftsman. The thesis to be developed here is that the attitude of the craftsman, as opposed to the artist, is perhaps the most fundamental aspect of his concept of philosophy and thus crucial to understanding both Wittgenstein's conception of philosophy and his view of art, including his own architecture. So our questions are: where does this unorthodox 'deflationary' view of philosophy arise? How does it determine his concept of clarity? How does it determine his relation to art? What is the relationship between art and philosophy in Wittgenstein? All of this has a great deal to do with Wittgenstein's philosophical debt to Heinrich Hertz which is the key to understanding the peculiarities of Wittgenstein's concept of philosophy, his philosophical style and its relation to art[3].

---

2   Richard Rorty, *The Consequences of Pragmatism* (Minneapolis: University of Minnesota Press, 1982).

3   I refer to Wittgenstein's works parenthetically in the text as follows. Ludwig Wittgenstein,
PI with paragraph number, *Philosophical Investigations*, trans. by G.E.M. Anscombe (Oxford: Basil Blackwell, 1958);
CV with page number, *Culture and Value*, trans. by Peter Winch (Chicago, University of Chicago Press, 1980);
F with letter number, *Briefe an Ludwig von Ficker*, ed. by G.H. von Wright (*Brenner Studien*, 1 (Salzburg: Otto Müller, 1969)),

2. Heinrich Hertz: philosophy as 'showing' on the basis of perspicuous contrasts

One of the many puzzles surrounding Wittgenstein is his disavowal of his own originality. It seems absurd that such a departure from the traditional way of doing philosophy as the work of the mature Wittgenstein represents could be anything but highly original. Nevertheless, Wittgenstein consistently denied that he was an original thinker. Only recently in the course of re-evaluating Heinrich Hertz's philosophy of science have we been able to grasp the sense of Wittgenstein's remarks[4].

In stark contrast to Ernst Mach and the Vienna Circle, which has been up till today erroneously taken to be the only rigorous approach to the philosophy of science à l'epoque, Heinrich Hertz developed a method of eliminating conceptual confusions in physics to rival theirs. Whereas the Vienna Circle proposed to deal with the problem of empty abstractions like 'absolute space, time and motion' or 'force' in Newton's physics on the basis of a radical, purging, purification of language, Hertz proposed something considerably more subtle on the basis of a more complex conception of what a presentation of a physical theory actually involves. Whereas Mach & Co. were content to evaluate presentations of theories on the basis of their empirical correctness, logical coherence and simplicity of presentation, Hertz complicated the matter by posing the question 'simple for whom?' Thus, in addition to their emphasis upon factual adequacy and structural elegance Hertz suggested that rhetorical appropriateness was

---

Fr with letter number, 'Gottlob Frege: Briefe an Ludwig Wittgenstein', ed. by Allan Janik and C.P. Berger, *Grazer Philosophische Schriften*, 33/34 (1989), pp. 3-33,
N with page number, *Notebooks 1914-16*, trans. by G.E.M. Anscombe (Oxford: Basil Blackwell, 1961), and
TLP with proposition number, *Tractatus Logico-Philosophicus*, trans. by D.F. Pears and B.F. McGuinness (London: Routledge & Kegan Paul, 1961).
I refer to Hertz parenthetically as follows:
PM, Heinrich Hertz, *Die Prinzipien der Mechanik in neuem Zusammenhange dargestellt* (Leipzig: Johann Ambrosius Barth, 1894).

[4] Allan Janik, 'Saying and Showing: Wittgenstein and Hertz', in *Wittgenstein's Vienna Revisited* (New Brunswick and London: Transaction: 2001), pp. 147-170.

also a philosophically significant aspect of any theoretical representation. Although this difference appeared so slight as to be overlooked by a commentator as astute as Ludwig Boltzmann[5], it was a difference that made a difference, as William James put it. Wittgenstein's conception of philosophy would be profoundly influenced by Hertz. There would hardly be a discussion of the nature of philosophy in which he would not make reference to Hertz. The Hertzian view of philosophy implied that there was a teleological and aesthetic moment in the development of physical theory that philosophers of science neglect at their peril. It would become the basis of Wittgenstein's mature thoughts on the subject in the *Philosophical Investigations* (I, §§89-133).

For Mach & Co, the difference between alternative presentations of the same theory was not an interesting question. Hertz insisted that it was absolutely essential to understanding them. He proceeds from the view that in science it is necessary to construct different representations of the same data depending upon whom you want to talk to. He offers us the analogy with presentations of grammar: pupils learning to master their mother tongue require an altogether different presentation of the rules of grammar than philologists do. The more we consider the analogy (as Hertz himself does not explicitly), the more complex it becomes; for it will soon become clear that students in the course of mastering their mother tongue will require a very different grammar from those foreigners who struggle with the same language, whereas different groups of foreigners will find different presentations of grammar more or less helpful depending upon the characteristic modes of expression in their own language, etc. For these different purposes we need different 'pictures' or models of the rules of grammar. The same is true in physics: a representation that is suitable for theorists is hardly suitable, say, for engineers or for chemists working with the same subject, let alone introductory students. Thus Hertz differs from Mach at the very outset by emphasizing how it is that the normal development of science *requires* a plurality of representations. He would employ the notion of alternative representation to illuminate the philosophical problems in classical physics.

---

5   Ludwig Boltzmann, *Populäre Schriften* (Leipzig: Johann Ambrosius Barth, 1905), p. 58.

He reasoned that if the conceptual problems that plagued classical physics arose in the mode of formulating the laws of classical physics as Newton did, an alternative way of presenting those laws could avoid those pitfalls. The point could be formulated in a Wittgensteinian mode as follows: if conceptual confusions arise in the development of the language of physics, they must be resolved within that language, not on the basis of a theory about it. This principle had already been applied by Wilhelm Ostwald and the so-called 'Energeticists' in their attempt to avoid the problems that the notion of force presents for classical physics by treating all observable changes as transformations of energy. This entails basing mechanics upon the concepts of space and time as mathematical quantities and mass and energy as physical quantities. For energetics the properties of force are derived from fundamental laws and definitions, which function as ways of simplifying notation such that it becomes clear that they are matters of the appropriateness of the theory. In Energetics there are no intangibles; there are no "arbitrary and ineffectual" hypotheses (*PM*, 22). However, the idea of a complex fundamental principle offends against our demand for simplicity with respect to principles in an analogous way to Newton's 'force', i.e., epistemologically rather than ontologically.

Hertz offers us a third possibility in the form of an axiom system which purports to deal with both of these problems in terms of what Helmholtz called 'concealed masses and motions' (*PM*, 31). In this third presentation of the principles of mechanics all mechanical phenomena are explained in terms of masses and movements, although the masses and movements that enter into explanations are not always perceived by us. Nevertheless, they are in principle identical with the sorts of masses and movements that we perceive and in no way 'occult' qualities. In short, Hertz offers a way of going beyond our actual experiences without going outside of experience, i.e., by modeling possible experiences mathematically. Thus to speak with Kant all of mechanics is represented within the limits (*Grenzen*) of the empirical, but not within the bounds (*Schranken*) of the empirically given[6]. Whether Hertz succeeds or

---

6   Immanuel Kant, *Prolegomena zu jener künftigen Metaphysik*, *Werke*, 3 vols (Berlin: Knauer, n.d.), II, 353.

fails in his efforts to axiomatize classical mechanics is a question that need not concern us here, for it is his *strategy* as a philosopher of science that is so important for Wittgenstein.

This axiomatization of mechanics is not an end in itself (as axiomatization would tend to become in logical positivism especially in the hands of Carnap) but part of a program for articulating the conceptual foundations of physical theory, whose sense is to be found in the ways in which that axiom system *differs* from the traditional Newtonian presentation and the alternative presentation developed within Energetics. Thus the task of his philosophical 'Introduction' to the *Principles* is to present the two currently available systems of mechanics as an introduction to his own, which in turn is a way of clarifying the conceptual foundations of physics without having recourse to a radical reform of language. It is prolegomena to all of Wittgenstein's philosophizing, which in effect extends what Hertz would say about representations of physical theories to language in general.

If we try to summarize the results of Hertz's achievement for philosophy, we end up with a view of philosophy startlingly like Wittgenstein's: Philosophy is an activity, not a theory. Philosophical problems are not solved but dissolved on the basis of an alternative representation of the problematic matter. Philosophy does not stipulate how language must be used but shows us on the basis of a perspicuous contrast how our conceptual confusions are attached to particular ways of representing things. These confusions are linked to different rhetorical aims in developing our representations of physical reality. Philosophy is a matter of inventing new and illuminating ways of representing matters that have hitherto confused us. Skill and imagination are thus absolutely essential to it.

3. *Wittgenstein's* Tractatus Logico-Philosophicus

Let us look at the development of the *Tractatus* from the point of view of Hertzian philosophy of science. The earliest surviving thought that went into 'Die Abhandlung' as Wittgenstein himself called it was the Hertzian notion that logic must take care of itself – as he puts it, at the very beginning of the notebooks

(*N*, 22.VIII.14). Logic must function without the help of a foundational theory. There is much to be said for the thesis that the published *Tractatus* represents a way of showing how that is possible without producing a theory (of course, it would require a far more substantial study than this to make a full case for the view developed here).

Let us examine the seven propositions that constitute the *Tractatus* alone (as the all important numbering system (*F*, 26, 5.XII.19) suggests to us) with a view to determining what is distinctively Wittgensteinian in it. When we do so we discover that only the last two are properly Wittgensteinian.

> 1. Die Welt ist alles, was der Fall ist.
> The world is all that is the case.
> 2. Was der Fall ist, die Tatsache, ist, das Bestehen von Sachverhalten.
> What is the case, the fact, is the existence of states of affairs.
> 3. Das logische Bild der Tatsachen ist der Gedanke.
> The logical picture of facts is the thought.
> 4. Der Gedanke ist der sinnvolle Satz.
> The thought is the meaningful proposition.
> 5. Der Satz ist eine Wahrheitsfunktion der Elementarsätze. (Der Elementarsatz ist einer Wahrheitsfunktion seiner selbst.)
> The proposition is a truth function of elementary propositions. (The elementary proposition is a truth function of itself).
> 6. Die allgemeine Form der Wahrheitsfunktion ist: $(\bar{p}, \bar{\xi}, N(\bar{\xi}))$.
> The general form of a truth function is: $(\bar{p}, \bar{\xi}, N(\bar{\xi}))$.
> 7. Wovon man nicht sprechen kann, darüber muss man schweigen.
> Whereof one cannot speak, thereof one must be silent.

The first four are identity statements that can be read as stipulating how a series of expressions define each other. They could be attributed to more or less any philosopher concerned with logic from Aristotle on. Proposition 5 states Frege's revolutionary view of complex propositions as functions of the truth values of their components and his Leibnizian notion that where there are complexes, there must be simples. These notions would become programmatic for analytic philosophy. Propositions 1 to 5 are thus by no means unique to Wittgenstein. Proposition 6 and 7 alone are distinctively Wittgensteinian. That fact has largely been overlooked by readers of the *Tractatus*. Those propositions tell us in effect that all of the propositions of logic can be derived from the Sheffer stroke, i.e., not both p and q, and that once we have grasped that point we shall understand that it is completely unnecessary to develop a *theory* of the nature of the proposition. This is entirely Hertzian: in fact with the invention of the truth-table we have an alternative means of representing what a set of axioms or a logical theory would clarify now on the basis of a foolproof *technique*. Wittgenstein the craftsman, the mechanical engineer, has invented an ingenious way to implement a Hertzian program for logic.

Proposition 6 asserts that there is a truth-functional connective that can represent every dyadic relation between propositions. Wittgenstein, the philosophical craftsman, invented a purely mechanical technique, the truth table, for demonstrating, 'showing', the logical status of propositions as tautologies, contradictions or empirical statements. One simply needs to know how to represent propositions and how to apply them to represent states of affairs. Truth tables are a technique for applying the Sheffer stroke to determine the nature of a given proposition. Thus application shows what the sign itself does not about the nature of a proposition (*TLP*, 3.262). With that the whole idea of a philosophy of logic became superfluous in Wittgenstein's eyes. There is simply no need to talk about the matter and certainly no sense in arguing about the status of specific propositions when we have a purely mechanical, crystal-clear, sure-fire means for showing it at our disposal.

At the same time this Hertzian notion of clarity implied that the *Tractatus* could not have the deductive form that Frege and Russell required of a contribution to the philosophy of logic. The 'truth' of the Hertzian notion of showing as reflected in the truth-table must itself be shown. This imposed what Frege termed an 'artistic' form (*Fr*, 19) on the *Tractatus*, which was as unacceptable to Frege as its numbering system would be to Ficker (*F*, 26). Briefly, the technical achievement in the *Tractatus*, which was philosophically inspired by Hertz, determined that it had to have a certain aesthetic form. This relation between craftsmanship, technique, and aesthetics determined everything about Wittgenstein's relation to art throughout his life.

4. *The Palais Stonborough: An example of the relationship between art and craftsmanship in Wittgenstein*

Paul Wijdeveld's trenchant analysis of Wittgenstein's achievement in the construction of the house for his sister is perhaps the most dramatic example of the way in which Wittgenstein's 'aesthetics' are determined by the concerns of a craftsman[7]. The story is a strange one in almost every respect. Paul Engelmann, who made the original drawings, was principally acting as a draftsman, rather than a full-fledged architect, for Wittgenstein's youngest sister, Margaret Stonborough. Mrs. Stonborough systematically frustrated Loos's student, Engelmann, by strictly ruling out a house built upon functional Loosian principles (the so-called *Raumplanung*). Instead she wanted to have a traditional semi-aristocratic city mansion. When Ludwig joined the project in late summer 1926 he was able to realize her wishes to build in a modern house in a traditional way. Only the smooth, unadorned façade is modern. The classical progression of the windows betrays the architect's traditionalism. As for the interior, Wijdeveld suggests that it is an effort to purify, to clarify, the essence of classical monumental architecture. So Wittgenstein would employ the *stucco lustro*, the favored material for churches and palaces since the baroque. The stone slabs of the floor, the unadorned pillars, the naked light bulbs and the two winged doors all reflect what we might consider Wittgenstein's Hertzian alternative realization of the traditional city mansion reflected in the concerns of an engineer and ultimately a craftsman. 'The lack of ornamentation and the austerity of exterior and interior did not result from the need to create a new architectural aesthetic form from the technical and constructional developments in the late 19th and early 20th centuries, but from the wish to clarify the roots of traditional monumental architecture as exemplified by

---

7   See Paul Wijdeveld, *Ludwig Wittgenstein, Architekt*, trans. by Ulrike Kremsmair and Heigelmaier (Basel: Wiese Verlag, 1994) and 'Engelmann and Wittgenstein: The Relevance of the Palais Stonborough to Contemporary Architectural Discussion', in *Architecture, Language, Critique: Around Paul Engelmann*, ed. by J Bakacsy, A.V. Munch and A.L. Sommer, 'Studien zur österreichischen Philosophie', vol. 31 (Amsterdam: Rodopi: 2000), pp. 105-113.

the work of Johann Bernhard Fischer von Erlach, whom he greatly admired'[8]. His own concern for craftsmanship is most clearly evident in the metal doors and door handles, which reflect the skill of the mechanical engineer. In short, the 'beauty' we perceive in Wittgenstein architecture is indeed a beauty that is the result of consummate craftsmanship, to be compared with the kind of beauty produced by American Shaker craftsmen as Elisabeth Veit has observed[9]. As Brian McGuinness has said, it is a beauty which requires an intellectual effort to grasp. To the end, Wittgenstein shared Loos's view that architecture was not art. His house, for its un-Loosian character bears that out.

5. *Wittgenstein's mature Concept of Philosophy*

Let us turn to Wittgenstein's mature conception of philosophy as presented in sections 89 to 133 of the first part of the *Philosophical Investigations* with a view to establishing once more the relationship between his Hertzian strategy and his tactical techniques in his mature philosophy.

Coming from the Introduction of Hertz's *Principles* to Wittgenstein's text we ought to be struck at once by a number of similarities both in philosophical strategy and mode of expression.

Like Hertz, who could marvel at 'how easy it is to attach to fundamental laws considerations which are quite in accordance with the usual modes of expression in mechanics, and yet which are an undoubted hindrance to clear thinking' (*PM*, 6), Wittgenstein is concerned with the problem that our usual ways of speaking, like Newton's, conceal as much as they reveal of reality rather like spectacles that allow us to read but are not themselves 'seen' (*PI*, I, 103). We are held captive by a picture (*PI*, I, 115) both in a general sense and in a specific sense.

Generally philosophers have a picture of language as exclusively a matter of representing the world, that at once 1) leads them to consider the logical basis of representation as constituting an

---

8   Wijdeveld, 'Engelmann and Wittgenstein', p. 112.
9   Elisabeth Veit, 'La Maison de Wittgenstein' (unpublished thesis, 'Unité Pédagogique d'Architecture', no. 6, Paris, 1984), pp. 335-340.

ideal language, and 2) systematically prevents them from seeing the most obvious fact about it, namely that there are a myriad speech acts which are both non-representational and irreducibly different from one another. Wittgenstein's discussion of the nature of philosophy thus begins with a consideration of how we tend to become fixated upon an ideal language when we do philosophy.

Moreover, we are all like philosophers inasmuch as we are so tied to specific, one-sided ways, of seeing things that we forget that it is legitimately possible to understand words in startlingly different ways than we normally do. So we associate the word 'cube' with the drawing of a cube, but there is also a very real sense in which it describes a triangular prism as well (*PI*, I, 139). Although the latter is always there, we need to be reminded of that fact occasionally.

Just as in Hertz an alternative to time-honored ways of thinking in physics shows us how those ways of thinking go astray, so Wittgenstein wants to 'teach us differences' to paraphrase Kent in *King Lear*, which was another of the mottos he considered for the *Investigations*[10]. Similarly the metaphor of being entangled in our own rules is no less suggestive of Hertz. Further, Wittgenstein likens the confusions of philosophers to people inexperienced with machinery who confuse an idling engine with one that is running (*PI*, I, 132); whereas Hertz will describe the role of 'forces' in physics as 'idling side-wheels' that have nothing to do with the machine's functioning (*PM*, 14). Thus on Wittgenstein's view the traditional philosopher is 'whipped' (*gepeitscht*) by questions that seem logical but in fact are not answerable (*PI*, I, 133), because they are not questions at all; whereas in the very passage that Wittgenstein contemplated as motto for the *Investigations* Hertz speaks of the mind of the physicist ceasing to be 'tormented' (*gequält*) by the contradictions in a concept like force or electricity (*PM*, 9). What the philosopher needs to discover is the spectacles on his nose to put his vain questioning to rest.

What we need in this situation is 'eine übersichtliche Darstellung' or a synoptic view (*PI*, I, 122), which shows us what other possibilities there are. We need a 'depth grammar' or logical grammar (*PI*, I, 664) that diverts our focus from the seductions of surface grammar and permits us to liberate ourselves from

---

10   William Shakespeare, *King Lear*, I, 4, 88.

our 'grammatical illusions' (*PI*, I, 110) and focus our attention upon a number of simple, commonplace truths, whose very obviousness prevents us from grasping them. In the preface to the *Investigations*, Wittgenstein had already compared his task to that of a draughtsman (the word 'Zeichner' would seem to emphasize professional skill in drawing rather than art) making sketches of a landscape from different directions in order to get a comprehensive overview of something that was most definitely visible but which could not be taken in with a single glance. It is precisely in aid of obtaining the already mentioned 'synoptic view' that Wittgenstein speaks of the needs to discover or invent intermediate cases (i.e., language games) to help lead the philosopher away from the confusing exceptional cases and back to the rule, i.e., away from the tendency to want to speculate about the nature of thought and reality and back to the things we actually do with words.

Thus Wittgenstein sought to develop techniques that would introduce such clarity into the question of, say, what it is to 'know' that question would simply cease to interest us as we gained insight into the natural history of an animal that speaks. However, it became increasingly clear to him that, contrary to the situation in the *Tractatus*, a single technique could never suffice to show us how language works; for it is as complex as the human organism itself. He would assemble all sorts of reminders of the complexity and nuances of human knowing and acting in aid of disabusing us of the desire to ask oversimplified questions, employ misleading examples and form crude judgments on the basis of misconstruing the logic of language.

Although an influence from Freud is perceptible here; for philosophy does not become therapy, but a therapeutic art (*PI*, I, 133) that seeks to develop a variety of techniques for attaining the goal of disabusing the philosopher of his obsession with seeing the relationship between language and world *exclusively* as a matter of representation[11]: "'It is high time for us to compare these phenomena with something *different*" – one may say – I am thinking, e.g., of

---

[11] On Wittgenstein's relationship to Freud see Brian McGuinness's excellent chapter 'Freud and Wittgenstein', in *Wittgenstein and His Times*, ed. by B.F. McGuinness (Chicago: University of Chicago Press, 1982), pp. 27-43; cf. my 'Wittgenstein on Madness, Mistakes, Metaphysics and Method', in Allan Janik, *Wittgenstein's Vienna Revisited*, pp. 213-24.

mental illnesses.' (*C V*, 55) In an unpublished early version of section 106 of part I of the *Investigations* Wittgenstein writes: 'One of our most important tasks is to express all false thought processes so characteristically that the other says: yes, that's just the way I meant it'[12]. He has to be put into a position where his difficulties cease to be difficulties and he finally attains peace of mind. Wittgenstein's Hertzian philosophical task was to develop spiritual techniques for doing so. His spiritual craftsmanship is eminently literary without being 'art'. What, then, is the relationship of art to philosophy in Wittgenstein?

6. Philosophy and Art in Wittgenstein's Thought

Wittgenstein considered that his philosophizing stood a definite relationship to art but was, nevertheless, to be distinguished from art. In 1930 the one-time follower of Schopenhauer would write:

> Now it seems to me that there is another way of capturing the world *sub specie aeterni* apart from the work of the artist. It is – I think – the way of thought, which can fly over the world as it were and then leaves it as it is – observing it from above in flight. (*CV*, 5)

The difference between the two is that philosophy is 'unpoetic' and therefore is not art. It is more like religion inasmuch as it simply unveils things as they are with a certain passion or sense of wonder (in this sense he could speak of his way of looking at things as religious, while denying being a religious man). In order to present such a Hertzian clear view of things Wittgenstein strove in the manner of a craftsman to develop a set of spiritual techniques for reminding us of all those incredibly important things, whose simplicity and familiarity prevent us from seeing them. These techniques amounted to a curious way of writing fiction with a view to reminding us of striking facts that the surface grammar

---

12   Ludwig Wittgenstein, *Philosophische Untersuchungen: Frühversion 1937-1938*, ed. by G.H. von Wright & H. Nyman (Helsinki: privately printed, 1979); I, 106.

of language tempts us to pass over – e.g., the plurality of activities that correspond to the many modes of 'thinking'. This is why he would insist that philosophy must be analytic without it being what is conventionally understood under the rubric analytical philosophy. This too was for him a matter of practicing a craft, one which, indeed, produced objects of great beauty which could only be grasped on the basis of great intellectual effort.

References

Boltzmann, Ludwig, *Populäre Schriften* (Leipzig: Johann Ambrosius Barth, 1905).
Hertz, Heinrich, *Die Prinzipien der Mechanik in neuem Zusammenhange dargestellt (PM)* (Leipzig: Johann Ambrosius Barth, 1894).
Kant, Immanuel, *Prolegomena zu jener künftigen Metaphysik, Werke*, 3 vols (Berlin: Knauer, n.d.).
Janik, Allan, *Wittgenstein's Vienna Revisited* (New Brunswick and London: Transaction: 2001).
McGuinness, Brian, 'Freud and Wittgenstein', in *Wittgenstein and His Times*, ed. by B.F. McGuinness (Chicago: University of Chicago Press, 1982).
—, *Wittgenstein, A life: Young Ludwig* (London: Duckworth, 1989).
Rorty, Richard, *The Consequences of Pragmatism* (Minneapolis: University of Minnesota Press, 1982).
Veit, Elisabeth, 'La Maison de Wittgenstein' (unpublished thesis, 'Unité Pédagogique d'Architecture', no. 6, Paris, 1984).
Wijdeveld, Paul, 'Engelmann and Wittgenstein: The Relevance of the Palais Stonborough to Contemporary Architectural Discussion', in *Architecture, Language, Critique: Around Paul Engelmann*, ed. by J Bakacsy, A.V. Munch and A.L. Sommer, 'Studien zur österreichischen Philosophie', vol. 31 (Amsterdam-Atlanta: Rodopi: 2000), pp. 105-113.
—, *Ludwig Wittgenstein, Architekt*, trans. by Ulrike Kremsmair and Heigelmaier (Basel: Wiese Verlag, 1994).
Wittgenstein, Ludwig, *Briefe an Ludwig von Ficker (F)*, ed. by G.H. von Wright, *Brenner Studien*, 1 (Salzburg: Otto Müller, 1969).
—, *Culture and Value (CV)*, trans. by Peter Winch (Chicago, University of Chicago Press, 1980).
—, 'Gottlob Frege: Briefe an Ludwig Wittgenstein' (*Fr*), ed. by Allan Janik and C.P. Berger, *Grazer Philosophische Schriften*, 33/34 (1989), pp. 3-33.

—, *Notebooks 1914-16 (N)*, trans. by G.E.M. Anscombe (Oxford: Basil Blackwell, 1961).
—, *Philosophical Investigations (PI)*, trans. by G.E.M. Anscombe (Oxford: Basil Blackwell, 1958).
—, *Philosophische Untersuchungen: Frühversion 1937-1938*, ed. by G.H. von Wright & H. Nyman (Helsinki: privately printed, 1979).
—, *Tractatus Logico-Philosophicus (TLP)*, trans. by D.F. Pears and B.F. McGuinness (London: Routledge & Kegan Paul, 1961).

Nicolás Sánchez Durá

WITTGENSTEIN, ETHICS AND LITERATURE
The case of Tolstoy's tale *Hadji Murat*

In his memoir of Wittgenstein, Paul Engelmann says that the conversations about literature that he had with him were the most profound influence that he received from the then young philosopher[1]. And Von Wright, in his early 'Biographical Sketch', declared that throughout his life Wittgenstein received deeper impressions from 'some writers in the borderland between philosophy, religion, and poetry' – such as Dostoyevsky and Tolstoy – than from the philosophers[2]. I think that in Wittgenstein, unlike other philosophers in his circle with whom he is usually associated, there is an internal relation between his philosophy and literature, and that the latter is not merely a source of illustrations of the former. For his style, his particular way of expressing himself, is not without importance in his philosophical 'substance', in his movements of thought.

In 1931 he noted:

> If it is said on occasion that (someone's) philosophy is a matter of temperament, there is some truth in this. A preference for certain comparisons (*Gleichnisse*) is something we call a matter of temperament & far more disagreements rest on this than appears at first sight.[3]

---

[1] Paul Engelmann, *Letters from Ludwig Wittgenstein with a memoir* (Oxford: Basil Blackwell, 1967), p. 82.
[2] Georg Henrik von Wright, 'Biographical Sketch', in Norman Malcolm, *Ludwig Wittgenstein. A Memoir* (Oxford: Clarendon Press, Oxford, 2001), p. 19.
[3] Ludwig Wittgenstein, *Culture and Value* (Oxford: Blackwell, 1998), p. 18 (1931).

The internal connection between literature and Wittgenstein's philosophy is especially notable in the case of ethics and religion. These aspects of his thought are not always discernible in someone who, according to the well-known testimony of his friend and follower Drury, said that although he was not a man of religion he could not help seeing any matter *from a religious point of view*[4]. Well, the aim of this essay is very limited: to show the relationship with literature adopted by Wittgenstein's moral temperament, for this purpose considering only Tolstoy's novella *Hadji Murat*, for which he always displayed a lively interest. I shall justify my choice.

There are already several studies that deal with Wittgenstein's interpretation of Tolstoy. But when it comes to considering the relation between them the exegesis tends to come to a halt and to elaborate on the influence that *The Gospel in Brief* had on the author of the *Tractatus* in the time of the Great War. However, Wittgenstein's dialogue with the Russian author goes far beyond that text of religious and moral criticism (which, for Tolstoy, are two sides of the same coin). In fact, there are various testimonies which show that Tolstoy's works were a constant point of reference for Wittgenstein's thinking and reworking of his moral and religious points of view throughout his life. In his recollections of their conversations about religion during the war (Olmütz, 1916), Engelmann describes the interpretation that the two of them made of the short story 'Two Old Men'. He confessed to Drury that recently only two European writers had had anything important to say about religion: Tolstoy and Dostoyevsky. He recommended Dostoyevsky's *The Brothers Karamazov* and also *Crime and Punishment*. And among Tolstoy's works he recommended the folk tales included in a book called *Twenty-Three Tales*, one of which is the story 'Two Old Men' to which Engelmann refers. When Drury later confessed to him that he preferred Dostoyevsky to Tolstoy, Wittgenstein disagreed vehemently and declared that Tolstoy's short stories would always survive, that they were written for everybody and that he preferred 'The Three Hermits'.

---

4   Maurice O'Connor Drury, 'Some Notes on Conversations with Wittgenstein', in *Ludwig Wittgenstein. Personal Recollections*, ed. by Rush Rhees (Oxford: Basil Blackwell, 1981), p. 94.

I am especially interested in the testimony of his friend Norman Malcolm in the mid 1940s. In a letter written at the end of the Second World War, Malcolm complained of the boredom of being mobilised on a warship. In his reply dated 26 June 1945 Wittgenstein compared the war to a school. If a pupil says that the school is boring it is because he is incapable of learning what is taught at the school.

> I can't help believing that an enormous lot can be learnt about human beings in this war – *if* you can keep your eyes open. And the better you are at thinking the more you'll get out of what you see. For thinking is *digesting*. If I'm writing in a preaching tone I'm just an ass! but the fact remains that if you're bored a lot it means that your mental digestion isn't what it should be.
>
> I think a good remedy for this is sometimes opening your eyes wider. Sometimes a book helps a little, e.g. T.'s 'Hadshi Murat' wouldn't be bad.[5]

In a later letter Wittgenstein is glad that Malcolm has obtained the novella *Hadji Murat* and tells him 'I hope you'll get a lot out of it, because there is a lot *in* it.' As for Tolstoy, he says: 'There's a *real* man; who has a *right* to write'[6]. Malcolm also says that Wittgenstein had an 'extremely favourable' opinion of Tolstoy's folk tales, that he was very pleased that he knew those stories, and that 'he questioned me closely to find out whether I had understood the moral of the one entitled "How Much Land Does A Man Need?"'[7] However, despite his very favourable opinion of Tolstoy, when Malcolm commented that he had been very impressed by a passage in *Resurrection*, Wittgenstein replied, at the end of 1945:

> I once tried to read *Resurrection* but couldn't. You see, when Tolstoy just tells a story he impresses me infinitely more than when he addresses the reader. When he turns his back to the reader then he seems to me *most* impressive. Perhaps one day we can talk about

---

5   Ludwig Wittgenstein, *Wittgenstein in Cambridge: Letters and Documents 1911–1951*, ed. by Brian McGuinness (Oxford: Blackwell, 2008), p. 379.
6   *Ibid.*, p. 383.
7   Malcolm, p. 45.

this. It seems to me his philosophy is most true when it's *latent* in the story.⁸

From all this we can draw some conclusions. Wittgenstein considered that Tolstoy's short stories expressed a moral teaching, that they could be read and understood by everyone, and that because of the teaching they conveyed their applicability was very wide. Moreover, Wittgenstein considered that this form of expression, in which the moral teaching was latent, was 'philosophy'. It is significant that immediately after the last sentence in the passage just quoted ('It seems to me his philosophy is most true when it's *latent* in the story'), Wittgenstein continues: '*Talking of philosophy*: my book is gradually nearing its final form ...', etc.

*

The case of the novella *Hadji Murat* is rather special. It is not a long novel like *War and Peace, Anna Karenina* or *Resurrection*, but it is also not a short story or tale in the form of a parable like the ones in *Twenty-Three Tales*. All the same, Wittgenstein read this novella and recommended it repeatedly throughout his life. In the summer of 1912 he wrote to Russell: 'I have just read *Chadschi-Murat* by Tolstoy! Have you ever read it? If not, you ought to for it is *wonderful*'⁹. And if he recommended it to Malcolm in time of war in order to help him to learn about human beings, he also suggested it to his sister Gretl, apparently too insistently, because in a letter probably written at the end of 1945 she replied: 'No my dear I am surely not going to read *Hadschi Murad* again. I could not stand it'¹⁰. There is no doubt that Wittgenstein read this novella several

---

8 Wittgenstein, *Wittgenstein in Cambridge*, p. 385. My italics. Malcolm had told him that he had been impressed by the start of chapter 59 in part I, in which Tolstoy criticises the idea that men are easy to classify morally once and for all: 'Every man bears within him the germs of every human quality, and now manifests one, now another, and frequently is quite unlike himself, while still remaining the same man.' Tolstoy, *Resurrection*, quoted in Malcolm, p. 99.
9 Wittgenstein, *Wittgenstein in Cambridge*, p. 35.
10 Unpublished letter from Gretl Wittgenstein to her brother Ludwig. Brian McGuiness, to whom I am grateful for providing me with it, dates it as 27

times. On 25 June 1945, many years after he had recommended it to Russell and at about the time of his correspondence with Malcolm and with his sister about it, he wrote to Rees: 'I read a wonderful book these days: *Hadshi Murat* by Tolstoy. Do you know it? If you don't I'll try to get a copy for you'[11].

What moral philosophy was expressed by this novella that Wittgenstein liked so much? It is not easy to ascertain, because, as far as I am aware, he did not make any substantive declaration about the teaching that it embodied. For the time being I shall not answer my own question – supposing that it has an answer. But I shall begin to do so indirectly by referring very briefly to other folk tales by Tolstoy that Wittgenstein is known to have recommended. At first sight, they are all in agreement with his religious and moral conceptions, but it is not easy to discern the teaching that, according to Wittgenstein, could be deduced from each of them.

In 'How Much Land Does A Man Need?', the main character falls into the hands of the devil as a result of considering the consumption of goods encouraged by modern cities to be an essential objective, and of his insatiable desire to earn more than is needed for a dignified, austere life and his compulsion to acquire property in order to attain higher social status, in other words, as a result of considering material riches to be an absolute value. All of which leads to conflict with his neighbours, a constant rootlessness, an insuperable dissatisfaction and a sense of ill-being and, finally, to his death. At the end of this story Tolstoy provides the answer: 'Six feet from his head to his heels was all he needed'[12]. The case of 'The Three Hermits' is similar. A bishop – in other words, an authority of the ecclesiastical hierarchy – finds three hermits who are living on an island for the salvation of their souls. They do almost everything in silence and need little more than a glance to understand one another. The people think they are stupid. The bishop declares that he is 'called, by God's mercy' to teach them. The hermits say that they do not know how to serve God. 'We only

---

    October, probably 1945 (published electronically in *Gesamtbriefwechsel* by Intelex).
11   Wittgenstein, *Wittgenstein in Cambridge*, p. 378.
12   Leo Tolstoy, 'How Much Land Does A Man Need?', in Leo Tolstoy, *Twenty-Three Tales* (London: Henry Frowde and Oxford University Press, 1906), p. 176.

serve and support ourselves,' they say. When they are asked how they pray they raise their arms and recite a cheerful refrain, 'Three are ye, three are we, have mercy upon us'[13]. The bishop, believing that they are referring to the Holy Trinity, gives them a lesson on theology and tries to teach them to say the Lord's Prayer in the prescribed form. Yet, however much they try, the hermits keep forgetting the prayer as soon as they stop repeating it. The story emphasises the fact that they are holy men by having them walk upon the water to catch up with the bishop and ask him to repeat the Lord's Prayer again to see if they can stop forgetting it. Now it might be said that Wittgenstein's liking for this story reflects the negative opinion that he had of an experience of religious belief in the form it takes in organized religion, and his conviction that 'looking after oneself', acquiring mastery of oneself, is an unavoidable moral imperative, and that in the case of religious expressions it is not a question of whether they are true, false or nonsensical[14], because what is important is not the literality of what they say but the attitude to life that they express.

In any case, it is not easy to define the moral teaching that these parable-like stories contain and that, according to Malcolm, Wittgenstein wished, by means of acute questions, to make sure that he had grasped. At this point, an example and a warning are provided by Engelmann's recollections of the comments that the two of them made about the story 'Two Old Men'. In principle, the moral has to do with the experience of religion as an ecclesiastic rite, and again with criticism of the way in which religious belief is administered politically, and with the wrongness of considering religious statements as historical truths about events that took place in a particular place in the remote past. The story describes the journey of two poor peasant pilgrims who set off for Jerusalem.

---

13   Leo Tolstoy, 'The Three Hermits', in Tolstoy, *Twenty-Three Tales*, p. 153.
14   In the conversation with Friedrich Waismann about Schlick's ethics Wittgenstein said: 'I can quite well imagine a religion in which there are no doctrines, and hence nothing is said. Obviously the essence of religion can have nothing to do with the fact that speech occurs – or rather if the speech does occur, this itself is a component of religious behavior and not a theory. Therefore nothing turns on whether the words are true, false, or nonsensical.' Wittgenstein, in Friedrich Waismann, 'Notes on Talks with Wittgenstein', *The Philosophical Review*, 74, no. 1 (1965), pp. 12-16 (p. 16).

When one of them arrives he finds a spectacle that provides considerable profit to those who are in charge of the holy places. The other one does not reach Jerusalem because he stops to help a family of peasants who are on the point of dying of hunger. The narrative, which implicitly contains many of Tolstoy's opinions about the genuine religious attitude, emphasizes that life and the preservation of humanity are sacred. However, the comment that Wittgenstein made – and that Engelmann transmitted – is disconcerting because it concerns a detail that is easy to overlook and that does not seem to be the centre of Tolstoy's moral and religious teaching. Before the two peasants separate, the one who does not reach Jerusalem takes out his snuff box to inhale some snuff. The one who completes the pilgrimage reproaches him for indulging in a vice that is not fitting for a pilgrim, and the first one replies: 'The evil habit is stronger than I'.[15] Engelmann says that in this acknowledgement Wittgenstein saw the true religious feeling: 'Instead of trying to excuse his action before himself and others as 'not really sinful', the peasant confessed having succumbed to sin'[16].

Therefore, although Wittgenstein considered that these stories could be read by everyone and that because of their moral teaching their applicability was very wide, it is not easy to ascertain what he thought about what this teaching was in each case. In fact, even the synopsis that I have given of the two stories described above does not do justice to many aspects that Tolstoy interweaves and that are in accord with other aspects of Wittgenstein's philosophy. For instance, the behaviour of the bishop and that of the peasant who is eager to increase his property are contrasted with attitudes and behaviour that, from the description of them, border on childishness or madness when viewed from the commonly accepted perspective of 'order'. This is the case with the nonsensical prayer of the hermits who are so bad at remembering, a prayer that does not even respect agreement of number in its invocation: 'Three are ye, three are we, have mercy upon us' (in the original Russian, the verb in 'Three are ye' is in the plural, whereas in 'have

---

15   Leo Tolstoy, 'Two Old Men', in Tolstoy, *Twenty-Three Tales*, p. 90. What Elisha says in Engelmann's version is not 'evil habit' but 'sin'.
16   Engelmann, p. 80.

mercy upon us' it is in the singular). But it is also the case with the Bashkirs in the story 'How Much Land Does A Man Need?' Their merry, jovial behaviour seems to reduce the idea of purchase and profit to absurdity, for they are willing to give away their land to the first person who asks for it as long as he is friendly and gives them presents. Thus both cases could express the opinion that Wittgenstein states in *On Certainty* §611: 'Where two principles really do meet which cannot be reconciled with one another, then each man declares the other a fool (*Narr*) and heretic'[17].

To put it briefly, these stories weave an intricate mesh of meaningful relations, of 'floating' significances, which go beyond what might at first sight seem a simple sermon and the meaning of which cannot easily be reduced. In the case of the relation of Wittgenstein's moral and religious philosophy to the novella *Hadji Murat*, I think there is a difference that must be taken into account, the difference that exists between, on the one hand, something that is inexpressible by its very nature or character and, on the other, something that is latent because the author writes it in a particular way, turning 'his back to the reader', as Wittgenstein put it in his letter to Malcolm. The first part of this distinction seems to correspond to the period of the *Tractatus*, the second to that of the *Philosophical Investigations*. However, despite the profound changes that his conceptions about meaning underwent, Wittgenstein did not substantially vary either his moral point of view or his way of approaching *Hadji Murat*, as I will try to show.

*

In the period of the *Tractatus* and its austere pictorial theory of meaning, which condemns any moral or religious statement to senselessness, Wittgenstein thought that the way of speaking about what could not be said meaningfully was a 'hopeless' approximation by way of similes and allegories. This is the strategy that he defends to make himself understood by his audience in his 'Lecture on Ethics':

---

17   Ludwig Wittgenstein, *On Certainty* (Oxford: Blackwell, 1998).

Now all religious terms seem in this sense to be used as similes or *allegorically*. For when we speak of God and that he sees everything and when we kneel and pray to him all our terms and actions seem to be parts of a great and elaborated *allegory* which represents him as a human being of great power whose grace we try to win, etc., etc. But this *allegory also describes* the experience which I have just referred to [To wonder at the existence of the world. N. S.]. For the first of them is, I believe, exactly what people were referring to when they said that God had created the world; and the experience of absolute safety has been described by saying that we feel safe in the hands of God. A third experience of the same kind is that of feeling guilty and again this was described by the phrase that disapproves of our conduct. Thus in ethical and religious language we seem constantly to be using similes.[18]

Wittgenstein considered that in ethical value judgements (and in religious expressions) we inadvertently make the mistake of thinking of absolute value judgements as being similar to relative value judgements. In relative value judgements we simply state a fact (a 'good' runner is one who runs at such and such a speed), whereas underlying absolute judgements there is a 'characteristic' misuse of these expressions: namely, using them as similes or allegories when there is nothing in the world to support the relation of similarity that they apparently establish. However, *it is no less true that, at the same time,* he thought that these pieces of nonsense bring us closer to, point to or show experiences of a kind that in turn draw limits to what, for him, constituted the sphere of ethics. Of the three experiences that Wittgenstein mentioned in that lecture – experiences of his, which were not the only ones and to which he did not seek to attribute the status of a universal principle – he considered the experience of wondering at the existence of the world as being 'my experience par excellence'. Yet in this there is a paradox which he himself acknowledges: these experiences of his can be located in space and dated; in other words, they are events that occurred or that occur. How could they have an absolute value if the world as it is conceived in the period of the *Tractatus* is no more than an occurrence of events and

---

18 Ludwig Wittgenstein, 'A Lecture on Ethics', *The Philosophical Review*, 74, no. 1 (1965), pp. 3-12 (p. 9). (My emphasis.)

there is no place for values? He himself says that he is 'tempted' to solve this paradox by saying that wondering at the existence of the world is similar to considering the world as a miracle. However, considering something as a miracle is, for him, simply considering a fact from a particular perspective, with a particular 'way of looking' (which is not science's way of looking).

Therefore, we can conclude that what Tolstoy's allegories offer us in the *Tractatus* period is not an explicit moral sermon but rather what is indicated by Wittgenstein's comment about Uhland's poem 'Count Eberhard's Hawthorn': 'if only you do not try to utter what is unutterable then *nothing* gets lost. But the unutterable will be – unutterably – *contained* in what has been uttered!'[19] And in his recollections Engelmann sums up as follows: '[...] the poem as a whole gives in 28 lines the *picture* of a life'[20]. So one might say that, in accordance with the conception of meaning in the *Tractatus* period, the inexpressible in language is offered in Tolstoy's stories as a way of seeing, as a picture that establishes a perspective which changes the way in which life is considered. And thus Wittgenstein recommended *Hadji Murat* to Malcolm, to help him to 'open his eyes' (i.e., to see in a different way) and to learn about human beings in and from the war. The point is not that there is no moral 'lesson', the point is not that one has to learn from what is 'absent' in the text[21]. Rather, we have to learn something that is 'contained' in Tolstoy's stories – or in Uhland's poem – but that is offered for our consideration *articulated* in a particular way, as a picture from which a perspective is established.

However, there is something intriguing here. Although Wittgenstein abandoned the restrictive theory of meaning that appears in the *Tractatus*, he did not therefore abandon his preference for the latency of philosophy in Tolstoy's narratives (and in general). In fact, his statement to Malcolm that the Russian writer seemed more expressive to him when he turns his back to

---

19 Wittgenstein, letter to Engelmann, 9-4-17, in Engelmann. (Wittgenstein's emphasis.)
20 Engelmann, p. 85. (My emphasis.)
21 On this point I do not agree with Cora Diamond. (Cf. Cora Diamond, 'Introduction to "Having a rough story about what moral philosophy is"', in *The Literary Wittgenstein*, ed. by John Gibson and Wolfgang Huemer (London: Routledge, 2004), pp. 128 ff.

the reader – the more latent the philosophy, the truer it is – was made in the period when he was working on the *Philosophical Investigations*. In other words, when he considered that the particular grammar of religious and ethical language games did not make them less meaningful than any other. Cora Diamond says that 'What Tolstoy does not tell us is how to think about Hadji Murat himself, his life and his death, or how to make what we think of Hadji Murat alive in our own lives'[22]. According to her, it is in this aspect that the Russian writer resembles the way in which Wittgenstein demanded that both the *Tractatus* and the *Philosophical Investigations* should be read. I do not agree with the statement about Tolstoy and *Hadji Murat*: the stories that Tolstoy wrote after *A Confession* are always didactically moralising. But what I am interested in emphasising here is that, although Wittgenstein maintained his distinction between 'saying' and 'showing' beyond the pictorial theory from which it originated, and although it is true that in the case of moral philosophy he maintained his preference for allegory and latency, this does not eliminate the possibility of reconstructing some of the main features of his moral philosophy from his constant interest in *Hadji Murat*.

Yet there is a clarification that has to be made. So far I have used the term 'moral philosophy' ambiguously, but at this point it is necessary to remove the ambiguity. One can in fact make a distinction, at least a distinction of reason, between a moralist and a moral philosopher. The moral philosopher (or ethics) devotes himself with a great degree of detachment and lack of involvement to conceptual analysis of the language of morality, or to establishing its most abstract principles. The moralist seeks a moral code on the basis of which he acts and makes judgements, with which he engages and which spurs him on, which represents a conception of the meaning of life or a specification of what he understands by a good life. So, did Wittgenstein recommend that novella in order to think about ethics or to show its moral teaching?

At the time of the 'Lecture on Ethics' Wittgenstein mixed the two aspects together. On the one hand, he devoted himself to a clear conceptual analysis of moral language, to defining what he

---

22   Diamond, p. 130.

considered in that period to be a typical misuse of the expressions of ethics which is basically caused by overlooking the false analogy that we inadvertently make between absolute value judgements and relative value judgements. Moreover, he sought to clarify conceptually what he understood by ethics 'in a slightly wider sense' than that used by Moore in his *Principia Ethica* (which conceived it as 'the general enquiry into what is good'). In order to indicate what he understood by ethics he offered a list of expressions that he considered equivalent: ethics is 'the inquiry into the meaning of life, or into what makes life worth living, or into the right way of living'[23]. It is at this point – in order to show what is indicated by this set of expressions that would broaden the field of ethics beyond Moore's concept – that he describes the three *personal* experiences that I mentioned earlier (wondering at the world, feeling absolutely safe, etc.). In other words, Wittgenstein stops speaking on the basis of a distanced conceptual analysis and chooses similes (many of a religious nature, as we have seen) that have to do with his personality and express his moral, rather than ethical, point of view. The conjunction of two texts from the same period, one written in 1930 and the other in 1931, shows what I am referring to. In the first, from the conversations with Friedrich Waismann about Schlick's ethics (1930), he says:

> At the end of my lecture on ethics, I spoke in the first person. I believe that is quite essential. Here nothing more can be established, I can only appear as a person speaking for myself.[24]

But I have already cited, at the beginning, what he wrote a few months later:

> If it is said on occasion that (someone's) philosophy is a matter of temperament, there is some truth in this. A preference for certain comparisons (*Gleichnisse*) is something we call a matter of temperament & far more disagreements rest on this than appears at first sight.[25]

---

23 Wittgenstein, 'A Lecture on Ethics', p. 5.
24 Wittgenstein, in Waismann, p. 16.
25 Wittgenstein, *Culture and Value*, p. 18 (1931).

Well, I think that these two aspects, ethical and moral, are also mixed together in his interpretation of *Hadji Murat* after the *Tractatus* period. Moreover, as I have already said, I think that if we make a hermeneutic combination of Tolstoy's story and the esoteric notes and jottings that Wittgenstein left it will be possible to discern his conception about the form of a correct way of living that would be worth living. So, *what is the 'picture of a life' that is expressed in* Hadji Murat *and that Wittgenstein found so interesting?*

*

The whole of Tolstoy's novella could be considered as a Western, a film genre that he was very keen on, as his friends and biographers were aware[26]. In this case, however, life on the frontier is set in the northwest Caucasus, in Chechnya and Dagestan. An interminable frontier war in which the confrontation is not between the redskins of the prairies and the settlers of the West but between the mountain people and the Tsar's army[27]. Yet in this confrontation between two worlds, two religions or two cultures there are many fractures and contradictions on both sides. Divisions that affect the various characters that appear in the story, people whose behaviour cannot be explained solely or mainly by the ethnic or religious community to which they belong. Although the gallery of characters is not as huge as that of *War and Peace*, it is nevertheless sufficient to show a range of individuals who, except on certain occasions, cannot easily be evaluated with regard to how they behave and the decisions that they take in such an extreme situation as war. It is true that from the outset there is an unjust situation: the invading army that considers the natives who live there as a bunch of savages and at times thinks of the war in terms of extermination, destroying entire villages and their

---

26 Engelmann, pp. 91–92.
27 'What the Far West and the Red Man were to American mythology, the Caucasus and its warring tribes, or the unspoiled communities of Cossacks and Old Believers on the Don and the Volga were to Pushkin, Lermontov and Tolstoy.' George Steiner, 'Nineteenth-century America and Russia', in *George Steiner: A Reader* (Oxford: Oxford University Press, 1987), p. 134.

environment; there is also laughable behaviour, such as the official war reports, which convert the futile, accidental deaths of soldiers into patriotic discourses about militarily disastrous imaginary battles. Not to mention the disputes of prestige and caprices between the generals which lead to military ineffectiveness, death, and destruction. But that army is made up of a mixture of people, ranging from soldiers who are serfs in the *izbas* they come from to officers such as Butler, who makes a point of dressing in the style of the mountain people, with *beshmet, cherkeska,* and leggings, an officer who experiences the war in terms of sport and adventure, as an opportunity to display his manliness, and who is capable of admiring the warrior Hadji Murat and establishing a sincere friendship with him. Which means, Tolstoy says, that it is not possible for him to imagine 'the other face' of war: 'To maintain his poetic view of war he even subconsciously avoided looking at the dead and wounded'[28]. On the other hand, a number of conflicts develop between different factions among the men of the mountains with the aim of gaining political leadership in their resistance against the Russians. We also find villages and individuals who avoid the fighting in order to achieve an easy-going modus vivendi and who therefore clash with the Muslim religious leaders, who understand their resistance as a *ghazavat* (holy war), and so on. In short, the story shows a wide range of conceptions of war and how it provides an extreme opportunity in which to consider the moral dilemmas that the characters have to face. So it is not strange that he recommended this book to Malcolm to help him to open his eyes and accept war as a privileged opportunity for learning 'a lot' about human beings.

 Well, just as in a Western, the story presents – with the coldness and distance of an anthropological study – hatred and ambition, a thirst for vengeance, a blind desire to inflict death or injury on the enemy, treachery, but also loyalties based on unconditional personal and family attachments. All these attitudes and actions are attributed to Hadji Murat but also to his main enemy, Shamil, who paradoxically is not a Russian but a Chechen, a legendary guerrilla hero who led the resistance against the Russo-Tsarist

---

28 Leo Tolstoy, *Hadji Murat*, in *The Cossacks and Other Stories* (London: Penguin Books, 2006), p. 420.

conquest. Hadji Murat is a profoundly religious guerrilla fighter, even in his name, for in Persian 'Hadji' is the title given to someone who has made the pilgrimage to Mecca at least once. He is a believer who nevertheless has changed the direction of his struggle many times. When Shamil rises up in a holy war against the Russians, the khans under whose protection Hadji Murat lives refuse to join in. But after becoming acquainted with the Russians in Tiflis (now Tbilisi), from whom he feels distant because he does not understand their ways of living, he advises his people to join the rebel leader. However, in order to gain total control over the villages under his command, Shamil disloyally and deceitfully kills the khans whom Hadji Murat considers his adoptive family. For this reason Hadji Murat goes over to the Russian side in order to protect his people and take vengeance on Shamil, and is appointed governor of Avaria by the invaders. Nevertheless, he soon changes this alliance. As a result of personal quarrels and questions of status, another mountain khan allied to the Russians, Akhmet-Khan, denounces him and falsely accuses him of disloyalty and betrayal. The Russians pursue him, and he takes vengeance on the khan by kidnapping his wife, whom he respects and returns after payment of a ransom. He does not trust the Russians to admit the falseness of the accusation against him; moreover, he is briefly taken prisoner and is defiled by a Russian soldier before escaping.

Thus he finds himself in a dilemma: he cannot join Shamil, who killed his people simply because of his ambition for power, and his customs require him to seek vengeance; he cannot join the Russians because they have dishonoured him (also, he does not trust their impartiality with regard to the unjust accusation that has been made against him)[29]. At this point, when he is fleeing from the Russians, the only thing that matters for him is to take vengeance on the person who accused him. Therefore he accepts the renewed invitation to join Shamil: this is the only way in which he will have a possibility of avenging himself on Akhmet-Khan, the ally of the Russian army. From then on, despite his lack of friendship or sympathy for Shamil, he becomes his second-in-

---

29   Tolstoy's story makes it clear that this dishonour has a religious component: the man who defiled him, as the text gives us to understand, was a *giaour*; in Persian, a Christian among Muslims.

command, fights ceaselessly against the invaders and carries out what his enemies consider as military feats. To such an extent that jealousy and the fear of losing power lead Shamil to wish to capture Hadji Murat alive or dead, and he forbids the Caucasian population, on pain of death, to provide him with aid.

Hadji Murat decides to go over to the Russians once again and he promises them that he will kill Shamil or die. During his flight, some villagers fulfil their duty of hospitality despite the prohibition, and four or five men loyally follow him despite the repugnance they feel towards the Russians and their sympathy for Shamil's cause. Thus another dilemma appears: as his mother, two wives and five children have been taken captive by Shamil, he cannot fulfil his promise until the Russians rescue them. But the invaders also do not keep their word: they do not trust the motive that causes Hadji Murat to join them and they do not have the military capacity for the rescue or any intention to exchange his family for prisoners. Once again Shamil offers to pardon him, but Hadji Murat decides to escape from the Russians to the mountains, fight against the rebel leader and rescue his family. So, during an excursion, he escapes with his loyal followers after mercilessly killing all but one of the few members of the small Russian escort that always keeps guard on him. He becomes a wanted man, a reward of a thousand roubles is offered for his head, and a hundred men, comprising Cossacks and local militia, set out after him.

Hadji Murat and his men entrench themselves on a small island among the rice fields. Just when it seems that they are going to escape, their route is blocked by a party of bounty hunters from the mountains led by an old friend and by the son of Akhmet-Khan, the man who falsely accused him. They charge with their swords drawn, Hadji Murat and his men fire repeatedly, and one of them sings 'La ilaha illa allah' ('There is no God but Allah'). The *murids* who accompanied him in his flight fall wounded and dead. He is hit by bullets twice, he gets up to charge with his dagger drawn, is felled, gets up again, and falls. Hadji-Aha, his former friend and now pursuer together with the Russians, strikes him with a dagger. Then, with his sword, he cuts off his head, which is to be passed from village to village. Thus ends Tolstoy's novella.

In 1947 Wittgenstein jotted down a reflection that I think is enlightening:

Someone reacts *like this*: he says 'Not *that*!' – & resists it. Out of this situations perhaps develop which are equally intolerable; & perhaps by then strength for any further revolt is exhausted. We say 'If *he* hadn't done *that*, the evil would not have come about.' But with what justification? Who knows the laws according to which society unfolds? I am sure even the cleverest has no idea. If you fight, you fight. If you hope, you hope.

Someone can fight, hope & even believe, without believing *scientifically*.[30]

This is precisely the situation in the case of Hadji Murat. Although the story of his life may seem incoherent and foolish, a second look enables us to see it as a fight against what he considers as intolerable in various situations. And there is no point in saying 'if you had fought against the Russians with your own people from the very beginning' and so on; or else, 'if you had remained faithful to your first alliance with the other side', etc. For he takes his decisions on the basis of unforeseeable 'social' factors: the political jealousy of Shamil, who orders the capture of Hadji Murat at the time of his greatest success as a fighter; the Tsar's absurd, cruel order to convert the campaign in the Caucasus into a war of extermination that affects his fellow countrymen, who do not understand his collaboration with the aggressors; the changing alliances of the invaders; and, finally, the failure of the Russians to keep their word about rescuing his family. Hadji Murat does not base his conduct on a calculation that presupposes the determination and predictability of human behaviour; instead, at each point he fights against what he considers intolerable, in principle on the basis of the moral code that he shares with his social milieu. The entire novella is studded with passages that emphasise this aspect, and at one point Hadji Murat expresses it in general terms when he is asked what he liked during the time when he was in Tiflis with the Russians:

> 'We have a saying ... A dog asked a donkey to eat with him and gave him meat, the donkey asked the dog and gave him hay: they both went hungry ... Every people finds its own ways good'.[31]

---

30 Wittgenstein, *Culture and Value*, p. 69.
31 Tolstoy, *Hadji Murat*, p. 435.

This reference to the moral code of the community to which one belongs implies other aspects that have to be taken into account, to which I now turn.

In his conversations with Rhees about ethics, Wittgenstein defended the fruitfulness of what might be called the 'anthropological method' in philosophy[32]. In other words, imagining a tribe that behaves in such and such a way as one case of moral systems among others. However, the sociological *description* of the actions and valuations of various groups cannot contain the statement 'such and such constitutes an advance'[33]; that is to say, it does not allow an external valuation from the perspective of our system. Moreover, in 1945 he declared to Rhees that describing the ways and customs of various tribes would not be an ethical discussion because 'studying ways and customs would not be the same as studying rules or laws'[34]; in other words, those descriptions do not tell us how we should behave and the decisions that we should take in specific situations in which it makes sense to ask certain questions. Because, for example, that resolute fight against the intolerable, without any calculation, is a necessary but not sufficient consideration for considering Hadji Murat's various actions morally.

There is a section of the conversations with Rhees that is particularly relevant on this point. When Rhees asked him if he considered Brutus's stabbing of Caesar a noble action (as Plutarch thought) or a diabolical one (as Dante thought), Wittgenstein replied that such a thing could not be discussed because 'You would not know for your life what went on in his mind before he decided to kill Caesar. What he would have had to feel in order that you should say that killing his friend was noble'[35]. Moreover, those feelings might have to do with a sense of belonging, a link with a particular ethical system that we do not know. Rhees and Wittgenstein argued about a case: a man had come to the conclusion that he should either leave his wife or else abandon his work of cancer research because he considered the two

---

32   Rush Rhees, 'Some Developments in Wittgenstein's View of Ethics', *The Philosophical Review*, 74, no. 1 (1965), 17-26 (p. 25).
33   Wittgenstein, in Waismann, p. 15.
34   Wittgenstein, in Rhees, 'Some Developments in...', p. 24.
35   *Ibid.*, p. 22.

things incompatible. Wittgenstein said that if the man acted in accordance with Christian ethics (which must be understood here as morality, in accordance with the distinction that I made earlier), then there was no dilemma: in no case should he leave his wife, and so the problems were different (e.g., how to continue with his work as well as possible, how to behave with his wife in such a difficult situation, etc.). But if the question were posed in relation to a man who 'does not have an ethics' (which must be understood as meaning that he does not adhere to an established moral code), then, taking into consideration all the possible situations (that he stays with her and his work suffers, that although he leaves his work and loves her he turns out to be a bad, resentful husband, that by giving up his life he also wrecks his wife's life, etc.), 'Here we may say that we have all the materials of a tragedy; and we could only say: "Well, God help you"'[36]. In other words: good luck.

We cannot know Brutus's speculations before he killed Caesar, but we do know Hadji Murat's thoughts because Tolstoy sets them down as he constructs his narrative. Thus the reader is confronted with actions that are similar in appearance but have different meanings. On one occasion, the very first time that he faces death with Shamil's followers, he sees his sworn brother fall dead and, fearing for his own life, he runs away. Later he says that he has only to remember that shame in order to fear nothing. Therefore every time that he flees subsequently it is not from fear but, for example in the final escape, in order to rescue his own people. On another occasion, however, Tolstoy takes care to specify that, before he flees from Shamil for the last time in order to go over to the Russian side, his lack of fear does not inspire nobler feelings in Hadji Murat: he does indeed imagine himself at the head of an army provided by the Russians with which to defend his life and avenge the deaths of his people in accordance with the code of his community, but he also cherishes the idea of a reward from the Tsar which will enable him to become governor of Avaria again and rule over the whole of Chechnya.

On the other hand, when he finally rejects Shamil's pardon, decides to fight him and rescue his family, fleeing from the Russians forever, and in the attempt meets his death, Tolstoy also

---

36 *Ibid.*, p. 21.

makes a point of describing Hadji's very different thoughts. He remembers his childhood and his mother, picturing her not as the toothless, shabby captive of Shamil that she has now become. He remembers her when he was a child, clinging to her trousers as she took him to the fountain or being put in a basket to go and see his grandfather, a pious old craftsman who taught him to work with his hands and to pray. He remembers the first time that she shaved his head, just like the first time that he shaved the head of his eldest child, now held captive by Shamil, who wanted to put his eyes out. And he remembers her singing a song when she put him in the bed beside her, a song about an event in the life of Patimat, who was stabbed in the chest by her wrathful husband when she refused to be separated from Hadji Murat in order to be the wet nurse of the son of a khan:

> 'Your damask blade slashed open my white breast, but I pressed to it my darling boy, and washed him in my hot blood, and the wound healed without help of herbs and roots. I did not fear death, no more will my boy-*djigit*.'[37]

To put it briefly, when he escapes for the last time in order to rescue his family Hadji Murat recalls the experience of feeling *absolutely* safe that Wittgenstein described in the 'Lecture on Ethics' as 'the state of mind in which one is inclined to say "I am safe, nothing can injure me whatever happens"'[38]. One of the experiences with which he attempted to indicate the sphere of ethics considered not as 'the general enquiry into what is good' (Moore) but rather as the enquiry into the meaning of life or into what makes life worth living. At the end, when he is fighting to rescue his family, when he no longer belongs to the Russians or the Chechens but only to himself, when he no longer adheres to any precise code of reference, that is what he is fighting for. As Wittgenstein says in his notes:

> Not funk but funk conquered is what is worthy of admiration & makes life worth having been lived. Courage, not cleverness; not even

---

37 Tolstoy, *Hadji Murat*, p. 449.
38 Wittgenstein, 'A Lecture on Ethics', p. 8.

> inspiration, is the grain of mustard that grows up to be a great tree. To the extent there is courage, there is connection with life & death. [...] But it is not by recognizing the want of courage in someone else, that you acquire courage yourself.[39]

This is a central aspect of the novella which I think attracted Wittgenstein's attention powerfully: the figure of the tragic hero depicted by Hadji Murat. In the 1930s, speaking of the fear that he experiences when he is slightly ill and the feeling of the 'breaking of a contract' that God had made to leave him undisturbed, Wittgenstein laments that he finds it hard to endure this fear, which is what he would recommend to others, and he says: 'One likes to see the hero in the other as a drama (that is performed for us) but to be even the least bit of a hero oneself leaves a different taste'[40]. So, as he writes a few years later, it is a weakness not to be a hero, but it is a much greater weakness

> to *play* the hero, thus not even to have the strength to clearly & without ambiguity acknowledge the deficit on the balance sheet. And that means: to become modest: not in a few words which one says once but in life.[41]

Once again, therefore, we find the lesson that he drew from the story 'Two Old Men', on which he commented to Engelmann in the years of the 1914–18 war: no excuses, either to oneself or to others. After the Second World War, probably thinking of his own experience of fighting, Wittgenstein returned to the theme of heroism:

> A hero looks death in the face, real death, not just a picture of death. Behaving decently in a crisis does not mean being able to act the part of a hero well, as in the theatre, it means rather being able to look death *itself* in the eye.[42]

---

39   Wittgenstein, *Culture and Value*, pp. 43–44 (1940).
40   Ludwig Wittgenstein, 'Movements of Thought', in Ludwig Wittgenstein, *Ludwig Wittgenstein: Public and Private Occasions*, ed. by James C. Klagge and Alfred Nordmann (Oxford: Rowman & Littlefield, 2003), p. 63.
41   *Ibid.*, p. 163.
42   Wittgenstein, *Culture and Value*, p. 58 (1946).

And that is precisely what Hadji Murat does after feeling ashamed at having run away when his sworn brother fell dead in an unequal fight with Shamil's men. That is his attitude once again when he decides to abandon the Russians and escape to the mountains in order to fight against that leader and rescue his family. And that is also how he dies, fighting without hope but with a feeling of indifference, and he remembers the song about a fighter, Hamzad, who before dying in a situation similar to his own sings about the radical nature of death:

> You birds of the air, fly to our homes and tell our sisters, our mothers and fair maidens that we died for the *ghazavat*. Tell them our bodies shall lie in no grave, our bones will be carried off and gnawed by ravening wolves and black crows will pick out our eyes.[43]

However, there is not only one way of embodying this heroic view. Wittgenstein considers it in a relative way, historically and individually. A deed performed in other times may now rightly be considered an act of heroism. But it does not depend on the practical aspects of the action which can be described externally, for what decides whether an action is heroic is its 'greatness', which is determined by its 'significance', 'by the pathos which is associated with the way of acting'. It is not the way of acting but the pathos associated with it that decides what is heroic. However, the fact is that different times and peoples (Wittgenstein speaks of 'race') associate their pathos with particular ways of acting, and people who are unaware of this are led astray and continue to think that what is decisive is the external description of the behaviour. Yet when a 'transvaluation of values' takes place and pathos is associated with another way of acting, then it can be seen that what was previously considered heroic is now no longer heroic, even though it may remain in circulation for some time, like 'worthless bills'[44].

I think that, for Wittgenstein, in the character of Hadji Murat there were – to continue with the simile – old bills – which he could use to practise his anthropological method – and bills still

---

43 Tolstoy, *Hadji Murat*, pp. 448–449.
44 Wittgenstein, *Public and Private Occasions*, pp. 31–33.

in circulation. Basically, one: his way of going on doggedly through life, the overcoming of fear, his calm, temperate attitude, cold and at the same time passionate, distanced and ultimately indifferent even to the challenges that death in its various guises presents to him. At the beginning of Tolstoy's story the narrator finds a Tartar thistle as he is walking and exclaims: 'But what strength and vigour, I thought, recalling the effort it had cost me to pluck it. How stoutly it defended itself, and how dearly it sold its life'[45]. And in the last chapter, referring to the slain warrior, the story ends with an evocation of a thistle that had been crushed by a cart wheel: 'This was the death that was brought to my mind by the crushed thistle in the ploughed field'[46].

Yet a further aspect of this character must have attracted Wittgenstein. For Hadji Murat is a man who has lost his roots, like the falcon in the tale told in the hills that, significantly, he remembers before his final departure in order to rescue his family. When the falcon returns to the free falcons in the mountains after the time that he has spent with human beings the other falcons will not accept him because of the silver bells on his legs; but the falcon that had been in captivity wants to stay in the mountains and his fellow falcons kill him. In the fragment *Licht und Schatten* Wittgenstein speaks of the case of a man who reaches the boundaries of his culture and confronts it: 'then it is that confrontation, its type and intensity, that interests us in him, that takes hold of us in his work. The more great the more intensely, the less great the less intensely'[47].

In his memories of his conversations with Wittgenstein, Engelmann speaks of the importance that Wittgenstein attributed to the 'happy end' in Westerns (and in films in general). A film seemed to him to be the acting out of a wish-fulfilment dream and therefore had to end with the satisfying of the wish expressed in the dream. However, in order to make Wittgenstein's opinion credible Engelmann adds something on his own account. Taking as his starting point Hölderlin's distich about Oedipus Rex – 'Many have failed to find words for highest joy's joyous expression, / Here

---

45   Tolstoy, *Hadji Murat*, p. 338.
46   Ibid., p. 464.
47   Ibid., p. 57.

we find it at last, here in sorrow expressed' – Engelmann compares the tragic end to what seems to be its opposite, the happy ending. For whether the transitory moving effect has to do with one type of human being or with the public in general, the tragic end shows, in the form of grief, that which is most joyous; in other words, 'the victory of man's loftiest aspirations over the base side of his nature, a victory he can attain and seal only through his own death'[48].

And this is so in the case of *Hadji Murat*, a dynamic series of pictures in prose that is almost like a Western from Hollywood's golden age.

References

Diamond, Cora, 'Introduction to "Having a rough story about what moral philosophy is"', in *The Literary Wittgenstein*, ed. by John Gibson and Wolfgang Huemer (London: Routledge, 2004).

Drury, O'Connor, Maurice, 'Some Notes on Conversations with Wittgenstein', in *Ludwig Wittgenstein. Personal Recollections*, ed. by Rush Rhees (Oxford: Basil Blackwell, 1981).

Engelmann, Paul, *Letters from Ludwig Wittgenstein with a memoir* (Oxford: Basil Blackwell, 1967).

Gibson, John, and Wolfgang Huemer (eds.), *The Literary Wittgenstein* (London: Routledge, 2004).

Malcolm, Norman, *Ludwig Wittgenstein. A Memoir* (Oxford: Clarendon Press, 2001).

McGuinness, Brian (ed.), *Wittgenstein in Cambridge: Letters and Documents 1911–1951* (Oxford: Blackwell, 2008).

Rhees, Rush, 'Some Developments in Wittgenstein's View of Ethics', *The Philosophical Review*, 74, no. 1 (1965), pp. 17-26.

—, *Ludwig Wittgenstein. Personal Recollections* (Oxford: Basil Blackwell, 1981).

Steiner, George, 'Nineteenth-century America and Russia', in George Steiner, *George Steiner: A Reader* (Oxford: Oxford University Press, 1987).

Tolstoy, Leo, *Hadji Murat*, in *The Cossacks and Other Stories* (London: Penguin Books, 2006).

—, 'How Much Land Does A Man Need?', in Leo Tolstoy, *Twenty-Three Tales* (London: Henry Frowde and Oxford University Press, 1906).

---

48   Engelmann, pp. 92-93.

—, 'The Three Hermits', in Leo Tolstoy, *Twenty-Three Tales*, 1906.
—, 'Two Old Men', in Leo Tolstoy, *Twenty-Three Tales*, 1906.
Von Wright, George Henrik, 'Biographical Sketch', in Norman Malcolm, *Ludwig Wittgenstein. A Memoir.*
Waismann, Friedrich, 'Notes on Talks with Wittgenstein', *The Philosophical Review*, 74, no. 1 (1965), pp. 12-16.
Wittgenstein, Ludwig, 'A Lecture on Ethics', *The Philosophical Review*, 74, no. 1 (1965), pp. 3-12.
—, *Culture and Value* (Oxford: Blackwell, 1998).
—, *On Certainty* (Oxford: Blackwell, 1998).
—, *Movements of Thought*, in *Ludwig Wittgenstein: Public and Private Occasions*, ed. by James C. Klagge and Alfred Nordmann (Oxford: Rowman & Littlefield, 2003).
—, *Licht und Schatten* (Innsbruck: Haymon, 2004).
Wittgenstein, Gretl, 27 October, probably 1945, published electronically in *Gesamtbriefwechsel* by Intelex.

Salvador Rubio Marco[1]
ON SEEING AND ASPECTS
Cometti, Wittgenstein, and *Don Quixote*

This text rests upon a triangle: Jean-Pierre Cometti's work, Ludwig Wittgenstein's ideas, and Cervantes's *Don Quixote*. In fact, the starting point is a quote from Cometti's *Ludwig Wittgenstein et la philosophie de la psychologie* which relates Wittgenstein's concepts of *seeing, seeing as* and *blindness about aspects* to a famous episode of *Don Quixote*.

It is very important for me to specify from the beginning that I am not pretending to compete with the vast and distinguished group of Cervantists and Quixotists. Rather, I am in debt to some of their recent works. Nor am I pretending to enter into discussion with the no less vast and distinguished group of Wittgensteinians despite the fact that I am currently developing, on another level[2], my own theories following in Wittgenstein's footsteps. I want instead to emphasize the third angle of this triangle, taking on the challenge of Jean-Pierre Cometti's comparison and trying to extend it my own way. Obviously, the aim of that undertaking is to pay a humble homage to Cometti's memory and to demonstrate the liveliness of his work in a practical way.

---

[1] Research work for this paper was funded by grants from FFI2015-64271 (MINECO, Spain-FEDER, UE), 18958/JLI/13 (Fundación SENECA, Plan Regional de Ciencia y Tecnología de la Región de Murcia, Spain) and 'Aesthetics Unlimited' (Government of Denmark).
The translations of the Spanish secondary literature on *Don Quixote* will be mine.

[2] This is the aim of a large part of my recent papers and a forthcoming book about the theory of aspects.

Cometti in his *Ludwig Wittgenstein et la philosophie de la psychologie*[3] puts Don Quixote's and Sancho's famous episode of the windmills in intimate connection with the Wittgensteinian concepts of *seeing, seeing-as* and *blindness about aspects*.

> Don Quixote does not see the windmills *as* knights and sometimes *as* windmills. He sees knights, unlike Sancho who sees windmills. Only by knowing that his master sees knights is Sancho possibly able to see windmills as knights, and perhaps he does. In those cases, we would not say that Sancho Panza is *blind* to aspects, nor would we say that Don Quixote does not see anything *except* aspects, which would probably not make much more sense either, and that a distinction between 'seeing' and 'seeing as' is really needed, in spite of the similarity between them. But is that not really a defective way to present the matter? Does this [way of presenting things] not inevitably come into conflict with some objections whose impact we have not really taken into account? What exactly corresponds to the fact of 'perceiving an object'? Is it not equivalent to perceiving it *as* this or *as* that?[4]

The immediate context of Cometti's quote is a well-known and classical philosophical example: the duck-rabbit. Cometti's conclusion is that Wittgenstein was not interested in perceptual trivialities, but rather in psychological and philosophical confusions arising from them[5].

My aim in this paper is not to develop the quote by Cometti (a wonderful commentator of Wittgenstein's work) in order to build a theory of aspects[6]. I prefer to follow along the lines of Cometti's quixotic *motto* by keeping close to a recent philosophical-Cervantist bibliography. Nevertheless, I need to explain Cometti's ideas about 'perceptual trivialities' and

---

3 Jean-Pierre Cometti, *Ludwig Wittgenstein et la philosophie de la psychologie* (Paris: PUF, 2004), p. 64.
4 Ibid., 64.
5 And even that interest was included in Köhler's original criticism of introspection. As we know, Köhler's *Gestalt Psychology* (Wolfgang Köhler, *Gestalt Psychology*, New York: Liveright, 1929; repr. 1970) is the source Wittgenstein's example of the duck-rabbit.
6 See footnote 2.

'psychological and philosophical confusions' before turning to the quixotic perspective.

> To say that I see the duck-rabbit *as* a duck does not make sense unless I admit the possibility of seeing it *also* – but not simultaneously – *as* a rabbit. On the contrary, to *see* a duck there and nothing more or nothing other (alternatively), is not to see it *as* a duck.[7]

So is every *seeing* a *seeing as*? The answer is 'no'. *Seeing* is not necessarily *seeing as*.

Obviously, *seeing as* implies the possibility of seeing the duck or else (but not simultaneously) the rabbit. To see a duck (without any possible alternative) is not *seeing as*, but just *seeing*. Here is another example of Cometti's: On the one hand, I'm admiring Monet's *La Gare Saint-Lazare* in the museum of Orsay. I can see a patch in the painting as smoke or as a locomotive. But on the other hand, 'There is a bench in the front of *La Gare Saint-Lazare*. I see that bench. I would never say that I see it "as" a bench'[8].

Here is the 'perceptual triviality'. Nevertheless, our triviality hides a 'psychological and philosophical confusion' insofar as two grammars of *seeing* are at stake here. Not for nothing, Wittgenstein's reflection on aspects was narrowly connected with the concept of experiencing the meaning of words, understanding music and physiognomy. We are tempted to say that all the confusion orbits around two meanings of seeing:

1) a *strong seeing* or straightforward seeing, which is involuntary ('I see that bench'), and

2) a *soft seeing* or complex seeing, a kind of interpretive-seeing, which is voluntary, even often metaphoric ('I see the patch as a locomotive', but also 'Now I see the funny point of the joke').

An attentive philosopher would quickly remark that

a) *seeing* 1 is not completely non-interpretive and purely perceptual (what does 'purely perceptual' really mean?) because it is mediated by concepts, by language and even by personal history[9],

---

7   Cometti, p. 65.
8   *Ibid.*, p. 66.
9   Vid. *Ibid.*, p. 65.

b) and *seeing 2* is not merely interpretive or voluntary 'I'm not just interpreting the patch as a locomotive, but rather, I see it as a locomotive' or 'I am not able to see it as a locomotive'.

'The straightforward seeing is not subject to the will. But what does that mean? This way of representing the matter is not free of misunderstanding'[10]. The psychological and philosophical confusion lies in trying to take account of the working of those ways of seeing in terms of 'different physiological or mental processes' (without denying the existence of the psychological and physiological phenomena involved):

> My manner of expression could perhaps incline us to think that the distinction between a straightforward seeing and a seeing-as is due to two physiological and psychological processes different in nature, even though the real matter here is only two different uses of the verb 'to see', that is, its grammar. Ought we to conclude that those kinds of 'phenomena' have no relationship, physiologically and psychologically, with that matter? Not necessarily, but the point of interest for Wittgenstein is the confusions to which psychology and philosophy may fall prey.[11]

There is room for a third component: blindness about aspects. Cometti thinks that it is a clear example of 'fictitious concept'[12], related to blindness about meaning or blindness about colours.

> A person who was 'blind to aspects' would see exclusively a rabbit or a duck there where we see now a duck, now a rabbit. In a sense, it is the same thing that happens to us every time when, in spite of the ambiguous nature of the objects with which we are concerned, our regard fixes on an object for what it is, without any alternative; for example, when we see a round tower in the distance as a square tower, as long as I am *just* seeing a square tower, plainly and simply.[13]

Of course, 'our regard fixes on an object for what it is' (or for what we are falsely convinced that it is, in the case of Don Quixote

---

10 Ibid., p. 67.
11 Cometti, p. 67.
12 Vid. Ludwig Wittgenstein, *Culture and Value* (Oxford: Basil Blackwell, 1977; repr. 1989), p. 74e.
13 Cometti, p. 64.

and the knights.) That is exactly Don Quixote's problem. But in terms of aspects and blindness about aspects, the relevant point here is that there is not an alternative way of seeing considered by the viewer. Now, it is time to come back to *Don Quixote* and the Cervantists.

For Serafín Vegas González (Vegas 2016), the episode of the windmills contributes to one of the main dualities of *Don Quixote*, closely linked to the *seeing*. That duality is the following:

(1) Don Quixote does not see, because what he claims to see does not exist or is false.

(2) Don Quixote sees, although what he claims to see does not exist or is false.

As is well known, the episode of the windmills (1, VIII) is preceded in the novel (1, II) by the episode of the inn (in Spanish: *la venta*). There is, according to Vegas, an important difference between the kind of seeing involved in the two episodes:

> i.e., while in the adventure of the inn, Cervantes shows specifically that the castle and the young women that don Quixote *sees* and the sound of the horn that he *hears*, 'seem to him' and 'he pictures it to himself as' being a castle, maidens and a horn played by a dwarf of the castle, in the adventure of the mills *when* ('as well as seeing them') don Quixote *sees* (*discover*) mills, he *sees* (*discover*) giants.[14]

It is clear that, in the episode of the inn, the author is involved in explaining and interpreting the perceptual experience of Don Quixote as representations and judgments without anchorage in reality. Nevertheless, in the episode of the mills, the author

---

14   Serafín Vegas González, *El Quijote desde la reivindicación de la racionalidad* (Alcalá: Centro de Estudios Cervantinos, 2006), p. 218. The passage in Don Quixote is the following: '[...] they *perceived* some thirty or forty windmills that are in the plain; and as soon as Don Quixote *spied* them, he said to his squire: "[...] *look* yonder, friend Sancho Panza, where you may *discover* somewhat more than thirty monstruous giants [...]"' (I, VIII). (Italics mine.) From now, the quotes from *Don Quixote* (Miguel de Cervantes Saavedra, *Don Quixote*, trans. by Charles Jarvis (Oxford: Oxford University Press, 2008) will be simply followed by I or II (part), the chapter number and (if needed) the page number, as is usual for Cervantist scholars.

disappears (he does not intervene by qualifying the character's experience) in order to leave the protagonist on his own in the story and thus Don Quixote's perceptual experiences are less easily interpreted or explained as mere suppositions or mistaken judgments[15].

Following Vegas again[16], Cervantes opens for the reader two different (even if compatible) interpretations of the episodes:

a) The first of these interpretations endorses (1), and is the one according to which Cervantes invites the reader to interpret the adventure of the mills after the adventure of the inn, and then to be inclined to conclude that the giants 'seen' by Don Quixote are the same kind of representations and imaginations as those of the episode of the inn.

b) The second line of reading endorses (2), and is the one according to which Cervantes offers enough clues to interpret the adventure of the inn in the light of the adventure of the mills, and then what Don Quixote 'claims to see' (either castles or giants) is what Don Quixote actually 'sees' (either castles or giants).

We may be tempted to think that the problem can be solved in terms of the distinction between 'objective seeing' ('I see X') and 'propositional seeing' ('I see that p'), in the tradition of Price, Ayer, Wittgenstein or Luntley. It may be considered, in fact, as a sophisticated version of the previous distinction between *strong seeing* and *soft seeing*. This would be to endorse (1).

> In that case, and emphasizing the visual experience as a pattern *par excellence* of perceptual experiences in general, Cervantes earns himself the right to conclude that Don Quixote's confusion between 'objective seeing' (seeing X) and 'propositional seeing' (seeing that p) implies that the knight of La Mancha did not really see what he thought (or judged, or imagined) he was seeing, for Don Quixote affirmed that he was seeing something that was in fact unreal, non-existent: 'seeing in his imagination what he did not see and what did not exist' (I, 18).[17]

---

15   Vid. Vegas, pp. 218-19.
16   *Ibid.*, p. 218.
17   *Ibid.*, p. 221.

Nevertheless, as we know, Wittgenstein insists in many places on the idea that all 'objective seeing' involves necessarily an intentional and conceptual component. Even if 'objective seeing' is a legitimate use of *seeing*, the notion of a passive and primitive 'objective seeing' is nonetheless a myth. At the same time, 'propositional seeing' ('I see that *p*') is a distinctive, primitive and active process (as is also, in a manner, a 'seeing X'):

> [...] we actually 'see' the rational relationships and connections which allow us by themselves to say that, in that specific case, I am seeing that this is a book; in a word, that I am seeing a book.[18]

But I have promised to keep close to the quixotic approach. Don Quixote is a very special kind of madman, because he is always loyal to a reality principle: the laws of chivalry derived from chivalric literature. Don Quixote is perfectly able to see mills, inns, flocks of sheep and village lasses (and not just giants, castles, armies and maidens). He is perfectly able to perceive the reality as does the common man. His exceptional nature appears when, and only when, something elicits the code of chivalry, and then 'the malignant enchanters' become the explanation of every possible hesitation.

Pedro Cerezo has cleverly described that idea concerning in particular the episode of the windmills:

> In Sancho's opinion, Don Quixote works with a code that has broken down and is obsolete:
>
> 'God save me,' quoth Sancho, 'did not I warn you to have a care of what you did, for they were nothing but windmills; and nobody could mistake them but one who had the like in his head.' [I, VIII, 96]
>
> Sancho's answer admits a double meaning: actually, Don Quixote cannot see any other thing than what he already has in his head: the mills invented for the occasion, according to the presuppositions of the code of chivalry; he sees, then, in line with those presuppositions. But for Sancho those presuppositions are supplied by

---

18   *Ibid.*, p. 225.

his madness, that is, the windmills of air in the head of madmen. The pattern is repeated in every adventure where there is a 'delusion of seeing' because the matter is a looking distorted by the code.[19]

Don Quixote's reality principle (his loyalty to the code of chivalry) is also charged with a moral intention, and probably also a social-critical intention, by Cervantes. The scholars generally agree on the idea that the altruistic and courageous attitude of Don Quixote represents a crude complaint against the 'despicable and stingy interests of the selfish and superficial society of the time in which Don Quixote and his contemporaries were living'[20]. More extremely, Manuel Gallego reminds us of Miguel de Unamuno's interpretation of that critical intention in order to endorse his anti-positivist reading:

> Where does the incomplete nature of good old Sancho lie, then? What pushes the squire to refute the knight's statements? What makes him so confident that he sees mills instead of giants?: '... the fear, and just the fear, made Sancho and the other mortals see windmills in the huge giants...'.[21] And that becomes a radical criticism of (according to Unamuno) the evil called progress [...].[22]

However, the giants are, for Unamuno, the mechanics and the chemistry, the bases of progress and of Europe, in a *fin-de-siècle* spirit. Unamuno's anti-positivist reading of Don Quixote, even if rather disputable, supports Don Quixote's approach ahead of Cervantes's approach concerning moral engagement.

Whatever the case may be, I find Vegas's hypothesis very exciting: that the whole novel is a contest between the epistemic fundamentalism[23] of Cervantes and the coherentism of Don Quixote. On the one hand, Cervantes's epistemic fundamentalism justifies

---

19 Pedro Cerezo Galán, *El Quijote y la aventura de la libertad* (Madrid: Biblioteca Nueva, 2016), p. 148.
20 Vegas, p. 281.
21 M. de Unamuno, *Vida de don Quijote y Sancho* (Madrid: Alianza Editorial, 1905; repr. 2015), chap. VIII.
22 Manuel Gallego Arroyo, *Filosofía en el Quijote* (Madrid: Síntesis, 2016), p. 56.
23 'Fundamentalism' translates the original Vegas's Spanish term 'fundamentismo'. The Spanish term avoids some inconvenient connotations that the English term cannot avoid.

his decidedly picking a side in favour of Sancho: Sancho is the only holder of the crude real approach to the phenomena and Don Quixote is described from the beginning of the novel as a madman (even though he is a very particular example of one). Obviously, it endorses thesis (1): Don Quixote does not see, because what he claims to see does not exist or is false. Cervantes operates in his text in order to prevent the reader, time and time again, from realizing that the logic of Don Quixote's discourse corresponds to mistaken visual experiences or hallucinated interpretations of reality.

On the other hand, Don Quixote's coherentism hinges on the idea that the primary elements of physiological perception are dependent on the configuration and organization of physical stimuli according to a linguistic component and the previous experiences, beliefs, and propositional attitudes of the observer. In the case of Don Quixote, the very role of foundations is played by the code of chivalry as a reality principle concerning all his behaviour and his explanation of behaviour throughout the novel, in contrast to the role played by the capacity to fit in with the sensory experiences of the ordinary man. "'One may easily see", answered Don Quixote, "that you are not versed in the business of adventures: they are giants'" (I, VIII). Consequently, Don Quixote sees in the inn a castle corresponding with the criteria of the books of chivalry:

> a castle, with four turrets and battlements of refulgent silver, together with its drawbridge, deep moat, and all the appurtenances with which such castles are usually described. (I, II)

Of course, this is to endorse thesis (2): Don Quixote sees, although what he claims to see does not exist or is false. In fact, there is no other concept for 'see' apart from (or before) this type of processing of linguistically organised and coherent stimuli.

> Don Quixote, in a contrary position to Cervantes, is convinced that the general framework of his chivalrous beliefs justifies the value of truth and the capacity of knowledge of his beliefs according to that framework, and consequently the gentleman of La Mancha feels it is legitimate to require reasonableness for his assertion that the knowledge of the chivalry book guarantees the fact of 'being

experienced in the things of the world' (II, XXIII) and the knowledge of reality.²⁴

Both sides in the discussion open their own particular Pandora's box: the danger of isolation and, ultimately, relativism and scepticism. For Vegas, Cervantes (but never Don Quixote) is clearly an anti-coherentist and anti-relativist. However,

> Classical anti-coherentism, in Schlick's and Cervantes's mode, makes the same mistake as that they attribute to the coherentist, that is, to embrace an absolute knowledge – the sensory one, in this case – as the yardstick that governs every aspiration to truth and knowledge.²⁵

Nevertheless, Don Quixote provides us with a new turn of the screw which adds a grade of complexity to the description of Don Quixote's and Cervantes's positions that we have not seen until now: at the end of the story Don Quixote decides to abandon his chivalrous endeavours and to return to his birthplace thanks to a trick played by the Knight of the White Moon (the bachelor Samson Carrasco in fact); once challenged and defeated, Don Quixote accepts coming back to the village 'for the space of one year' (II, LXIV) and this is the beginning of his presumed *recovery* from madness. Samson Carrasco insists on the idea that Don Quixote could never break his promise of return out of respect for his loyalty and swearing to the Code of knights-errant. We have here, then, a kind of vengeance on Don Quixote's part against Cervantes, for Don Quixote's coherentism is still alive. Consequently, following Vegas:

> [...] the development of the Don Quixote story turns against the fundamentalist approach of Cervantes, for the gentleman of La Mancha never stops to insist convincingly throughout all *Don Quixote* on the idea that the sensory-perceptual experience cannot be considered as a field of self-sufficiently absolute knowledge. The whole of Don Quixote's discourse aims to show very clearly the inconsistency of Cervantes's fundamentalism based on an

---

24 Vegas, p. 274.
25 *Ibid.*, p. 275.

unsustainable conception of knowledge and reality, governed by everyday familiar criteria about what has to be recognized as 'knowledge'.[26]

The solution proposed by Vegas involves a distinction between a surface structure of *Don Quixote*, governed by Cervantes's fundamentalism, and a deep structure of *Don Quixote* which makes room for the coherentist possibility of Don Quixote and, more importantly, for a Cervantes-subject of enunciation (i.e. an implied author, responsible for the whole work) being above the Cervantes-narrator who puts a systematic stop to Don Quixote's coherentism inside the novel[27].

From that point of view, it is possible to understand Vegas's final thesis (in that chapter at least):

> Don Quixote ends up being a valuable tool as a wake-up call about the problems involved in the most common formulations of epistemic fundamentalism, and at the same time Cervantes's novel shows the inconvenience of classical coherentism which, in a similar way to Don Quixote's coherentism, cannot escape the objection of isolation.[28]

It is time to come back to the initial quote by Cometti.

Obviously, the case of *Don Quixote* may be translated or applied only metaphorically to ordinary situations of seeing. It is true that the necessary association of perceptual elements and cognitive elements must be shared by both domains (*Don Quixote* and the usual situations of seeing), but (fortunately) we rarely behave in our lives as radical coherentists governed by strict (literary or not) codes, and our current divergences are far from Don Quixote's windmill-giant duality.

Even so, *Don Quixote* offers us a detailed and lucid deconstruction of that propinquity of diverse 'seeing' and the complexity of perceiving-knowing-feeling-interpreting-understanding of the language games played with the word 'see'

---

26   Ibid., pp. 275-276.
27   Vid. Ibid., p. 258 and following.
28   Ibid., p. 276.

which has been and is a constant source of philosophical and psychological confusion.

An account in terms of aspects is absolutely necessary ('a distinction between "seeing" and "seeing as" is really needed'[29]) in order to account for a good part of our common and hugely diverse situations involving 'seeing' (and hearing or tasting, usually as well), and not just being able to explain the duck-rabbit and other Gestaltist phenomena. Nevertheless, as Cometti notes, it is very significant that not everything about seeing can be explained in terms of aspects and blindness to aspects:

> we would not say that Sancho Panza is blind to aspects, nor would we say that Don Quixote does not see anything *except* aspects, which would probably not make much more sense either.[30]

Effectively, as we have remarked, the problem of Sancho (if he has any problem...) is not that he is blind to aspects (because consequently he would be unable to see giants in the case at hand). Nor can Don Quixote's tendency to see giants be explained in terms of an *aspect-mania*. And even though, the extreme case of Don Quixote's-Sancho's divergence, impossible to reduce to a matter of aspects, tells us crucial things about the grammar of more ordinary *seeing*: for instance, the abuse of the explanatory power of *seeing as* (why we do not usually see a bench *as* a bench).

And recalling Cometti's quote again: 'Does this [way of presenting things] not in fact come into conflict with some objections whose impact we have not really taken into account?'[31]. The perceiving-knowing duality does not work the same way in *Don Quixote* as it does in daily situations involving 'seeing', but the common merit of both (*Don Quixote* and Wittgenstein's work) is that it gives us a wake-up call about the necessary balance between the two, the variations of that balance, and the confusions (philosophical confusions mainly) derived from misunderstandings related to it.

---

29   Cometti, p. 64.
30   Ibid., p. 64.
31   Ibid., p. 64.

Curiously enough, *Don Quixote* is very useful for showing the complexity and diversity of 'seeing', which is the very interest of Cometti – and of course, of Wittgenstein. My text is not much more than an attempt to further develop Cometti's observations by means of some Cervantists ideas, aiming to pay Jean-Pierre a simple and heartfelt homage.

References

Cerezo Galán, Pedro, *El Quijote y la aventura de la libertad* (Madrid: Biblioteca Nueva, 2016).
Cervantes Saavedra, Miguel de, *Don Quixote*, trans. by Charles Jarvis (Oxford: Oxford University Press, 2008).
Cometti, Jean-Pierre, *Ludwig Wittgenstein et la philosophie de la psychologie* (Paris: PUF, 2004).
Gallego Arroyo, Manuel, *Filosofía en el Quijote* (Madrid: Síntesis, 2016).
Köhler, Wolfgang, *Gestalt Psychology* (New York: Liveright, 1970).
Unamuno, Miguel de, *Vida de don Quijote y Sancho* (Madrid: Alianza Editorial, 2015).
Vegas González, Serafín, *El Quijote desde la reivindicación de la racionalidad* (Alcalá: Centro de Estudios Cervantinos, 2006).
Wittgenstein, Ludwig, *Culture and Value* (Oxford: Basil Blackwell, 1977; repr. 1989).

TOWARD AN ANTHROPOLOGICAL AESTHETICS. IN CONVERSATION WITH JEAN-PIERRE COMETTI

Jacques Morizot
COMETTI'S LATE THOUGHTS
Some Notes on Contemporary Art and Agency[1]

As everybody knows (or not), Jean-Pierre Cometti's relation to writing was insatiable. In fact he was something of a bulimic: more than one hundred books, either as an author, translator, editor, director of a collective publication, without even counting his multiple activities as consultant for publishers. Quite rightly, he was not reluctant to qualify himself as a Stakhanovite. And even if it is easy to find numerous resurgences in this ever-growing mass of writings, there is nowhere the mark of sheer repetitions or the symptom of an endless litany. On the one hand, these are rather inventive variations on obsessive themes. On the other hand, they do not converge toward a unique centre, for his oeuvre has always been in progress, and was at the same time burdened by tensions he was quite indifferent to overcoming. And probably he would not have perceived things under this description.

When I first met him at the end of the eighties, his major philosophical reference was Ludwig Wittgenstein, and more precisely, the developments that appeared after 1925 or so that show evidence of a growing distance from the *Tractatus*[2] and formal thinking. Just as Wittgenstein never fully broke with the masterpiece of his youth, despite continually revising the contents and modifying the original inspiration, Cometti never renounced his deep affinity with Wittgenstein's later philosophy, especially as regards forms of life and what is most elusive in our cultural

---

1   I would like to thank Jerrold Levinson for his careful reading of my text, which undoubtedly has improved it.
2   Ludwig Wittgenstein, *Tractatus Logico-Philosophicus* (London: Routledge & Kegan Paul, 1922).

practices. But the growing importance taken by the American pragmatists, first and foremost John Dewey, tended to displace the centre of gravity toward more social issues, where the interplay of art with the various dimensions of society and pedagogy becomes prominent.

In fact, from the start, Cometti kept close contact with art and the world of the arts. He began as a guitarist performing in jazz groups, but also maintained a strong complicity with the poets grouped together in the *Cahiers du Sud* in Marseille; moreover, he spared no effort to support young artists, by writing in catalogues or organizing discussions with them. During a long period, philosophy of art was present only indirectly, through a dialogue with themes borrowed from Robert Musil, Martin Heidegger, or Wittgenstein on architecture. It manifests itself in *L'art sans qualités*[3], through the pages devoted to Kandinsky, Mondrian or Soun-Gui Kim, and similarly in *Art, modes d'emploi*[4]. However, Cometti never wrote as an art critic, even though the nature of criticism was a constant concern for him.

It is later that a corpus emerges explicitly centred on the phenomenon of art as a major expression, not of humanity in the abstract but of the multiplicity of our collective behaviours. It is the subject of his trilogy: *La force d'un malentendu*[5], *Art et facteurs d'art*[6] and *La nouvelle aura*[7], to which one must add *Conserver-Restaurer*[8]. The present paper focuses on this last phase of Cometti's heritage, a set of books with rather definite limits but of course not without tight relations with other writings dealing with democracy, literature, and norms.

This late phase of reflection is dominated by the idea of modernity and contemporary art, through Cometti's strong conviction that aesthetic autonomy is not only a delusion but also

---

3   Jean-Pierre Cometti, *L'art sans qualités* (Tours: Farrago, 1999).
4   Jean-Pierre Cometti, *Art, modes d'emploi* (Bruxelles: La Lettre volée, 2000).
5   Jean-Pierre Cometti, *La force d'un malentendu* (Paris: Questions théoriques, 2009).
6   Jean-Pierre Cometti, *Art et facteurs d'art* (Rennes: Presses Universitaires de Rennes, 2012).
7   Jean-Pierre Cometti, *La nouvelle aura* (Paris: Questions théoriques, 2016), p. 219.
8   Jean-Pierre Cometti, *Conserver/restaurer. L'œuvre d'art à l'époque de sa préservation technique* (Paris: Gallimard, 2015).

a noxious ideology that pervades every aspect of art's conception. The notion of autonomy in relation to art combines an aesthetic component, mainly of Kantian origin (disinterestedness, etc.), and an artistic one, according to which art is its own definition and consequently, that any possibility of interpreting it functions within the limits of its own genealogy, since it consists of this network of formal transformations or cross-references). Often this period is identified as a troublesome effort to achieve liberation, through a situation of independence from the straightjacket that imposed external constraints, such as social or moral ones, on artistic production, and sometimes as the fulfilment of the romantic ideal of an artist's being able to claim responsibility for his free creation instead of being subjected to the will of his patrons, despite the growing power of gallerists and curators. Contrary to that, Cometti regards artistic autonomy as but 'a contingent product of history', if not a vulgar by-product, motivated from the outside by an exercise of selective memory – as in fact nothing more than an intellectual cement, largely independent from artistic materials. The real fact is that a work of art has no stable identity through time and that the distinction between aesthetic and artistic is either factitious, or deceptive and perverse. For all these reasons, Cometti was inclined to stress the structures of the 'art-institution' and the intricate circumstances that rules over its reception.

For Cometti, two episodes in the course of modern history have a special sort of significance when viewed from the standpoint of art's functioning: the thunderbolt of Dada and the adventure of the Black Mountain College, some decades later. These involve complementary and perhaps cumulative insights, not only in the intrinsic content of their activities but also in some major aspects brought to bear by selected readings, and in particular, the figures of Bürger and Dewey.

Dada's only privilege lies in exhibiting the most aggressive clash of rebellion against the common values accepted to that time in the main areas of society. In the artistic field, a prominent expression is the growing split between the classical notion of an artwork, defined by its internal composition and structure, and the avant-garde notion of a work open to badly matched connections with the exterior and unforeseeable settings that prevent it from reaching any sustainable unity. This loss of identity between form and content has as a result to keep such work away from any received stereotype, and correspondingly, to bring it into the conflicting and experimental space of theory. But one should never forget that this apparent vogue of destruction is also the reverse side of a tentative construction that had to wait for half a century to find a satisfactory interpretation[9].

Bürger's indispensable merit lies in his 1974 attempt to provide a critical and social reading of art at a time when formalist approaches were dominant[10]. But while Cometti supported with enthusiasm Bürger's plan to elaborate the 'categorial framework' of twentieth century art, personally I have always thought that he was paying too little attention to certain blind spots in *Theory of the Avant-Garde*. To my eyes at least, Bürger's analysis suffers from several kinds of limitation or drawbacks that weaken its useful scope. First, the book's strong dependence on the Marxist concept of ideology is too simplistic and uniform to provide valuable insights, particularly during a troubled historical period. Second, the choice of literature as the main point of reference, and in particular the surrealist nexus, is dubious, since it is more likely that cubism in the plastic arts, even more than abstraction, was the leading artistic movement at the time. Third, the area covered seems too restricted at the cultural and intellectual level, since it borrows almost exclusively from research published in German. I remember I had with Jean-Pierre a long discussion in a terrace café near the Canebière in Marseille, where I tried to push my arguments forward. Though he agreed on several points, I don't think I was able to convince him altogether of the weakness of Burger's brief.

Regarding Black Mountain College, it would seem at first sight that the stakes are not so dissimilar, but the fact is that a very different context modifies the whole phenomenon. For this

---

9   See Hal Foster, *The Return of the Real* (Cambridge, MA: MIT Press, 1996), chap. 1.
10 Peter Bürger, *Theorie der Avantgarde* (Francfort am Main: Suhrkamp Verlag, 1974); in English, *Theorie of the Avant-Garde,* trans. by Michael Shaw (Minnesota: University of Minnesota Press, 1984); the French translation due to Cometti, *Theorie de l'avant-garde* (Paris: Questions théoriques, 2013). An insightful perspective is offered in Olivier Quintyn, *Valences de l'avant-garde* (Paris: Questions théoriques, 2015), chap. 1.

episode takes place in a University, so that questions of education and training become much more important than incitement to social provocation. We must recall that John Andrew Rice founded that college in 1933 as an open institution delivering no diplomas but involved in any and all innovative methods pertaining to the arts. The underlying model was without a doubt the Bauhaus, with its continuous exchange between theory and practice and its insistence on explanatory programs applicable to distant areas. So it is no surprise that, after its closing in 1932, former teachers from Dessau decided to emigrate to North Carolina (Josef Albers, Walter Gropius, Marcel Breuer, among others), joining some of the most advanced American artists. Throughout its existence – that is, until 1957 – Black Mountain College was indeed an exceptional laboratory for all forms of creation. This ran from the most daring and unexpected, for instance *4'33"*, a silent piece performed by David Tudor with the complicity of John Cage and Merce Cunningham, or the *White Paintings* by Rauschenberg, to pioneering studies devoted to architecture, such as Buckminster Fuller's invention of the geodesic dome, to technology marking a significant step toward the E.A.T.[11] in the 60s[12].

The intellectual inspiration comes obviously from Dewey, particularly his William James Lectures delivered at Harvard in 1931 and published in 1934 under the title *Art as Experience*[13]. They resulted largely from reflection on the modernist works of the Barnes Collection, and Dewey's lessons tried to provide a thorough description of the various stages of the artistic process and reception. The ambition of Black Mountain College was to

---

11 E.A.T. is the acronym of 'Experiments in Art and Technology', an initiative taken by Rauschenberg and the engineer Billy Klüver to help artists in the use of technical solutions for works or shows. One of its major interventions was *9 Evenings: Theater and Engineering* and took place in New York, 13-23 October 1966.
12 For an overall survey, see Jean-Pierre Cometti and Éric Giraud (eds), *Black Mountain College* (Rennes: Presses Universitaires de Rennes, 2014); Mary Emma Harris, *The Arts at Black Mountain College* (Cambridge, MA: MIT Press, 1987); Vincent Katz (ed.), *Black Mountain College. Experiment in Art* (Harvard: MIT Press, 2002).
13 John Dewey, *Art as Experience* (1934), reprinted in *John Dewey: The Later Works, 1925-1953*, vol. 10, ed. by Jo Ann Boydston (Carbondale: Southern Illinois University Press, 1989).

expand this type of inquiry from the artisanal and philanthropic level that took place in Merion to a full experimental view of the creative powers involved in art. In Dewey's words, the issue lay in the experience of democracy and democratic meaning in the arts, for he was confident that art is the paradigm of creative democracy. We find here all the common ingredients of a classical utopia in the cultural field, with its double valence: a fascination for something that looks like a sort of miracle and in the same time a distant uneasiness when this compelling seduction gives way to the feeling of a lost paradise. However, in *La démocratie radicale*[14], Cometti commits himself to a re-examination of Dewey's ideals in a more comprehensive survey, with questioning of liberalism applied to a world of individuals. He does not renounce his initial diagnosis, the will to expand culture to society as a whole instead of restricting it to a minority, but the tonality is somewhat disenchanted, as if the resources of the Enlightenment project were now exhausted. He writes that moments like the one at Black Mountain College are rather 'like parentheses in history, after which they have been shut out again'[15]. Their potential strength remains available, but the conditions of their actual development are scarce and subject to a happy coincidence.

I have already said that Cometti's two intellectual landmarks were Wittgenstein's later philosophy and Dewey's pragmatism, the influence of Peirce and James being far less pronounced. When pondering on the forms of life – interestingly, Wittgenstein hesitates in German between *Lebensform* and the more commonplace term of *Lebensweise* – there is every chance to get involved in naturalizing or socializing the relation between human beings and their environments, both as a natural species and as more or less lucid members of a community. Through the key notion of experience, Richard Shusterman remarks, Dewey is in full agreement with Emerson when he wrote: 'there is something better to do for art than the arts [...] Nothing less than the creation of man and nature'[16]. Art is an essential link and a

---

14 Jean-Pierre Cometti, *La démocratie radicale* (Paris: Gallimard, 2016).
15 *Ibid.*, p. 243.
16 In his Preface to the French translation of John Dewey, *L'art comme expérience* (Tours: Publications de l'Université de Pau/Farrago, 2005), p. 9.

powerful accelerator between our distant Darwinian roots and the prospect of reconstructing philosophy, or even the entire system of culture. Cometti is a direct descendent of this inspiration, in my view much more so than he is of Rorty's ironism, even if the two men were close friends. But how can we locate the specifics of this common area designated as 'art'?

Wittgenstein's seminal insight about language games was his refusal to adopt as a starting point the datum that words have a permanent identity, deposited in dictionaries, and that propositions have a definite meaning revealed by their logical analysis. Much more important are imports from contexts of use, differences in usage or background assumptions, or continuous discrepancies in the way of comprehending them. The same is true in relation to art matters. Ernst Hans Gombrich is famous for his statement that art does not exist but only individual artists, whose activities and production may exhibit similarities and analogies, although it is impossible to describe them all as members of a distinctive class[17]. The next step taken by Cometti leads him to insist that works themselves – the putative common denominator among artists of whatever sort – do not exist either but that they gain some identity, if any, through the type of appropriation involved – hence the place given to audience, galleries, exhibitions, and so on. The most remarkable situation is probably that of interactive works whose status is no longer that of an object and where the players are mere agents in the course of the game instead of subjects in the full sense of the term.

To conceive of this new frame of understanding, Cometti has coined the concept of *artmakers* (in French 'facteurs d'art') on the model of *truthmakers* in epistemology. A truthmaker is that in virtue of which something is true, or the kind of entity in the world that can act as a bearer of truth. Although there is still no universally accepted theory of truthmaking – the most common proposals include entailment, necessitation, and projection – the suggestion has had a strong impact on the topic of the ontology of truth. If we take the idea of artmakers seriously, it is probable that the whole practice of describing and interpreting art phenomena

---

17   Cf. the introduction in Ernst Hans Gombrich, *The Story of Art* (London: Phaidon, 1972).

will also be open to a complete reappraisal. Cometti himself has given many insights and instances in the books mentioned above, with regard to aesthetic notions and the network of artistic properties and contexts involved, so I will not offer any additional development here.

Instead, I want to focus on several philosophical commitments at the heart of his enterprise. (1) The first issue deals with realism, a position that is coming back fiercely after its decline in modern times. It goes without saying that Cometti had not the least sympathy for the very notion of an aesthetic property, either viewed as inherent to something's mode of being or as a result of some consensus. (Regarding the latter, if the convergence of opinion does not prove the reality of an underlying property, the denial of any assumption of that type tends to make the agreement at least opaque if not arbitrary). Too often this debate is complicated by quarrels about terminology or inconsistencies in definitions. The gist of the problem is indeed elsewhere.

From Cometti's standpoint, realism relies heavily on two presuppositions whose effect is to issue in a dead end[18]. The first one is to make us believe that realism is the only actual alternative to relativism, and since relativism is hampered by so many drawbacks, that it is sensible to adhere to realism. In fact, realism and relativism are unholy accomplices, if not the two faces of the same coin, because they share the same beliefs regarding the objective- subjective duality. From this follows the difficulty of giving a satisfactory treatment of expressive properties (such as emotional ones) and of aspects. The second one is realism's claim to enjoy a dominant position over any other, since it represents *par excellence* the drive of the closest desirable contact with reality, instead of any artificial or *ad hoc* construction. It is true that a realist anchoring secures against dissolution of the world in favour of sheer versions or descriptions, and also a proliferation of possible worlds, but in aesthetic matters it amounts to a shrinking of the space of conceptualisation. To protect oneself from the risks of projection or evaluation, one is compelled to conceive of several levels connected by subtle relationships, such as by appeal

---

18   The most meaningful passages are taken from Cometti, *Art et facteurs d'art*, chap. III.

to supervenience. Besides, it is widely acknowledged that such a tendency is a common accompaniment of the metaphysical revival (as opposed to proposals from cognitive sciences), without excluding theological extensions (such as Roger Pouivet's appeal to the Thomist anthropology of which Cometti was so critical). I can only agree with him that this is not the best news for the prospects of aesthetics.

(2) A convergent sort of questioning arises in relation to ontology. Under Cometti's pen, the word serves as a repulsive token in favour of a philosophy of usage. For he had the strong conviction that it is derived from the paradigm of the object, so that any work is supposed to contain in itself all that defines its identity as a work, independently of any link to a context or audience. This essentialist prejudice, that has remote roots in Ancient Greece, is particularly noticeable in what Schaeffer dubs the 'speculative theory of art', whose most fertile terrain has been German idealism. Of course a pragmatic approach is forced to be at variance with the central tenets of such philosophy.

Is it necessary, for all that, to give up any idea of an ontological support? Cometti knows too well that this is an additional illusion. But there is still a challenge to be met: the decision to broach ontology in a more modest setting, at an existential rather than a formal level. Art must not be viewed as 'a separate kingdom', a situation that inevitably fosters aestheticism and formalism. By contrast, what is really at stake is the endless diversity of the arts, as Peter Kivy and Dominic Lopes, among others, have championed[19]. Cometti's crusade may also be summarized by Noël Carroll's agenda, when he notes that 'all we will be forswearing is the responsibility we never mastered anyway, the definition of art with a capital "A"'[20]. For his part, Cometti likes to speak of crumbly or precarious ontologies, by which he means ontologies with a limited and varying scope, or which grasp only one aspect to the detriment of others, and are thus open to unending revision according to new circumstances or other appropriations. In a nutshell, what is

---

19 Peter Kivy, *Philosophies of Arts* (Cambridge, Cambridge UP, 1997); Dominic McIver Lopes, *Beyond Art* (Oxford: Oxford University Press, 2014), which argues for 'a buck passing theory of art'.
20 Noël Carroll, *Art in Three Dimensions* (Oxford: Oxford University Press, 2010), p. 15.

criticized is less ontology as a neutral and intellectual tool than the abusive absolute use of it that philosophers are prone to.

It is nevertheless regrettable that Cometti largely neglected the ontological revival of the last half-century, from a descriptive and sometimes a revisionist viewpoint. (This is all the more surprising, since Cometti had himself translated David Lewis's masterwork in that vein.) At the centre of these reflections lay the question of the ontological basis, with the proviso that a material basis is no more compulsory. It should be remarked that a material basis is neither restricted to unique works since it makes sense to consider copies, versions, reproductions of pictures as a legitimate counterpart of musical performances (see Eddy Zemach for instance), nor prohibited for hybrid and more complex works. But the important fact is the availability of competing hypotheses, in the first place of which one may mention ontologies based on action, by way of tokens and even types of it. The idea is to treat any work as an event, giving prominence to the on-going process rather than the fully accomplished result. The best-developed proposition is supplied by David Davies who characterizes a work as an artistic statement articulated in a suitable medium so as to specify what he calls 'a focus of appreciation'[21]. According to him, aesthetic empiricism and even refined contextualism are unable to explain the success of perception as regards what ought to be appreciated in a given performance, because they fail the 'work-relativity of modality' and hence the comprehension of artworks as 'doings'. Even if Cometti is more concerned by the environmental aftermath of works rather than by their internal structure, it is still regrettable that a potentially rich dialogue with Davies failed to emerge, through lack of discrimination between work-performances and performance-works[22].

(3) A last topic worthy of notice relates to the *aura*. Since Benjamin, it is common to repeat that a typical feature of modernity is the decay of a privileged dimension of any work, namely what is part of a ritual constitutive of its uniqueness and authenticity, the

---

21 David Davies, *Art as Performance* (Oxford: Blackwell, 2004).
22 See the disputatio on Davies's book in *Philosophiques*, 32/1, 2005, Société de Philosophie du Québec, especially Cometti's remarks (pp. 220-224) and Davies's answers (pp. 243-245).

aura characterized as a phenomenon of appearance and 'distance however close it may be'[23]. In other words, the modern techniques of reproduction jeopardize a work's 'unique existence at the place where it happens to be' – and ultimately, the work's belonging to a tradition. Often these remarks are interpreted as reflecting a nostalgic mood, but Benjamin does not forget that then new forms of art, such as film, accommodate these situations and modify the development of aesthetic experience. From some decades on, a manifestation Benjamin could not have anticipated is going to shatter his own conclusions. Cometti agrees with Maurizio Ferraris that the media coverage of contemporary art creates an all-new context that begets paradoxically a new sort of aura, still more powerful that the former fetishism of masterpieces. 'The idea defended in this book consists in the thought that the aura attached to objects like artworks is one component of its value in the economic sense of the term, and secondly that the conditions that are today part of their mode of production and distribution are also the source of a specific aura'[24]. This occurs when the work becomes the subject, if not the hostage, of a spectacular stage setting, hands itself over to luxury, or enters in famous art collections located in prestigious places. The kind of 'super-auratisation' that follows has a contagious effect, not only via plain connection with other works but indirectly, by means of transfer that eventuates in a process of heritage or better, 'an instrumented and generalized process of patrimonialising', a situation that fascinated and repelled Cometti in the same time.

It is essential to keep the preceding remarks in mind as we turn our attention to Cometti's ultimate book, *Conserver/Restaurer*, the fruit of a seminar given at the École Supérieure d'Art in Avignon. Cometti was himself quite aware of potential problems with it, writing that 'conservation [/restoration] borrows probably too much from spectator theory and too little from a philosophy of usage, hence its troubles with notions of work, intentionality,

---

[23] Walter Benjamin, *The Work of Art in the Age of its Technological Reproducibility*, trans. by Michael W. Jennings (Cambridge, MA: Belknap Press, 2008).

[24] Cometti, *La nouvelle aura*, p. 219. See also Maurizio Ferraris, 'Esthétique naturalisée et art culturalisé', in *Naturaliser l'esthétique?*, ed. by Jacques Morizot (Rennes: PUR, Æsthetica, 2014).

and identity'[25]. At the heart of his analysis is the notion of a condition report (in French 'constat d'état') that takes stock of the material state of an object or work so as to decide what operations are suitable to keep it in order and repair possible damages. Of course, Cometti has nothing to object to the general methodology, but insists on interpreting it along pragmatist lines as a genuine inquiry that should aim at the largest available framework. So he underlines that a 'condition report appeals implicitly to background conditions and categories that forbid thinking it is only a matter of describing as precisely as required the material data'[26]. The challenge is to make explicit most of those background considerations, the purpose being to arrive at an efficient and original solution, proceeding by abductive reasoning, for there is no ready-to-hand rule for applying any general law.

Cometti's enemy in this domain is Cesare Brandi – probably the most famous theoretician on restoration at least in Italy and France – who sticks to the principles of an organicist and aestheticist policy. It is indeed advisable when a work prominently features a *Gestalt*, but erasing a layer of blackened varnish or even mending a gap on a damaged fresco does not offer any manageable strategy when confronted with, say, an assemblage or installation work. One interesting example evoked in the book is Ruggirello's composite work (*Untitled*, 1989) than includes more than three thousands dry bees thumbtacked with regularity on a white panel with addition of photo prints. When examined in 2012, the support appears to be dusty, a lot of bees are damaged, and numbers of them are missing. What kind of decision is appropriate to the situation? (To replace all the bees? To replace just the damaged ones? To make use of facsimiles instead?) Technical constraints and proposals are just one factor; aesthetic appearance and the conformity to the artist's priorities also play an important role – in the present case, the artist did not dismiss the possibility of creating this work anew if damaged – along with the history of its reception[27]. By the way, it is interesting to notice close relationships and even some

---

25 Cometti, *Conserver/restaurer*, pp. 71-72.
26 *Ibid..*, p. 268.
27 Vid. *Ibid.*, p. 21. This work was the subject of a DNSEP Master by Y. Dechezlepretre (2012, dir. C. Jarton) available on the ESAA site.

intellectual spin-off with the questioning nowadays focused on exhibitions and museums policies.

If the book had a rather unfavourable reception among professionals, that was not so much due to their radical hostility to its contents – for very few people today contest the need to anchor properties in real contexts of use – than because of the narrowness of the documentary basis that chose to overlook the greatest part of the current studies in this field. Unfortunately Cometti missed the opportunity to profit from lots of recent developments that indeed offer insightful lines of thought[28]. Moreover, technologies derived from informatics can now offer sophisticated solutions that correct visible deficiencies without modifying the physical state of the object under consideration[29]. Lots of these innovative researches and initiatives move the boundaries in a direction rather favourable to the issues of the book. So one is inclined to think that the ascendance of a putative official theory of restoration over the whole profession is less the case than Cometti seems to imply, and that the selection of Brandi as an opponent and stalking horse was somewhat ad hoc. Yet it remains a daring move of Cometti to propose that the route is straightforward from a philosophy of usage to a policy about restoration.

To sum up, this last phase of Cometti's multifarious oeuvre offers considerable spurs for rethinking aesthetic theory and practice, provided one does not search in them for what they are unable to offer. He had no taste at all for questions of definition, the critical starting point for most post-Wittgensteinan aesthetics, and almost none for the protocols of description and justification that Sibley took to be the main concern in aesthetics. According to Cometti,

---

28 As a very short sample: Alfredo Vega Cardenas, 'Restauration épistémologique. Vers une méthodologie transdisciplinaire pour la conservation-restauration', *CeROArt* [en ligne], 6 (2011) <http://ceroart.revues.org/2120> [accessed 4 February 2019]; Yaël Kreplak, 'Voir une œuvre en action. Une étude praxéologique de l'étude des œuvres', *Les Cahiers du CAP*, 4, Publications de la Sorbonne (2017), pp. 189-213.

29 The best example I know of is Rothko's *Harvard Murals* in Boston, restored by C. Mancusi-Ungaro's team; see 'Light Repairs', A roundtable on the restoration of Mark Rothko's Harvard Murals, *Artforum international* (summer 2015) <https://www.artforum.com/print/201506/light-repairs-a-roundtable-on-the-restoration-of-mark-rothko-s-harvard-murals-52269> [accessed 4 February 2019]

most of what goes under the label of analytic aesthetics was but a pretentious scholasticism that obstructs rather than facilitates an understanding of artworks. Apart from the pragmatist literature at large in its political dimension, he was at the end leaning more and more towards authors who focus attention on the creative part of art due to either the artist or the spectator. This explains why he remained committed to the Goodman of *Ways of Worldmaking*[30], the three-dimensional framework of Carroll's late writings, and the emergence of relational aesthetics. It also explains why he never broke altogether with Heidegger's ghost, an inspiration he shared with Rorty.

Whether or not one feels a strong sympathy for the kind of philosophy Cometti supported, it is legitimate to put forward two types of limits regarding the very notion of usage, the first internal and the other external. The first one has to do with the conceivable links between pragmatism and illocutionary logic. Creating a work can be seen as an extended sort of speech act, so similar questions could arise on that subject: What felicity conditions apply? Is the notion of failed art still admissible, and if so, how should it be managed?[31] Also, apart from differences in reception, is there a clear distinction between an imaginative interpretation and a mere misunderstanding of a work of art? What individual responses rightly testify to the shareable value of a work?

The other one is about the sense of the paradigm itself. It is undoubtedly right that focusing exclusively on the object as a material entity severs the work from its functioning modalities. But it seems also legitimate to ask a reciprocal question: if and when everything is dissolved in a maze of usages, it becomes more and more difficult to say what there is usage *of*. It is unlikely that usage is an intransitive term, and it is always at risk of being an empty nutshell without a definite correlate. These notions deconstruct one another, maybe endlessly.

---

30 Nelson Goodman, *Ways of Worldmaking* (Cambridge, MA: Hackett, 1978).
31 Some of these questions are tackled from the point of view of intention-dependence in Christy Mag Uidhir, *Art and Art-Attempts* (Oxford: Oxford University Press, 2013). Jerrold Levinson, David Davies, and Dominic Lopes have also devoted remarks to that topic.

References

Benjamin, Walter, *The Work of Art in the Age of its Technological Reproducibility*, trans. by Michael W. Jennings (Cambridge, MA: Belknap Press, 2008).
Bürger, Peter, *Theorie der Avantgarde* (Francfort am Main: Suhrkamp Verlag, 1974); in English, *Theorie of the Avant-Garde*, trans. by Michael Shaw (Minnesota: University of Minnesota Press, 1984); in French, *Theorie de l'avant-garde*, trans. by Jean-Pierre Cometti (Paris: Questions théoriques, 2013).
Carroll, Noël, *Art in Three Dimensions* (Oxford: Oxford University Press, 2010).
Cometti, Jean-Pierre, *Art et facteurs d'art* (Rennes: Presses Universitaires de Rennes, 2012).
—, *Art, modes d'emploi* (Brussels: La Lettre volée, 2000).
—, 'Disputatio on David Davies', *Philosophiques*, 32/1 (2005), pp. 220-224.
—, *L'art sans qualités* (Tours: Farrago, 1999).
—, *Conserver/restaurer. L'œuvre d'art à l'époque de sa préservation technique* (Paris: Gallimard, 2015).
—, *La démocratie radicale* (Paris: Gallimard, 2016).
—, *La force d'un malentendu* (Paris: Questions théoriques, 2009).
—, *La nouvelle aura* (Paris: Questions théoriques, 2016), p. 219.
Cometti, Jean-Pierre et Éric Giraud (eds), *Black Mountain College* (Rennes: Presses Universitaires de Rennes, 2014).
Davies, David, *Art as Performance* (Oxford: Blackwell, 2004).
—, 'Disputatio on David Davies', *Philosophiques*, 32/1 (2005), pp. 243-245.
Dewey, John, *Art as Experience* (1934), repr. in *John Dewey: The Later Works, 1925–1953*, vol. 10, ed. by Jo Ann Boydston (Carbondale: Southern Illinois University Press, 1989); in French, *L'art comme expérience*, trans. by Jean-Pierre Cometti (Tours: Publications de l'Université de Pau/Farrago, 2005).
Ferraris, Maurizio, 'Esthétique naturalisée et art culturalisé', in *Naturaliser l'esthétique?*, ed. by Jacques Morizot (Rennes: PUR, Æsthetica, 2014).
Foster, Hal Foster, *The Return of the Real* (Cambridge MA, MIT Press, 1996).
Gombrich, Ernst Hans, *The Story of Art* (London: Phaidon, 1972).
Goodman, Nelson, *Ways of Worldmaking* (Cambridge, MA: Hackett, 1978).
Harris, Mary Emma, *The Arts at Black Mountain College* (Cambridge, MA, MIT Press, 1987).
Katz, Vincent (ed.), *Black Mountain College. Experiment in Art* (Harvard, MIT Press, 2002).

Kivy, Peter, *Philosophies of Arts* (Cambridge, Cambridge UP, 1997).

Kreplak, Yaël, 'Voir une œuvre en action. Une étude praxéologique de l'étude des œuvres', *Les Cahiers du CAP*, 4, Publications de la Sorbonne (2017), pp. 189-213.

Lopes, Dominic McIver, *Beyond Art* (Oxford: Oxford University Press, 2014).

Mancusi-Ungaro, Carol et al, 'Light Repairs', A roundtable on the restoration of Mark Rothko's Harvard Murals, *Artforum international*, (summer 2015), <https://www.artforum.com/print/201506/light-repairs-a-roundtable-on-the-restoration-of-mark-rothko-s-harvard-murals-52269> [accessed 4 February 2019]

Quintyn, Olivier, *Valences de l'avant-garde* (Paris: Questions théoriques, 2015).

Uidhir, Christy Mag, *Art and Art-Attempts* (Oxford: Oxford University Press, 2013).

Vega Cardenas, Alfredo 'Restauration épistémologique. Vers une méthodologie transdisciplinaire pour la conservation-restauration', *CeROArt* [en ligne], 6 (2011), <http://ceroart.revues.org/2120> [accessed 4 February 2019]

Wittgenstein, Ludwig, *Tractatus Logico-Philosophicus* (London: Routledge & Kegan Paul, 1922).

Roberta Dreon
AESTHETIC CONSUMPTIONS AND ANTHROPOLOGICAL NEEDS

1. *A prelude of sorts*

A few years ago I organized a one-day workshop in Venice together with some colleagues and friends[1], entitled 'What is art for?'. Its rather over-ambitious aim was more or less explicitly represented by the discussion of one of the crucial assumptions regarding the modern art system as an autonomous realm, which Jean-Pierre Cometti did not hesitate to call a 'myth'. This assumption had to do with

> the old idea we inherited from the XVIII century, that was expressed in Kant's work and later elevated to a superior power by the Romantics – namely the idea that the arts have their own purpose *in themselves* and that they do not answer any exterior *interest*.[2]

In those years Cometti's long-standing interest in the arts and the aesthetic debate had been shifting toward the social and political bearings of the institutionalized practice of art, probably under the influence of his research on the avant-garde

---

[1] I would like to mention the names of the colleagues who took part in the Venetian gathering together with Jean-Pierre Cometti: Daniele Goldoni, Gian Luigi Paltrinieri, Jacinto Lageira and Maria Luisa Ciminelli gave papers, while Arnold Davidson and Luigi Perissinotto acted as chairs and actively contributed to the discussion. The meeting took place on May 13th and 14th, 2013 at the Department of Philosophy and Cultural Heritage at Ca' Foscari University.

[2] I am quoting a passage from Cometti's contribution to the Venetian meeting, whose title was 'De *Brillo Box* à *Puppy*. La fin de l'art et sa capitalisation dans la culture'.

and his translation of Peter Bürger's book into French[3]. In *Art et factors d'art*[4], he claimed that the autonomist pretensions of contemporary fine art had been nourishing a form of false consciousness: on the one hand, the price paid for those pretensions was a lack of significance of art when dealing with political, social, and ethical matters, authorizing administrations to cut funds for cultural and artistic activities and policies in times of economic crisis. On the other hand, the alleged autonomy of art eventuated in an extensive subjection of the arts themselves to the art market and to the system of those actors – artists, art merchants, curators and critics – who can judge the artistic value of things; consequently, the allegedly independent and purely aesthetic consciousness is not the real subject of judgments of taste[5]. In the paper he presented in Venice, Cometti argued that the present state of the arts could be understood only by acknowledging the failure of the avant-garde project to abolish the autonomy of art and the economy of desires connected with it. Current artistic productions – from Warhol's *Brillo Box* to Jeff Koon's *Puppy* – ironically bridged the chasm between art and life, by integrating artistic practices within the capitalist system of production, distribution, and fruition. These topics are which were to become the center of one of Cometti's posthumously published books, *La nouvelle aura. Économies de l'art et de la culture*[6].

Nevertheless, I think that also Dewey's work in the philosophy of art represented a crucial influence in pushing Cometti's

---

[3] Peter Bürger, *Théorie de l'avant-garde*, trans. by Jean-Pierre Cometti (Paris: Questions Théoriques, 2013).

[4] Jean-Pierre Cometti, *Art et facteurs d'art. Ontologies friables* (Rennes: Presses universitaires de Rennes, 2012).

[5] See Cometti, *Art et facteurs d'art*, particularly the 'Introduction' and the first chapter, 'L'autonomie artistique et ses conséquences'. On the concept of 'aesthetic consciousness' and its relevance for the emergence of the idea of an aesthetic *Erlebnis*, different from other kinds of experiences, see Hans-Georg Gadamer, *Truth and Method*, trans. by Joel Weinsheimer and Donald G. Marshall (London: Continuum, 1975), particularly the following sections: 'The dominance of the concept of genius' and 'Critique of the abstraction inherent in aesthetic consciousness'.

[6] Jean-Pierre Cometti, *La nouvelle aura. Économies de l'art et de la culture* (Paris: Questions Théoriques, 2016).

interests toward the political dimension of artistic practices[7]. His intellectual engagement seems to answer John Dewey's rather polemical idea that

> [...] a philosophy of art is sterile unless it makes us aware of the function of art in relation to other modes of experience, and unless it indicates why this function is so inadequately realized, and unless it suggests the conditions under which the office will be successfully performed.[8]

It is by setting out from this point that I wish to further develop the argument which I outlined for the first time during that workshop with Cometti.

2. What are our current aesthetic conditions?

The passage from *Art as Experience* I quoted above involves three demands: it suggests to us that the arts have a function, or more than one function, in relation to other modes of experiencing the surrounding world (1); it urges us to consider the present situation in its specific features (2); and (3) it leads us to pose the question of whether the current conditions are capable of realizing the above-mentioned functions.

Cometti gave an insightful picture of the current situation of the arts (2), with particular reference to the area of visual arts. Nevertheless, I think that the field of artistic production *strictu sensu* is far from covering the whole present situation, which involves multiple varieties of aesthetic practices, generally disregarded by professional philosophers – from watching and seeing films on TV to taking pictures, creating or listening to

---

[7] Among other things, I recall that Cometti coordinated the translation of Dewey's *Art as Experience* into French (Paris: Gallimard, 2010), that his book *Qu'est-ce que le pragmatism?* (Paris: Gallimard) dates back to 2010, and that in the last year of his life he was working on the book *La démocratie radicale. Lire John Dewey*, published posthumously in 2016 (Paris: Gallimard).

[8] John Dewey, *Art as Experience* (1934), in *John Dewey: The Later Works, 1925–1953*, vol. 10, ed. by Jo Ann Boydston (Carbondale: Southern Illinois University Press, 1989), p. 17.

commercial or popular music in a supermarket parking lot as well as in one's own car, decorating one's own residence, adorning faces and bodies, etc. Most high-brow artistic production follows a more or less strategic trajectory, whereby new artistic proposals first shock the public, then are rejected by the system because they break previous rules, and finally are integrated into the institutions and welcomed by them[9]. However, other products and activities serve the purpose of satisfying the 'aesthetic hunger' of most people, very often through unpretentious, everyday experiences, as Dewey reminds us in *Art as Experience*. Cometti was probably considering this kind of issue when speaking about the economy of desires connected to a particular way of producing and disseminating culture. I think that we should philosophically consider the complex variety of broadly aesthetic practices to which Hegel's famous thesis of the end of art does not apply, because we immediately recognize ourselves in those forms of aesthetic consumption, without the need for any intellectual mediation. These are familiar fruits from our own tree, so to speak, even when we strongly reject them because of their implications. This is a largely neglected field of inquiry for traditional aesthetics that I consider worth philosophically investigating, for the above-mentioned reasons.

Moreover, if we look at the few philosophical inquiries into this field and to the far more numerous sociological interpretations – from Bourdieu onwards – we can see that most of them tend to interpret these practices as a sort of transfer of different needs, such as identity or social needs (1), as well as considering the broadly aesthetic needs underlying them as being entirely configured and induced by cultural and social processes (2).

I do not wish to deny that this is often the case, but I think that we cannot generalize these assumptions – anthropological needs are also based on naturally human ways of interacting with an environment, including culture and sociality as constitutive ingredients of our modes of being as living organisms. Finally, I think that we should maintain a plurality of answers to the question of the role that artistic practices and aesthetic consumptions play in

---

[9] On these dynamics see Nathalie Heinich, *Le triple jeu de l'art contemporain. Sociologie des arts plastiques* (Paris: Les Éditions de Minuit, 1998).

human interactions, as well as the question of the anthropological needs they arise from and the complex range of modes they can be satisfied by[10]. I will start by drawing a rough distinction between philosophical and sociological contributions to the subject.

3. *The state of the debate: philosophical approaches*

Though philosophical discourse on aesthetic needs and consumptions is not plentiful, one of the main lines of thought can be found in the pragmatist tradition, particularly in Dewey and George Mead, which will be the focus of the final section of this paper. The other line is represented by critical theory, especially that of Adorno and Marcuse.

A good starting point is provided by the debate on mass culture, entailing a more or less explicit reference to aesthetic consumptions. Noël Carroll published an interesting book on this subject almost two decades ago, *A Philosophy of Mass Art*[11], which can be helpful to emphasize some features that are relevant to our present discussion.

The first point I wish to focus on can be summarized by the question of whether aesthetic consumption – at least aesthetic consumption in much of the contemporary world – consists in and is exhausted by the consumption of mass products. A variant of this question is whether the consumption of mass artistic production is the primary current response to human aesthetic needs. My opinion is that many aesthetic practices in contemporary Western societies partially consist in the consumption of products and services from the so-called cultural industry; nevertheless those aesthetic activities cannot be entirely reduced to capitalist economy, neither as regards the objects that are experienced nor as regards the ways in which they are experienced.

A couple of examples will help clarify that we cannot simply classify a certain practice as aesthetically confirming an economy of desires entirely subservient to the free market system. A dinner

---

[10] This point is emphasized in Abraham Maslow, 'A Theory of Human Motivation', *Psychological Review*, 50 (1943), pp. 370-396.
[11] Noël Carroll, *A Philosophy of Mass Art* (Oxford: Clarendon Press, 1998).

with some friends at home entails a wide use of tasteful mass products, but these can be part of shared social practices (cooking together, chatting, reinforcing intimate personal bonds) that can be enjoyed for free[12]. By contrast, so-called 'relational artists'[13], such as Rirkrit Tiravanija, while suggesting the possibility of sharing the pleasure of a common social space through food, do not consider the social asymmetries that lie at the basis of visits to art galleries. A trip to the seaside in the south of Italy during the early warm days of summer could be artificially staged as a pre-cooked experience designed by the so-called experience economy created by ultra-capitalist strategists Pine and Gilmore[14]. Nevertheless, it can be something very different, depending on the people with whom we share the experience, the means we use, the expenses we have to cover and how we cover them: only some of the objects and phases of the whole process are subject to monetary exchanges and the significance of the whole experience usually involves a more complex intertwining of components than those that can be translated into costs and benefits. I do not wish to underestimate the importance of these aspects, especially in scarcity conditions: I only wish to point out that even in contemporary industrial or post-industrial societies consumption is not entirely interpretable according to the logic of mere profit, but is rather more polyvalent.

Carroll has the merit of having shown that mass art is a legitimate topic for philosophical aesthetics: the fact that most people have access to aesthetic experiences primarily or even exclusively through forms of mass art consumption should be considered very seriously from a philosophical point of view, and this is the reason why Carroll chose to develop a philosophical theory of mass art. But Carroll adopts an approach that aims to define mass art products as a particular field of things: in other words, he aims to formulate an ontology of mass art. He does not seem interested either in the practices connected with mass art production and fruition or in the possible anthropological, social

---

12 I have intentionally chosen examples similar to the cases suggested as forms of consummatory experience by Dewey in *Art as Experience*, chap. 3, 'Having an Experience'.
13 See Nicolas Bourriaud, *Relational Aesthetics* (Paris: Presses du reel, 2002).
14 Joseph Pine and James Gilmore, *The Experience Economy* (Boston: Harvard Business School Press, 1999).

or cultural reasons behind them. So, I would like to draw attention to precisely those aspects.

As is well known, the very idea of mass art has long been under discussion. Carroll explicitly refers to a conception of mass art as the kind of artistic production in a broad sense that is characteristic of modern industrial societies, where artworks are produced through recourse to technologies of scale designed for mass consumption, and delivered to a huge number of consumers. He includes as mass art photography, commercial movies, television and radio programs, consumer literature, and commercial music.

In an essay dating back to 1967 and re-published in English in 1975 under the title of *Cultural Industry Reconsidered*[15], Adorno claims that the label mass art or, better, mass culture, is misleading. Mass culture can still be understood as being analogous to popular culture, in the sense that mass culture could mean a culture that spontaneously arises from the masses – it would be the contemporary version of popular culture. On the contrary, the cultural industry is something structurally different, because it is produced for mass consumption from top down, according to economic and political strategies. From Adorno's point of view, 'the masses are not primary, but secondary, they are an object of calculation; an appendage of the machinery'[16]. Moreover, from his point of view the cultural industry looks like a unitary system in which the various branches of production are systematically ordered.

It is clear that Carroll does not share such a passive conception of the masses or the idea that mass production is systematically and strategically aimed at commercial exploitation as a means to maintain economic and political asymmetries. On the contrary, he adopts an anti-dogmatic and pluralist attitude with which I agree.

As far as practices of aesthetic consumption are concerned, a very interesting thesis comes from the field of Cultural Studies and in particular from John Fiske, who argues that there is no such thing as mass art[17]. On the contrary, there are many

---

15 Theodor Adorno, Cultural Industry Reconsidered, *New German Critique*, 6 (1975), pp. 12-19.
16 *Ibid.*, p. 12.
17 John Fiske, 'Cultural Studies and the Culture of Everyday Life', in *Cultural Studies*, ed. by Lawrence Grossberg, Cary Nelson, Paula Treichler (New York: Routledge, 1992), pp. 154-165.

kinds of popular art where 'popular' is not so much a property characterizing the origin of the products themselves, but their use – including the use we can make even of typically industrial products. Of course, there are uses that basically confirm social divisions as well as the asymmetric power of the financial and political elites; nevertheless, there are also uses endorsing forms of resistance to the existing social, political and economic order as well as favoring more complex – ambiguous or divergent – behaviors. Maybe Rauschenberg and the Arte Povera movement were trying to say something similar by means of a new, divergent reuse of industrial products. What is interesting for me in Fiske's position is that he shifts the focus, moving from mass production objects to the uses we can make of them. I also find the examples of aesthetic consumption he suggests insightful – for example, he mentions the use that can be made of plastic flowers by a low-income couple in a suburban American district, who try to enjoy their own home and to create a more intimate connection with the place they are living in. Another interesting example he offers is represented by the use of television narratives such as soap-operas and TV-series as an opportunity for members of a generally uneducated public to rethink their own stories and relationships.

A second important aspect I would like to emphasize in relation to Carroll's book is constituted by the series of arguments he presents for or against mass art, together with their implications for the advocates and detractors of mass art. I will briefly summarize some of these arguments, because they are useful to understand at least some of the reasons for the general philosophical mistrust or indifference towards aesthetic consumption.

In his famous *Avant-Garde and Kitsch* essay the influential art critic Clement Greenberg[18] characterizes 'kitsch' (including, in his opinion, Tin Pan Alley songs as well as Gershwin and academic art) in contrast to avant-garde creations. As noted by Carroll, one of Greenberg's arguments against kitsch is that it induces passivity in spectators: in order to be accessible to the vast majority of

---

18 Clement Greenberg, 'Avant-Garde and Kitsch', *Partisian Review*, 6, 5 (1939), pp. 34-49, reprinted in Clement Greenberg, *The Collected essays and Criticism*, vol. 1 (Chicago: Chicago University Press, 1986), pp. 5-22.

people, industrial art production should provide its public with pre-digested products. Kitsch productions spares the public any intellectual effort, whereas avant-garde creations push the spectator's activity to the maximum, forcing him or her to engage in a strenuous exercise that seems almost ennobling. Carroll is right to argue that this is an oversimplification: accessibility does not rule out an active role on the part of the observers, but in many cases (consider certain detective novels, or even early rap music)[19] it requires a process of co-construction of meaning on the part of the reader or the listener.

However, Carroll does not consider one interesting aspect in Greenberg's essay: for him, kitsch is easy in the sense that it easily meets the public's need for 'diversion'. Kitsch is a form of *Ersatz culture*, a substitute culture, because it is 'destined for those who, insensible to the values of genuine culture, are still hungry for the diversion that only culture of some sort can provide'[20]. Greenberg does not explicitly tell us what it is that we are distracted by, but he was probably conditioned by his idea that the avant-garde is dominated by an aspiration towards the absolute which only an art for art's sake could fulfill, by imitating divine creation, as something valid 'solely on its own terms'[21]. Here is a first example of the tendency to think about consumption and 'aesthetic hunger' as a kind of compensatory satisfying of the different needs I mentioned at the beginning of this paper: kitsch would cheaply replace the tension towards the absolute with an effortless diversion. In Cometti's words[22], it deals with an economy of desires which is managed by other means, different from those traditionally attributed to the ennobling power of culture[23].

---

19   Consider the case of Norbert Davis's *Rendezvous with Fear* for Wittgenstein (cf. Sara Fortuna, *Il giallo di Wittgenstein. Etica e linguaggio tra filosofia e detective story* (Milano-Udine: Mimesis, 2009) or Richard Shusterman on rap music (Richard Shusterman, The Fine Art of Rap, in *Pragmatist Aesthetics. Living Beauty, Rethinking Art* (London: Rowman & Littlefield, 2000)).
20   Greenberg, 'Avant-Garde and Kitsch', p. 12.
21   Ibid., p. 8.
22   See footnote no. 2.
23   On this aspect see Herbert Marcuse, 'The Affirmative Character of Culture', in *Negations. Essays in Critical Theory* (Boston: Beacon, 1968), pp. 65-98, and John Dewey, 'Individualism Old and New', in *The Later Works, 1925-*

In Adorno's case, Carroll rightly emphasizes the freedom of art from external purposes as a crucial issue: though no artwork is capable of really opposing existing regressive conditions, only an art that is *ohne Zweck* can have any hope of offering resistance. The problem of objects produced by the cultural industry is that, on the contrary, they are 'purposeful': they are created for commercial exploitation and an unbridled search for profit. At a deeper level, they are geared towards the preservation of inequalities and existing asymmetric powers relations. The lack of any autonomy among the products of the cultural industry structurally undermines them, regardless of their use. According to Adorno, they condemn the public to an absence of freedom, basically because they close the doors of the human imagination: they tend to merely confirm political and economic conditions, preventing those who enjoy them to think otherwise. With regard to this point Carroll asks if we should consider the chance to imagine other possibilities and other worlds as a prerogative of negative art. In my opinion, an attempt to answer this important issue requires us to question the alleged ontological difference between products of the cultural industry and purely authentic art, by looking at the uses and the practices people make of them.

There is also one further point in Adorno's position that deserves some attention here: on the one hand, in the *Dialectics of Enlightenment*[24] and in the late *Aesthetic Theory*[25], the cultural industry is accused of strategically guiding and exploiting aesthetic consumption, as well as of creating artificial needs – obviously the reference here is to the hypertrophic consumerism of advanced industrial societies. Adorno and Horkheimer formulated the thesis that the cultural industry does not only configure human needs but is able to artificially create them. However, in the 1975 essay we find the thesis that the cultural industry provides a 'substitute gratification'[26] of more authentic

---

1953, vol. 5: 1929-1930 (Carbondale and Edwardsville: Southern Illinois University Press, 1988), pp. 41-123.

24 Max Horkheimer and Theodor Adorno, *Dialectics of Enlightenment: Philosophical Fragments* (Standford: Standford UP, 2002).

25 Theodor Adorno, *Aesthetic Theory* (Minneapolis: University of Minnesota Press, 1970).

26 Adorno, *Cultural Industry*, p. 18.

needs, distracting individuals from the 'real interests of humans'[27] – hence, there must be anthropological needs that are not artificially induced. Commercial art 'prevents the development of independent individuals who judge and decide consciously for themselves', which is to say that it impedes the realization of a crucial 'precondition for a democratic society'[28]. Consequently, we could say that, on the one hand, even Adorno's negative art is not entirely without purpose, because it aims to create free and independent individuals as a precondition for a non-regressive society. Hence, it raises the question of whether the dichotomy between the purposeless and the purposeful in art is the most adequate distinction we can draw. On the other hand, I would point out that this ideal development of free individuals has an ascetic aspect, as it does not include individuals who may enjoy their interactions with others and the situations they are in. It remains basically alien to a positive affirmation of life, to a chance for flourishing and happiness[29].

Furthermore, Carroll raises some reasonable criticisms against the alleged potentially emancipatory character of mass consumption (with reference to Benjamin and McLuhan): the need to refine the analysis of individual cases shows that we need subtle discrimination here, rather than pre-constituted theses and categories. Carroll's approach is anti-dogmatic and honestly pluralistic, but it overlooks a different approach to interpreting mass art, namely one based on the idea that more crucial discriminations may concern the possible *practices* related to mass culture, the cultural industry, and fine or avant-garde art, rather than the type of *objects* we are dealing with in such practices[30].

---

27 Ibid., p. 17.
28 Ibid., p. 19.
29 On this issue cfr. Roberta Dreon, 'The Aesthetic, Pleasure and Happiness: or why Freedom is not Enough', *Pragmatism Today*, 6 (2015), pp. 8-21.
30 Another research line, which I never discussed with Cometti, could be an exploration of the recent production in so-called Everyday Aesthetics (for a first introduction see Yuriko Saito, 'Aesthetics of the Everyday', *The Stanford Encyclopedia of Philosophy* (Winter 2015 Edition), ed. by Edward N. Zalta, <https://plato.stanford.edu/archives/win2015/entries/aesthetics-of-everyday/> [accessed 30 January 2019]).
  In particular, it could be interesting to investigate the political consequences derived from an emphasis on aesthetic practices in ordinary

4. Sociological approaches

On the contrary, sociological approaches to aesthetic consumption are typically focused on uses and practices rather than the kinds of objects dealt with – either mass art products or works of fine art.

A second common feature in sociological inquiries on the subject is that most scholars read aesthetic consumptions as serving further purposes, very often different from those that are superficially visible. For Bourdieu, for example, aesthetic practices are never disinterested but rather respond to the largely unconscious or habitual need for social distinction and acknowledgment[31]. According to Bauman, they respond to the need to build new individual identities in a society characterized by the erosion of any stable reference to moral values and tending to remove any awareness of our miseries and our mortal destiny[32].

Ian Woodward has argued that sociological inquiries on consumption, and particularly on aesthetic issues, generally follow two basic directions exemplified by the above-mentioned authors[33]. The first direction of research, whose leading figure is still Bourdieu, focuses on social distributions and homologies in aesthetic consumption, basically downplaying the role of subjectivity: both the explicit and implicit choices of individuals are interpreted as being always mediated by the *habitus* characterizing the social group to whom one belongs. The second, post-modern, line of research, whose main figures are Zygmunt Bauman, Ulrich Beck and Anthony Giddens, conceives consumption as a highly individualized activity, where the real issue at stake is the building of an individual identity. I agree with Woodward's attempt to look for an intermediate and contextual

---

experience, although avoiding any ideological interpretation of aesthetic consumptions in everyday life.

31 Pierre Bourdieu, *Distinction. A Social Critique of the Judgement of Taste*, trans. by Richard Nice (Cambridge: Harvard University Press, 1987).
32 Zygmunt Bauman, 'Consuming Life', *Journal of Consumer Culture*, 1 (2001), pp. 9-29.
33 Ian Woodward, 'Investigating the Consumption Anxiety Thesis: Aesthetic Choice, Narrativisation and Social Performance', *The Sociological Review*, 54/2 (2006), pp. 263-282.

approach, because the shaping of a more or less continuous narrative identity always takes place in social situations where individuals are exposed to the judgments and actions of others. This point was already made, in my opinion, by Alan Warde when he claimed that researchers on consumption should consider consumers not as 'displaced and disembedded person[s]'[34]. He also claims to acknowledge that ambiguities are inherent in consumption: aesthetic consumption is a multifaceted phenomenon, it does not always respond to the need for individualization and the building of an identity narrative, it is often not a matter of free choice and can be significant for various reasons. Aesthetic consumptions do not always and necessarily generate anxiety; on the contrary, many times they give pleasure or have a calming effect.

Bourdieu meritoriously inaugurated a new research field on consumptions of cultural and luxury goods, whose boundaries transcend the usual distinction between the arts *strictu sensu* and aesthetic practices – even if we should at least mention the pioneering work done by Thorstein Veblen at the end of the 19th century with his *Theory of the Leisure Class*[35]. As relevant features for the shaping of a certain lifestyle, Bourdieu considers not only the kind of music or the type of theater preferred by Parisians in the 1970s, but also their choices in terms of clothing, interior décor, and even partners. He also emphasized the crucial importance of so-called symbolic capital in the consumption of cultural goods in post-industrial societies – which is to say, the relevance of being recognized and recognizable as occupying a specific point in the social field by means of each individual's aesthetic practices and preferences.

As is well known, the central thesis in *Distinction. A Social Critique of the Judgement of Taste* is that the alleged aesthetic distance from usefulness, the presumed autonomy, and the disinterested nature of artistic appreciation, are all profoundly socially conditioned. Allegedly 'pure' aesthetic contemplation is

---

34 Alan Warde, 'Consumption, Identity-Formation and Uncertainty', *Sociology*, 28/4 (1994), pp. 877-898 (p. 891).
35 Thorstein Veblen, *The Theory of the Leisure Class* (London: Allen & Unwin, 1924).

far from disinterested, useless, and autonomous: on the contrary, according to Bourdieu's analysis, the development of an allegedly pure aesthetic attitude is a more or less unconscious response to the agonistic dynamics of the social space through a quasi-naturalized habitus.

As regards the relationship between needs and consumption, it is particularly interesting to note one difference between Bourdieu's position and Adorno's approach. According to Adorno, the alleged power of the cultural industry is so systematic and monolithic as not only to promote conformity in aesthetic consumption, but also to create the artificial need for products of the cultural industry. By contrast, Bourdieu considers the fields of the production and consumption of cultural goods as having two relatively independent logics, *de facto* converging because each consumer can ensure the satisfaction of his own needs through the homology of the social habitus guiding his own behaviors as well as a specific field of cultural production. Consequently, the allegedly purely aesthetic taste reveals itself as a sense of social orientation allowing subtle, though mainly unconscious or habitual, discriminations.

Bauman's argument about consumerism is very different. He believes that the current form of consumption is the result of a historical discontinuity, even though he starts from a physiological conception of consumption:

> Indeed, if reduced to its archetypical form of the metabolic cycle of ingesting, digesting and excreting, consumption is a permanent and irremovable condition and aspect of life, bound by neither time nor history; one of the inseparable elements of biological survival which we, humans, share with all other living organisms. Seen in that way, the phenomenon of consumption has roots as ancient as living organisms.[36]

Nevertheless, he claims that the current form of consumption is the ultimate result of a profound revolution, which has brought consumption to the core of the social organization and of human relations. More specifically, Bauman believes that this revolution

---

36   Zygmunt Bauman, *Consuming Life* (Cambridge: Polity P., 2007), p. 25.

has led to a new alienating relationship between consumptions and needs. At the dawn of modern industrial societies consumption tended to satisfy pre-existing human needs, whose nature could be consequently envisaged as a state of tension and urge to find gratification. Nowadays, according to Bauman, we have replaced needs to be satisfied with a morbid desire to consume; the current form of desire should be considered morbid because it tends towards the artificial preservation of a state of tension which can never be satisfied and consequently justifies a never-ending form of consumption – 'consumption for its own sake', we might say. The search for a happy life is the merely superficial imperative of contemporary consumer society, while its hidden need consists in trying to put together rather fragile identities out of narrative fragments of consumption. Related to this is a profound anthropological need that pushes people toward unbridled consumerism in current societies: the search for distraction from our precarious human existence. It might be suggested that the consumption of cultural or aesthetic goods is a crucial ingredient for shaping weak imaginative identities, as well as for entertaining and distracting consumers from their existential uncertainty.

Nevertheless, I harbor some doubts about these rather monolithic explanations, though I have no ambition here to deconstruct Bauman's theory or to criticize Bourdieu's position. My point is that we should probably adopt a more careful, nuanced, and context-dependent interpretation of our aesthetic consumptions, which usually present a complex intertwining of different factors and consequences, and which respond to the most diverse needs and to more than one need at the same time, as Warde and Woodward seem to emphasize.

Another neglected point is that the current multiplication of stimuli and consumption possibilities can not only induce a form of anxiety, but also a kind of indifference already stigmatized by Simmel through the metaphor of the *blasè*[37]. The present tendency to supplant 'distinct consumption' with

---

37 Georg Simmel, 'The Metropolis and Mental Life', in *The Sociology of Georg Simmel*, ed. by Kurt H. Wolff (New York; Free Press, 1976), pp. 409-426.

'omnivorous consumption'[38] could also helpfully open up some uncertain situations where different habits collide producing new possibilities.

Lastly, there is one more important factor to be taken into account: if consumption – especially aesthetic consumption – is often pleasant and is connected to prosperity, why should we always think that pleasure and happiness are merely superficial or only apparent traits, while its deepest roots should be searched for somewhere else?

5. On aesthetic consumption as a natural feature and its consequences

In his essay on hedonism, a relatively young Marcuse stigmatized the general distrust of the mainstream philosophical tradition towards pleasure and the sensual dimension of happiness. He emphasized that we should acknowledge the basic value of historical hedonism, which was to oppose the general tendency to spiritualize and interiorize happiness by understanding it as uniquely possible in an extra-material world[39].

In contrast to this main trend, Dewey's approach to pleasure can be described as naturalistic, although in a non-reductive sense of the term. According to him every human interaction with the natural and social environment has a more or less pronounced aesthetic quality, first of all because our lives are far from detachable from their surroundings, as we tend to suppose if we assume that we are a disembodied consciousness instead of living organisms. It is because we are basically exposed to the actions of other human beings and the effects on us of the natural environment, as being against us or in our favor, that we primarily perceive occurrences as comfortable or dangerous, enjoyable or painful. From this point of view, consumption is physiological for Dewey, as it is for Bauman, but it is also naturally social. Indeed, we are peculiarly relational or

---

38 Richard A. Peterson and Roger M. Kern, 'Changing Highbrow Taste: From Snob to Omnivore', *American Sociological Review*, 61 (1996), pp. 900-907.
39 For a comparison between Marcuse's perspective and Dewey's inquiry on this issue, see Roberta Dreon, 'Aesthetic Issues in Human Emancipation: Between Dewey and Marcuse', *Pragmatism Today*, 6/2 (2015), pp. 74-85.

social beings, because we depend quantitatively and qualitatively on the social environment we belong to – and this dependence extends from our mere need for nourishment to our hunger for more abstract and refined meanings. Every human interaction with the environment could be described as 'consuming' from this point of view – even if Dewey does not use the term 'consumption' – because it never leaves the resources and energies as they were prior to the interaction itself. We humans are aesthetically hungry, to use Dewey's expression, because the world around us has a qualitative impact on our lives, because it can give us comfort or make us suffer.

But Dewey doesn't stop at this naturalistic account of our interactions with the environment. We can find a key element for developing a more open stance towards consumption practices in his approach to experiences that can be described as 'consummatory'. Particularly when speaking about 'an experience' in *Art as Experience*, he makes it clear that not all forms of consumption are dissipative and inevitably exhaust natural, individual, and social energies: there are forms of interaction producing an intensification or expansion of energies. Significantly, one of the issues faced by evolutionary aesthetics, when following an explanatory logic based exclusively on the struggle for existence, is that it cannot understand the reasons why humans 'waste' such an enormous amount of material, energy, and time in cultural and artistic activities apparently having no adaptive meaning.

Dewey was deeply aware that not every experience produces an enhancement of life, particularly in current industrialized society, as my opening quotation reveals. It was also for this reason – which, one might say, has political consequences, broadly speaking – that he introduced the notion of consummatory experience, where consummation means bringing a specific intercourse to its fulfillment and completion, as well as favoring a kind of careful perception of the various processes of doing and undergoing which are involved in it[40]. Dewey uses the term 'consummatory

---

40 See George H. Mead, 'The Nature of Aesthetic Experience', *International Journal of Ethics*, 36/4 (1926), pp. 382-393. For a more detailed analysis of the concept of 'consummatory experience' in Dewey, see Roberta Dreon,

experience' both to characterize an eminently artistic or aesthetic experience, and to distinguish more ordinary yet significant and fulfilling experiences from mainly inconclusive everyday exchanges that proceed indifferently, without leaving any trace and giving any satisfaction.

I think that from all this we can derive a possible criterion for distinguishing and evaluating aesthetic practices and consumptions of a primarily non-object-centered sort. Instead of drawing an ontological and honorific difference between high art and mass cultural products, we could draw open, time- and context-dependent distinctions between interactions that are capable of intensifying human existence and forms of consumption that tend to impoverish it. Of course, this is only one type of criterion, which should be integrated and balanced with the evaluative stance we can derive from the critical theory approach to the arts – roughly, the idea of distinguishing human aesthetic practices either as regressive ones that confirm unfair social relations, political injustices and serious economic inequalities, or as critical practices of resistance that are based on a reflective distance from and awareness of the negative features afflicting contemporary societies.

My point is that by adopting a Deweyan perspective, there is room also for more fruitful aesthetic practices, beyond either regressive or critical interactions: the aesthetic choice to enjoy our interchanges with the world appears to be a safe anthropological attitude in the light of which properly artistic experiences can be considered enhancing developments. We should acknowledge that it is natural for human organisms not only to pursue balanced, enriching and more meaningful interchanges with their natural and naturally social environment, but also to enjoy these interchanges as enhancements of living processes. To deny these anthropological needs would be to remove them, uncritically transferring them to other objects and practices – as Dewey's argument on the 'aesthetic hunger' of most people implies. The fact of separating artworks through museums and galleries, so as to make them something to be eminently enjoyed by either

---

'How to do Different Things with Words: Why Dewey's Aesthetics is Peculiar', *Pragmatism Today*, 4/1 (2013), pp. 74-84.

an intellectual or an economic elite, has the consequence of condemning most people to search for surrogates. Replacements can be found not only in the consumption of mass cultural products but also, across different fields, in every artistic practice that leads to a depletion of vital energies, to a dissipative consumption of the various features involved in a specific intercourse. Mead rightly reminds us that even the worship of the old painting masters can be regressive, because it can nourish the prejudice that the aesthetic cannot have any legitimate place in our ordinary life, but should be confined to specific places and times[41].

References

Adorno, Theodor W., *Aesthetic Theory* (Minneapolis: University of Minnesota Press, 1970).
—, 'Cultural Industry Reconsidered', *New German Critique*, 6 (1975), pp. 12-19.
Bauman, Zygmunt, 'Consuming Life', *Journal of Consumer Culture*, 1 (2001), pp. 9-29.
—, *Consuming Life* (Cambridge: Polity, 2007).
Bourdieu, Pierre, *Distinction. A Social Critique of the Judgement of Taste* (Cambridge-London: Harvard University Press, 1987).
Bourriaud, Nicolas, *Relational Aesthetics* (Paris: Presses du reel, 2002).
Bürger, Peter, *Théorie de l'avant-garde*, trans. by Jean-Pierre Cometti (Paris: Questions Théoriques, 2013).
Carroll, Noël, *A Philosophy of Mass Art* (Oxford: Clarendon Press, 1998).
Cometti, Jean-Pierre, *Art et facteurs d'art. Ontologies friables* (Rennes: Presses universitaires de Rennes, 2012).
—, *Qu'est-ce que le pragmatisme?* (Paris: Gallimard, 2010).
—, 'De "Brillo Box" a "Puppy". La fin de l'art et sa capitalisation dans la culture', unpublished paper, 2013.
—, *La nouvelle aura. Économies de l'art et de la culture* (Paris: Questions Théoriques, 2016).
—, *La démocratie radicale. Lire John Dewey* (Paris: Vrin, 2016).
Dewey, John, *Art as Experience*, in *The Later Works, 1925-1953, vol. 10: 1934* (Carbondale and Edwardsville: Southern Illinois University Press, 1987).

---

[41] Mead, pp. 387-388; see also Dewey, 'Individualism Old and New', p. 103.

—, *Individualism Old and New*, in *The Later Works, 1925-1953*, vol. 5: 1929-1930 (Carbondale and Edwardsville: Southern Illinois University Press, 1998), pp. 41-123.

Dreon, Roberta, 'How to do Different Things with Words: Why Dewey's Aesthetics is Peculiar', *Pragmatism Today*, 4/1 (2013), pp.74-84.

—, 'The Aesthetic, Pleasure and Happiness: or Why Freedom is not Enough', *Pragmatism Today*, 6/1 (2015), pp. 8-21.

—, Aesthetic Issues in Human Emancipation: Between Dewey and Marcuse, *Pragmatism Today*, 6/2 (2015), pp. 74-85.

Fiske, John, 'Cultural Studies and the Culture of Everyday Life', in *Cultural Studies*, ed. by Lawrence Grossberg, Cary Nelson, Paula Treichler (New York: Routledge, 1992), pp. 154-165.

Fortuna, Sara, *Il giallo di Wittgenstein. Etica e linguaggio tra filosofia e detective story* (Milano-Udine: Mimesis, 2009).

Greenberg, Clement, 'Avant-Garde and Kitsch', *Partisian Review*, 6, 5 (1939), pp. 34-49, repr. in Clement Greenberg, *The Collected essays and Criticism*, vol. 1 (Chicago: Chicago University Press, 1986), pp. 5-22.

Heinich, Nathalie, *Le triple jeu de l'art contemporain. Sociologie des arts plastiques* (Paris: Les Éditions de Minuit, 1998).

Horkheimer, Max, and Theodor, W. Adorno, *Dialectic of Enlightenment: Philosophical Fragments* (Stanford: Stanford University Press, 2002).

Marcuse, Herbert, 'On Hedonism', in *Negations. Essays in Critical Theory* (Boston: Beacon, 1968), pp. 119-150.

—, 1968 b, 'The Affirmative Character of Culture', in *Negations. Essays in Critical Theory*, (Boston: Beacon, 1968), pp. 65-98.

Maslow, Abraham, 'A Theory of Human Motivation', *Psychological Review*, 50 (1943), pp. 370-396.

Mead, George H., 'The Nature of Aesthetic Experience', *International Journal of Ethics*, 36/4 (1926), pp. 382-393.

Peterson, Richard A., and Roger M. Kern, 'Changing Highbrow Taste: From Snob to Omnivore', *American Sociological Review*, 61 (1996), pp. 900-907.

Pine, Joseph, and James Gilmore, *The Experience Economy* (Boston: Harvard Business School Press, 1999).

Saito, Yuriko, 'Aesthetics of the Everyday', *The Stanford Encyclopedia of Philosophy* (Winter 2015 Edition), ed. by Edward N. Zalta <https://plato.stanford.edu/archives/win2015/entries/aesthetics-of-everyday/> [accessed 30 January 2019]

Simmel, Georg, The Metropolis and Mental Life, in *The Sociology of Georg Simmel*, (New York; Free Press, 1976), pp. 409-426.

Shusterman, Richard, 'The Fine Art of Rap', in *Pragmatist Aesthetics. Living Beauty, Rethinking Art* (London: Rowman & Littlefield, 2000).

Veblen, Thorstein *The Theory of the Leisure Class* (London: Allen & Unwin, 1924).
Warde, Alan 'Consumption, Identity-Formation and Uncertainty', *Sociology*, 28/4 (1994), pp. 877-898.
Woodward, Ian, 'Investigating the Consumption Anxiety Thesis: Aesthetic Choice, Narrativisation and Social Performance', *The Sociological Review*, 54/2 (2006), pp. 263-282.

Bertrand Rougé

ON BEING ABOUT WHAT COUNTS
Art, Money, Value, and Figurative Distance as Artistic Quality

> Dans sa nouvelle : 'Sur la difficulté de dialoguer avec les morts', Giorgio Manganelli décrit les innombrables stratagèmes inventés par les vivants pour entrer en communication avec les défunts, lesquels rivalisent d'ingéniosité pour s'y soustraire. Comme souvent chez Manganelli, les vaines péripéties auxquelles ces efforts donnent lieu baignent dans la nuit d'un doute irrésolu qui contraste ironiquement avec les certitudes que la philosophie s'épuise à édifier... Ce que les vivants de Manganelli tentent avec les morts, nos vivants à nous s'y emploient de mille autres façons et avec mille autres choses, dont l'art fait éminemment partie.
>
> Jean-Pierre Cometti[1]

As Charlotte and I went to the Venice Biennale, in November 2017, we visited Damien Hirst's double exhibition entitled 'Treasures from the Wreck of the Unbelievable' at the Palazzo Grassi and the Punta della Dogana. This reminded us of April 2012, when we shared a flat near Venice with Jean-Pierre Cometti and discovered with him the renovated Punta della Dogana – we had agreed on the extravagance of the place and on the inanity of the exhibition that was on despite its promising title, *In Praise of Doubt*. This also reminded us of the many fireside conversations

---

[1] Jean-Pierre Cometti, *De la difficulté de dialoguer avec l'art*, p. 3. This text can be found on Cometti's webpage, https://sites.google.com/site/jipcompage/home, where many of his published and unpublished writings are accessible.

we had had at his house and ours since he had moved close to our home south of Carcassonne. We used to sip a few glasses of Blanquette de Limoux – the local ancestor of champagne Cometti had become fond of –, and we talked about art, politics, family and friends. About art and politics we often disagreed, but our frank dialogues were friendly, open-minded, thorough and often full of humor and irony[2].

This paper unilaterally attempts to pursue these conversations on one topic that was central to Cometti's understanding of art and on which we also disagreed, i.e., his staunchly anti-essentialist views that objects can be called art only under certain conditions that allow them to be activated as such; that without these conditions they cannot be called art; and that art consequently cannot be defined and lacks specific artistic qualities, properties or value – inspired by Robert Musil, he called this art's *Eigenschaftslosigkeit*[3].

For instance, as we once discussed the visiting conditions newly imposed for preservation purposes at the Scrovegni Chapel in Padua, I remember him arguing that artworks should not be the object of such maniacal attention and should be left to deteriorate and ultimately disappear because they were no different than any other type of object or living being. I always suspected his target was not artworks or essentialism as such but the essentialists, first and foremost, and any position – or pose – that could offend his deeply felt egalitarianism, which he equally applied to objects,

---

[2] Cometti and I also disagreed about tourism, which he described as superficial and useless. He did not like to travel abroad unless he had something to do there, such as teaching, reading a paper or giving lectures. Since this paper pursues our ironic conversations, I chose to found it on recent experiences as a tourist in Venice, Saint Petersburg and Granada.

[3] Cf. Jean-Pierre Cometti, *L'Art sans qualités* (Tours: Farrago, 1999). Cometti sometimes attenuated his thesis' radicality, as when for instance, speaking of the conditions that determine the status of masterpieces – he did not like the idea of the masterpiece –, he wrote that 'Elles sont loin de dépendre exclusivement des qualités intrinsèques des œuvres qu'elles honorent' (Jean-Pierre Cometti, *La Nouvelle aura. Économies de l'art et de la culture* (Paris: Questions théoriques, 2017), p. 118), thus suggesting that such works do have intrinsic qualities that contribute to their identification as masterpieces.

animals[4] and humans[5]. Ironically, he later taught several years at the Avignon art school that specialized in art restoration and this led him to write one of his posthumously published books on a subject he certainly never would have thought of dealing with before, *Conserver/restaurer: l'œuvre d'art à l'époque de sa préservation technique*[6].

Damien Hirst's two 2017 Venice exhibitions also immediately called to mind Cometti's growing focus on the contemporary relationship between art, money and the world of fashion and luxury – which he denounced as 'les solidarités que l'art a nouées avec l'argent et le "nouveau capitalisme"'[7] and extensively analyzed in *La Nouvelle aura*, another late and posthumously published book where he developed remarks about art's price and value previously made in 2009[8].

---

4   In his later years, he often mentioned his compassion for animal suffering and developed a specific interest for the fate of stray cats. Although I remember several conversations we had about the subject, this never really led him to become a vegetarian...

5   It may be symptomatic, in this respect, that in defence of his anti-essentialism he compared what he described as the art object's transitivity – or its indiscernibility from everyday objects constituting what he called the 'artistico-cultural continuum' (Cometti, *La Nouvelle aura*, pp. 36-40) – to Aristotle's comments in *Politics* (I, 5) about slaves being different from freemen only because of cultural circumstances: 'Il en va de même pour l'art. Si vous voulez savoir à quelles conditions un individu devient un esclave, il vous faut décrire tout une culture et en juger à la lumière de l'histoire, de l'anthropologie ou de la sociologie. Si vous voulez savoir à quelle condition un objet "est" de l'art, il vous faut examiner l'ensemble des croyances, des dispositifs et des institutions dont il est solidaire et qui assurent la possibilité d'un tel statut' (Cometti, *La Nouvelle aura*, p. 130).

6   Jean-Pierre Cometti, *Conserver/restaurer: l'œuvre d'art à l'époque de sa préservation technique* (Paris: Gallimard, 2017).

7   Jean-Pierre Cometti, 'L'art riche. Faits et méfaits de la main invisible', in *L'Art et l'argent*, ed. by Jean Pierre Cometti and Nathalie Quintane (Paris: Editions Amsterdam, 2017), pp. 78-98 (p. 81).

8   Jean-Pierre Cometti, *La Force d'un malentendu. Essais sur l'art et la philosophie de l'art* (Paris: Questions théoriques, 2009), pp. 35-81. In the volume that Cometti co-edited with Nathalie Quintane entitled *L'Art et l'argent*, he also re-published a 2009 text entitled 'Onze thèses sur l'art et le marché de l'art' and published the new piece entitled 'L'art riche. Faits et méfaits de la main invisible' (cf. foonote no. 7). Nathalie Heinich, the French sociologist of art and culture, has described this growing association of wealth, luxury, celebrity and art in international art fairs,

1. *Art's Price, Value and* Eigenschaftslosigkeit

Hirst's archaeological fiction of a freed slave's huge art collection being shipwrecked off the coast of Africa in the early 2nd century AD and then retrieved by Hirst himself who exhibits the fictive items in François Pinault's galleries in Venice[9] is a perfect illustration of how the worlds of art and money interact for their mutual benefit. Indeed, it has been suggested that the whole project – costing perhaps as much as £100 million – was co-financed by Hirst and Pinault in order to boost the sales and recently declining market value of Hirst's work – of which Pinault himself is a major collector[10]. In many respects, Pinault and Hirst – and their pseudo-archaeological exhibition of a fictive ancient and luxurious art collection – perfectly illustrate Cometti's sociological thesis about how the aura of art today, which he calls 'the new aura', is determined by its relationship with the auras of wealth, fashion and luxury:

> Il y a une équation très claire entre la valeur attribuée à un objet et la notoriété de *qui* s'en est porté acquéreur. La condition – problématique, à vrai dire – d'une telle opération réside dans un transfert d'aura de l'un à l'autre. L'aura a cette particularité de se diffuser et de se communiquer par contiguïté.[11]

---

openings and social gatherings as the 'Longchamp effect'. Warhol was a pioneer of this evolution, Hirst now is one of its most spectacular examples (Nathalie Heinich, *Le Paradigme de l'art contemporain. Structures d'une révolution artistique* (Paris: Gallimard, 2014), pp. 82-85).

[9] A complete documentation on this exhibition, with a downloadable guidebook and audio guides can be found on the Palazzo Grassi's website.

[10] *Cf.* Tiernan Morgan, 'Damien Hirst's Shipwreck Fantasy Sinks in Venice', *Hyperallergic* (August 10, 2017) <https://hyperallergic.com/391158> [accessed 29 January 2019]
Lawrence Weschler's account of how the art market sometimes was able to fight off the effect of the 1987 Black Monday crash clearly describes the same process: 'There was a great unspoken agreement: people would continue to bid incredible sums of money for various works on offer [...] in part to sustain the value of other similar works they themselves already owned' (Lawrence Weschler, *Boggs. A Comedy of Values* (Chicago: Chicago University Press, 1999), pp. 91-95 (pp. 93-94).

[11] Cometti, *La Nouvelle aura*, p. 177. They also seem to more or less support his notion that 'c'est la collection qui fait la valeur de ce qui est collectionné, et non l'inverse' (*ibid.*, p. 179). *Cf.* also 'la collection est un facteur auratique

The transmissibility of the aura is a social phenomenon Emile Durkheim already described as 'la contagiosité du sacré'[12], and money, according to sociologist Bernard Lahire, is a decisive factor in what he calls the 'social magic' that auratizes art[13]. Jean Dubuffet denounced this 'collusion' of art and the market in 1968 and consequently called for a radical abandonment of the very notion of value[14].

Cometti agreed with this consequence, as he often mentioned Pinault and Hirst in his later works[15] and focused more and more on the relationship between art and money. Hirst's use of precious or semi-precious stones and metals – *cf. For the Love of God* (2007) made of platinum and over 8,000 diamonds, or the hundreds of items in the Venice exhibitions made of gold, silver, jade, platinum, malachite or lapis lazuli –, his status as an art collector and speculator and his association with Pinault make him a good example of how the value of art may seem to have become indistinguishable from its market value – and from the market value of its precious components. Indeed, in one of his most provoking formulations about the state of art today, Cometti has stated that artistic value and market value are not distinguishable. Since money and art both are commodities whose value is nothing

---

[...] Les œuvres ou les objets collectionnés acquièrent une valeur qui se transforme en prix' (*ibid.*, p. 214).

12   Émile Durkheim, *Les Formes élémentaires de la vie religieuse* (Paris: PUF, 1985), p. 457.

13   Bernard Lahire, *Ceci n'est pas qu'un tableau: essai sur l'art, la domination, la magie et le sacré* (Paris: La Découverte, 2015), p. 481.

14   'Les marchands s'appliquent, pour leur profit, à obtenir des prix élevés, lesquels sont ensuite générateurs de prestige. Très étroite, très intime est la collusion entre le commerce et la culture; l'un et l'autre mutuellement s'épaulent et se fortifient; ils ne vont pas l'un sans l'autre; chacun des deux est relais de l'autre. On ne se libérera du poids pernicieux de la culture qu'en supprimant la notion de *valeur* des productions mentales' (Jean Dubuffet, *Asphyxiante culture* (Paris: Minuit, 2007), pp. 34-35; see also pp. 62-67, 98-99). Dubuffet denounces as 'culture' the institutionalized forms of art corresponding to a socially accepted definition that marginalizes individualist artistic endeavors. On the collusion of art and the market, see also Heinich, *Le Paradigme de l'art contemporain*, pp. 223-233, 255-263.

15   Cometti, *La Nouvelle aura*, pp. 59, 60, 170, 200; Cometti, *L'art riche*, p. 92.

but an exchange value determined by the market, he concluded that 'la valeur d'une œuvre, c'est le prix qu'elle coûte'[16].

If such a statement is to be understood as non-tautological, then Cometti means that an artwork's value *as an artwork* is its market price – which of course is meant to go hand in hand with his notion of art's *Eigenschaftslosigkeit*: since art has no specific artistic qualities or properties, it has no artistic value *per se* because there is no such thing as artistic value.

However, this view is problematic. For instance, it means that the market is the only scale that allows to evaluate a work of art, since art's only value – or its only measure – is its price. It also makes light of artworks one may appreciate as art and yet not find on the market – art that, for one reason or another, is not or cannot be sold.

In a way, Cometti absolutizes the widespread notion that market value and artistic value become less and less distinguishable. Indeed, as Heinich writes, 'elles tendent à s'alimenter l'une l'autre, soumises à des instances de reconnaissance de plus en plus interdépendantes'[17], but while Cometti rightly analyzes the speculative phenomenon in the artworld as exemplified by Hirst and Pinault, I feel he overgeneralizes this example when he presents it as a case for art's ultimate worthlessness. Speculation on bread does not mean bread is useless, nor does speculation on gold or tulips in a given society mean that gold or tulips are ultimately worthless in that society. Cometti does not – and perhaps does not wish to – take into account the difference Heinich makes between 'the plane of the real' and 'the plane of representations':

> Le *prix* d'un objet est bien un fait (quantifié, variable, et réfutable au sens poppérien), tandis que sa *valeur* est une représentation (qualitative, variable et discutable, mais non réfutable) – autrement dit une conception plus ou moins partagée de ce qu'il vaut.[18]

---

16 Cometti, *La Force d'un malentendu*, p. 66.
17 Heinich, *Le Paradigme de l'art contemporain*, p. 227.
18 Nathalie Heinich, *Des valeurs. Une approche sociologique* (Paris: Gallimard, 2017), p. 370.

These two sliding scales allow us to understand 'le sentiment d'une déconnexion entre le prix et la valeur artistique'[19] – as when artworks made of worthless materials attain very high prices –, whereas Cometti's view makes this impossible, unless one considers he is speaking of art having no *real* value. But art is no different than any other object or commodity in this respect, for no object or commodity has *real* value, because value being a representation, there is no such thing as *real* value. And yet this does not mean that value doesn't exist or that it has no *real* effect – as a representation in the relevant human cultures.

Perhaps Cometti became aware of this as he later penned a more cautious thesis on the price and value of art which begins by contradicting his initial phrasing:

> La valeur d'une œuvre n'est peut-être pas son prix et l'une ne détermine pas l'autre, mais toutes deux [sic] entrent dans des rapports qui ne sont qu'en apparence étrangers à la sphère des échanges économiques.[20]

By asserting that art and value are related and that the value of art is not measured by its price – although economic factors may interfere –, Cometti now suggests that art does have a value different from its price[21]. Acknowledging the existence of such an artistic value seems to impugn his theory of art's *Eigenschaftslosigkeit*, for it raises anew the question of art's qualities or properties that may thus be evaluated or valued.

Only Cometti's response would allow us to pursue this conversational thread. However, since the question of art's value rests unanswered, I would like to take it up starting with the comparison Cometti made between art and money. Using Karl Marx's analysis of commodity – and money – as fetish, he described art and money as both acquiring value only through exchange[22]. Indeed, Marx described money as the 'universal equivalent' which

---

19 Heinich, *Le Paradigme de l'art contemporain*, p. 259.
20 Cometti, *La Nouvelle aura*, p. 213.
21 Cometti's sentence is slightly ambiguous. I take 'mais toutes deux' to mean art and value – which is syntactically awkward but the only logical interpretation.
22 Cometti, *La Force d'un malentendu*, p. 63.

has no specific quality, property or use value – and showing that art is the same as money certainly is desirable *Eigenschaftslosigkeit*-wise. But is money's *Eigenschaftslosigkeit* relevant art-wise?[23] And what does the comparison between art and money tell us about art and value? I wish to address this question from a different starting point – where art and money also seem to be indistinguishable.

2. Art and Money: The Boggs case

Indeed, artworks have often dealt with money[24] – to such an extent that, as Marc Shell has noted, 'some artworks verge on becoming money'[25]. Representing money has often been a way of dealing with money, art and value as representation, fiction or illusion. Notably, 19th-century American painters William Harnett, John Haberle, Victor Dubreuil painted trompe-l'œil pictures of dollar bills meant to fool the eye in a context in which the question of gold- and/or silver-backed representative money was at the heart of the American political debate that culminated in William Jennings Bryan's 1896 famous 'Cross of Gold' speech[26]. As

---

23 Heinich stresses the inalienability and non substitutability of artworks (Heinich, *Des valeurs*, pp. 158-161), as opposed to money, and defines artworks as 'objets-personnes' in a 'regime of singularity' which is utterly foreign to the realm of money as 'universal equivalent' (*ibid.*, pp. 161-163). Unsurprisingly, contrary to Cometti, Heinich concludes 'L'on voit ainsi combien il serait dommageable de réduire la question de la valeur à celle du prix' (*ibid.*, 165).

24 Marc Shell has attempted to explore 'the monetary aura of artwork in the West', the relations of coin, icon and Eucharist wafer – among other examples of objects bearing meaning, presence or value —, as 'manifestation[s] of an ideal *and* a real thing' in the image of 'Jesus as god-man' (Marc Shell, *Art & Money* (Chicago: Chicago University Press, 1995), pp. 7-54 (p. 7). He has also analyzed the representation of paper money in American art (*ibid.*, pp. 57-117; cf. also Marc Shell, 'Argent et art: la question de la représentation dans la finance et la culture', *Revue d'économie financière*, 22 (1992), pp. 207-221), the 'modern iconological vacillations between art as money and money as art', and has attempted to 'map out the relation of monetary tokens that are wholly works of art (like Duchamp's notoriously fungible *Tzanck Check*) with artworks that are wholly monetary tokens or processes' (Shell, *Art & Money*, p. 58).

25 Shell, *Art & Money*, p. 58.

26 *Ibid.*, pp. 72-86; Weschler, *Boggs*, pp. 86-91,

many feared the increasingly fictive value of money that could be created or changed by mere political decisions, the confrontation of artistic and monetary representation was topical – although it seems the distinction often was blurred for the authorities themselves, as when William Harnett was arrested by the Secret Service for counterfeiting in 1886 and had to promise he would never again paint a trompe-l'œil dollar bill[27].

However, while painting dollar bills can be about the value of money, it can also be seen as one way for artists to question, test or demonstrate the market value of art compared to the 'universal equivalence' of the money it represents. Clearly, a silk-screened one-dollar bill signed by Warhol is worth far more than one dollar.

J.S.G. Boggs (1955-2017) has brought this process to a point where, like Harnett in 1886, he was arrested, prosecuted and tried for the same reasons in the United States and Britain in the 1980s[28]. Boggs very meticulously drew dollar bills, leaving the reverse blank and changing many details – such as substituting his signature for that of the Secretary of the Treasury and drawing a precise rendering of the U.S. Supreme Court in place of the U.S. Treasury on the back of a ten-dollar bill[29]. Boggs's currency is thus very far from counterfeit. But his art goes beyond the simple fact of drawing. He uses these drawings to pay restaurant bills, buy a pen or a pair of shirts after drawing attention to the fact that his bills are art and not real money, and that they may ultimately be worth more than their face value. When the transaction is refused he pays with real money. When it is accepted, he has a picture taken of the transaction, and he informs one of his collectors that he may get in touch with his drawing's new owner to buy it back from him. If the owner accepts to sell the drawing at a negotiated price, a contract is signed and the work is complete when all the elements involved in the transaction are available to be exhibited as one complete work documenting the whole process.

Arthur Danto has commented that:

---

27 Weschler, *Boggs*, p. 87.
28 *Ibid.*
29 *Ibid.*, p. 130.

> The happening climaxes when the drawing, in becoming art, confers the status of art on a number of things not ordinarily thought to enjoy that exalted position. [...] It is a kind of magic. [...] To understand the transaction is to appreciate the transfigurative power of the institutions of the art world. [...] I have often thought of the performance artist as a kind of priest [...] Nothing secular has an aura more seductive than money.[30]

Danto here supports the notion shared by Lahire, Dubuffet and Cometti that there is a 'magical' virtue in exchange that creates value – both for money and art[31]. However, while Boggs is fascinated with how money becomes valuable, he is aware that the value of money is 'all an act of faith'[32] – which is a better definition than 'magic' –, and it seems that his whole point is not really about money but about art, as he makes clear when he describes what happens to him when he tries to kick his habit of drawing dollar bills:

> I'll resolutely start out on some new tangent – a series of abstract canvases, for example – but then somebody always comes along and asks something like 'Well, what do you think that painting's worth?' and I find myself being drawn right back in. Because what does anybody mean by 'worth'? And how's that different from 'value'? And what precisely is it that we value in value? What is giving good value or getting it? And before I know it I'm right back in that hall of mirrors, with the mirrored door clicking shut behind me.[33]

---

30 Arthur C. Danto, 'Trompe-l'Œil and Transaction: The Art of Boggs', in *Embodied Meanings. Critical Essays and Aesthetic Meditations* (New York: Farrar, Straus & Giroux, 1994), pp. 109-110.

31 Weschler concurs: 'all art is magic (we *knew* that), and so is all money' (*ibid.*, p. 23). The recurrent mention of magic, transfiguration and transubstantiation identifies the weak points in the discourses that use them. Figuration and its *enargeia* seem to me to be more suitable substitutes (see Bertrand Rougé, '"*La (per così dire) energia delle figure*". Transporter, figurer, ou *l'enargeia/energeia* des œuvres. Pour une énergétique de l'art', *Aisthesis: Pratiche, linguaggi et sapere dell'estetico*, 2 (2012), pp. 175-211 (p. 175ss) <http://www.fupress.net/index.php/aisthesis/article/view/10996/10416> [accessed 29 January 2019]

32 Quoted in Weschler, *Boggs*, p. 12.

33 *Ibid.*, p. 123.

What triggers Boggs's interest is not a critique of money but the more general question of value as instantiated in art and his fascination with art's power to create value – which for him is best embodied in its confrontation with paper money. This points to the fact that the intimate relationship between money and art which was at the heart of Cometti's thoughts may have been a consequence of a more permanent or structural dimension of art. How art relates – or somehow equates – to money is a relevant 'sociological' question, but there may be other, non-sociological ways of dealing with it.

3. Art and Value: Being About What Counts

A few weeks after the Hirst show in Venice, I was in the Hermitage Museum in St Petersburg unsuccessfully looking for works that would trigger thoughts about art and money for this piece when I happened on a small picture by Willem Van Mieris (1662-1747). A young and an old woman are seated in a room. The young woman looks at the old woman who holds at arm's length not a mirror but a small portrait of herself slightly turned outward for the beholder to see. The painting is entitled *Old Woman Remembering her Youth*. This *vanitas* also seemed irrelevant to the question of art and money unless one was studying its strictly socio-historical dimensions – the representation of Netherlandish wealth, the patronage system, who bought the picture, how much was paid for it, etc. – but all the artworks in the museum and all other types of objects around it could have undergone the same type of historical and sociological analysis. Then it suddenly dawned on me that the poignancy of Van Mieris's picture, like all *vanitas* and perhaps like all art, was due to its being about the irreparable passing of youth, time and life – and that these are arguably among the most universally *precious* and *valuable* things in the world. Cave paintings then came to my mind as also being about life, natural forces and survival in the shape of lively representations of cows, horses and buffaloes that could be perceived as beautiful and powerful competitors in the struggle for life, sacralized totemic animals or prospective meat. As I turned around to see other works in the gallery around me and thought of the whole winter palace, I saw a Roman Charity, crucifixions, portraits of czars, kings and aristocrats, I remembered tables, vases, Fabergé eggs and clocks made of precious stones and metals, scores of luxuriously decorated rooms, and all suddenly seemed to perfectly fit in the same common perspective, also shared by Hirst's works about money, luxury and wealth – the preeminent values in his life and society. Whether they are about subsistence, moral values, religion, power or wealth, whether they are representations or not, artworks are artifacts so much individual or collective time, care, skill and/or wealth goes into the making of that they cannot be dissociated from the general question of what counts for the individual or the group concerned – i.e. value or values.

Suddenly, the question of art and money revealed itself to be but the visible tip of the whole artistic iceberg. Boggs's example showed that dealing with money in art was not about money but about art, Van Mieris's *vanitas* revealed how art is about what individuals or groups value the most – which essentially is life or life-related. In brief, being valuable or having a price or worth is a side-effect, a secondary quality of art. It is but one – sociologically describable – way art is about what counts... And what counts is life or life-related, even when it is determined or its representation is filtered by a set of socio-historical conditions.

Danto once described *aboutness* as one necessary condition for art's being art. Perhaps it would be useful to explore the more specific condition of art's *value-aboutness* – or, *being about what counts*[34]. For being about what counts may help account for a number of art's specificities in terms of value. The question is, what is art's value, and where does it come from? We will then address the question of how aboutness itself comes about.

---

34 In a similar but different vein – perhaps in another part of the iceberg –, Célestin Bouglé described art as 'le créateur des valeurs idéales par excellence' (quoted in Heinich, *Des valeurs*, p. 203). Willy-nilly, Cometti seems to be thinking about yet another piece of this iceberg when he writes: 'L'aura, dont les œuvres d'art ont cessé d'avoir le privilège, est confusément liée, au moins subjectivement, à la valeur que nous leur prêtons' (Cometti, *La Nouvelle aura*, p. 211). Indeed, the value we ascribe these artworks may very well happen to be the value they were about in the first place. And in any case, their being about value or life – even under specific socio-historical conditions – may be precisely what is centrally and definingly constitutive of their aura.

4. The 'Magical' Value-Adding Power of Art?

In Duccio's contract for the Siena *Maestà*, the price of panel and pigments was all paid for by the commissioners and Duccio was only paid a salary for the amount of work he put into the painting: 'Duccio shall be bound to put nothing into it except his person and his work'[35]. Duccio was paid for his craftsmanship, his painting was perceived as a commodity – 'crystallized labour', to use Marx's phrase. But was he paid for his art? Duccio's painting today would go for an incommensurably higher price, because it has acquired a place in the history of art and, as art, is perceived as much more valuable than its initial 'use value' as an altarpiece. The altarpiece as art is worth more than the altarpiece as commodity. It seems like art makes this difference, but how is this possible?

When Boggs pays for his lunch with a hand-drawn twenty-dollar bill and then has a collector buy it back for several hundred dollars, he tests this capacity art has to create – and question – value. Duchamp's *Tzanck Check* and Warhol's series of dollar bills have performed the same test. One here falls back on the usual metaphors of the 'magic' and 'alchemy' of art performing the 'miracle' of instant added value: turning worthless material into gold. Jasper Johns tells a story about his *Beer Cans* (1960) which raises the same questions:

> I was doing at that time sculptures of small objects – flashlights and light bulbs. Then I heard a story about Willem de Kooning. He was annoyed with my dealer, Leo Castelli, for some reason, and said something like, 'That son-of-a-bitch; you could give him two beer cans and he could sell them.' I heard this and thought, 'What a sculpture – two beer cans.' It seemed to me to fit perfectly with what I was doing, so I did them and Leo sold them.[36]

---

35 Quoted in Hayden B. J. Maginnis, *The World of The Early Sienese Painter* (University Park: The Pennsylvania State University Press, 2001), p. 63.
36 Gene R. Swenson, 'What is Pop Art ?' (Part II), *Art News* (Feb. 1964), pp. 40-43, 62-66 (p. 66) (Interviews of Stephen Durkee, James Rosenquist, Jasper Johns, Tom Wesselmann). Repr. in Carol Anne Mahsun, *Pop Art. The Critical Dialogue* (Ann Arbor: U.M.I. Research Press, 1989), pp. 111-137.

Other examples abound, such as Piero Manzoni turning his *Merda d'artista* into potentially valuable works of art, Daniel Spoërri exhibiting as art the leftovers of his girlfriend's breakfast or of a lunch eaten by Duchamp, or the case of so-called Junk Art[37]. Warhol has partially systematized and theorized this in his description and redemption of a variety of objects or images he called 'leftovers'[38]. Of course, all these examples are variations on Duchamp's readymades, which transform banal industrial objects with no artistic value into artworks. The idea is not to demonstratre the ultimate worthlessness or *Eigenschaftslosigkeit* of art but to exert the value-adding power of art: the baser and less valuable the materials used, the greater the artwork's value differential; the closer to total worthlessness the material, even if symbolically (shit, dirt, leftovers, junk), the more absolute by contrast the added artistic value.

Conversely, artists have defaced or destroyed objects of value or representing values. Pianos have been dismantled, Jean Tinguely built a self-destroying machine, Yves Klein several times performed his *Zones de sensibilité picturale immatérielle* (1959-62) that involved the destruction of gold, and in his famous *ekphrasis*, Homer described how Hephaestus 'magically' transformed the shining gold of Achilles's shield into the dark soil of a ploughed field. But in the end, all are ways of being about what counts – productivity or anarchy, gold or sensitivity and a fertile field – and the artwork or the performance is perceived as possessed of a value transcending the value of its components, however valuable they may be deemed.

These examples show that whether they – metaphorically – turn dirt, garbage or shit into gold or gold into dirt or nothing,

---

37 The idea of art transforming shit into gold was there from the beginning as 'Manzoni sold each can by weight at gold's daily market price, [and] the shit literally became worth its weight in gold' (John Miller, 'Excremental Value: Piero Manzoni's *Merda d'artista*', Tate, etc. 10 (summer 2007) <http://www.tate.org.uk/context-comment/articles/excremental-value> [accessed 29 January 2019]). But Manzoni's shit far outvalued gold in 2016 when one of his thirty ninety-gram cans was auctioned for a record €275,000.

38 See Bertrand Rougé, 'Warhol, Duchamp, le geste ironique de l'art et le design comme rien. In-différence, inframince et *leftover* dans *Fountain* et les *Boîtes Brillo*', *Figures de l'art*, 35 (2017), pp. 213-234.

artists always exert their 'magical', value-adding artistic power to transform – or to 'transfigure', as Danto would say. Sociologically-minded analysts like Lahire or Cometti consider that this is conditional 'social magic'. But is there some non-magical way to describe what is thus performed by art?

Obviously, artists do not have the magical-alchemical power to really transform, transfigure or transubstantiate mere objects into gold – even Boggs just transforms paper into an imitation of paper money, which itself is but a representation and a substitute. Yet they actually do create value which differs from – and often exceeds or transcends – the 'crystallized work' described by Marx or the value of the precious or vile materials used. Where does this value come from?

Heinich suggests that value depends on complex social processes by which an object is being ascribed a quality[39]. What then is the quality of art behind art's being about what counts?

The paradox is that, whether artworks are useless or not, whether they are made of valueless or extremely valuable materials, they still have a value-adding power which may be translated – or not – into market value, that is, a price[40]. The question is, if artworks made of valueless material are useless, result from a workless process and yet are valued at a more or less high price, then where does this value come from? I suggest that if they are useless and worthless, they do have value – whether it is acknowledged by a high price or not – because *they are not pointless.* They are about what counts –

---

[39] 'La valeur est la résultante de l'ensemble des opérations par lesquelles une qualité est affectée à un objet, avec des degrés variables de consensualité et stabilité. Ces opérations sont fonction à la fois de la nature de l'objet évalué, de la nature des sujets évaluateurs et de la nature du contexte d'évaluation' (Heinich, *Des valeurs*, p. 167). She thus defines measurable value, measuring value being only one way value can be attributed. For Heinich, there are three types of criteria according to which value can be attributed, i.e. measure, attachment and judgment (*ibid.*, pp. 25-32). Heinich considers quality to be determined by complex sociologically describable social processes.

[40] That this price may be justified or not is not really relevant here. Once the artwork is on the market, it also becomes a commodity and its price is also determined in a varying proportion by the art market laws, i.e. to a certain extent by market laws in general – including speculation – that tend to neglect the artistic value in order to focus on the market value.

and *art's value-adding power* comes precisely, not from *being what counts* – as directly valuable or precious – but from its being *about* what counts. This is why it is important to make the distinction between the value of art and the value of money.

5. Art's Added Value: Being About (How To Be About) What Counts

Actually, the problem of artworks about money and the notion of art's exchange value being its only value ('la valeur d'une œuvre, c'est le prix qu'elle coûte') are only indirectly linked to the question of art's value as art.

In his account of Boggs's fascinating 1987 trial at the Old Bailey, London, Weschler[41] recounts how, after 'Boggs insisted that the law couldn't possibly apply to his work', Robert Harman, the prosecuting barrister, asked him 'Are you suggesting that because your drawings are works of art, they are incapable of being reproductions?', to which Boggs replied: 'I suppose so because once you crossed over the line into reproduction, it would no longer be a work of art'[42]. Boggs's barrister, Geoffrey Robertson, later concurred: 'Has anyone here ever heard of a reproduction being worth more than its original'[43]?

These exchanges show that the issue is not only not counterfeiting, it is not even reproduction. It is more something like reflection. As Boggs says,

> It's all an act of faith. Nobody knows what a dollar is, what the word means, what holds the thing up, what it stands in for. And that's also what my work is about. Look at these things, I try to say. They are beautiful. But what the hell *are* they? What do they do? How do they do it? Take this one here. Five dollars. But what's a dollar? By

---

41   Weschler, *Boggs*, pp. 95-116.
42   *Ibid.*, p. 109. Boggs was not prosecuted for counterfeiting: 'Harman informed the jury that this case was being brought under Section 8 of the 1981 Forgery and Counterfeiting Act, but the prosecution would be alleging neither counterfeiting nor forgery – only the act of reproduction' (*ibid.*, p. 102).
43   *Ibid.*, p. 110.

now, it's just an idea. For that matter, what's 'five'? It doesn't exist either ... five itself doesn't exist, except as a concept. So you've got these two ideas joined together and they represent something else: they stand in for something you might eventually buy, for instance, but nothing in particular. And then I make a drawing of a five-dollar bill, and that's *another* order of representation: it's something that represents something that represents something but not anything in particular.[44]

Indeed, Boggs's goal is not to create market value but to address the notion of value, to focus attention on the question of value by producing an artwork that looks like a banknote but is not a banknote – 'an entity of a logically distinct order' as Danto would say[45] – that triggers reflexive thought *about* value as here instantiated by money.

In other words, like all art about money, it is reflexive art about art's being about what counts in a context in which what counts tends to be measured by the 'universal equivalent' known as money, for indeed, in some contexts – and this includes Hirst and Pinault's international world of art, luxury and fashion –, there is this idea that if you deal with value you have to address money and the market. Yet this is but one contextually-determined form of being reflexively about what counts. In other contexts, art will be about religion or political power or natural forces when these are perceived – and possibly socially-constructed as – what counts. The value of art is then reflexively related to the contextual system of values it is about – whether it supports or criticizes it, whether it aims to extol or to vilify its values and valuables – because it

---

44 *Ibid.*, pp. 12-13. The question raised here should be seen in relation with the debate that opposed Erle Loran and Roy Lichtenstein in 1963 over whether Lichtenstein's ironical remakes of Loran's analytical diagrams of two of Cézanne's paintings – and most Pop Art for that matter – did transform the images used or not, in which last case they could be described as mere non-artistic copies subject to copyright laws. Loran's lawsuit was dismissed, despite the fact that Lichtenstein refused to plead transformation. In other words, the only substantial difference there remained between Loran's diagrams and Lichtenstein's paintings was that Lichtenstein's paintings were *about* Loran's diagrams – and their value(s).

45 Arthur C. Danto, *The Transfiguration of the Commonplace. A Philosophy of Art* (Cambridge: Harvard University Press, 1981), p. 84.

is in part concerned with how it relates to what counts, whatever it is, contextually, that counts. For being concerned with how art relates to what counts is necessarily part of what it is to be about what counts.

A few examples may illustrate this point. Daniel Arasse, for instance, has devoted a whole book to how major Quattrocento painters of Annunciations 'ont utilisé la construction géométrique de la perspective elle-même pour [...] rendre visible cette venue de l'incommensurable dans la mesure'[46]. These artists created works about what perhaps counted most in their Christian world – Incarnation – that also were about how pictorial representation could represent the irrepresentable Mystery, about how the Incommensurable could paradoxically – some would say 'miraculously' or 'magically' – be made to fit in the beholder's experience of the measured realm of geometric perspectival space. In other words, all their efforts aimed to make it possible for art – then defined as the pictorial perspectival representation of the world – to be about what counted most for them, i.e. the Mystery of Incarnation that transcends space and measure. More specifically, there had to be some intimate structural relation between the basic principle of religion they were representing and the basic principle of their art defined as perspectival representation[47]. Similarly, portraits of Louis XIV were about what politically counted most in seventeenth-century France; cave paintings of cows, horses and lionesses evoked perceptions, feelings or conceptions that counted for those who

---

46 Daniel Arasse, *L'Annonciation italienne. Une histoire de perspective* (Paris: Hazan, 1999), p. 13.

47 I have stressed in 'Annonciation/Visitation...' how the Mystery of Incarnation became the model for painting thus grounding the distant power of art in the incommensurable power of God – or vice versa, grounding the devotee's spectacular experience of the Annunciation in the specific *non-address* devised by the painter (Bertrand Rougé, 'Annonciation/Visitation: la distance ou l'étreinte. Vers une poétique picturale?', *Figures de l'art* 16 ('Autour de Daniel Arasse') (Pau: PUP, 2009), pp. 81-110). I have tried to show how Visitations have also often been the occasion for painters to stress painting's 'visitational dimension' leading to an aesthetic *encounter* similar to the meeting of Mary and Elizabeth – the experience of the Visitation itself thus becoming a mere side-effect of painting's visitational powers. In which case it becomes clear that 'being about what counts' is a way art has to position itself as being at the heart of 'what it means to be what counts'.

painted them and one may presume they painted them so that the dimensions they valued most would appear to best effect.

Even non-representational artworks such as readymades are about the questioning of art's limits, which undoubtedly was of great significance to Duchamp, and abstract artists put at the heart of their works what to them counted most, be it color, rhythm, musicality, personal expressivity, and so on. In this respect, ornamental art may be a telling test case of what is at stake in art's being about what counts. Indeed, although non-representational ornamental art cannot directly refer to specific evaluable content, ornamentation is most specifically and almost exclusively about what counts, in the sense that social groups, cultures and individuals usually choose to adorn objects, buildings, places and people that count in their worldviews – usually according to a hierarchical system of ornamental rules where the most elaborate and complex often signals the most valued. In other words, non-representational ornamental art's presenting itself as being exclusively and hierarchically an indication or a signal of what counts may be the primary fundamental way art is about how art is about what counts. For instance, in the Alhambra's very intricate and elaborate web of mostly geometric stucco decoration, which was meant to signal and enhance the value of the Sultan's palace and power, a few calligraphic elements praising Allah are found as well as poems that praise the palace itself, thus self-referentially making explicit the ornamentation's implicit enunciation and function as epideictic[48]: being – in this case indexically – about what counts and making it explicit. Furthermore, as the spectacular ornamentation in the Alhambra was made in a period of political and economic crisis for the Nasrid second dynasty, plaster was used rather than more precious stone, thus increasing the value differential between the cheap material it was made of and the added value resulting from its ornamental-epideictic function.

As Byzantine icons and iconolatry would also contribute to demonstrate, icons acquiring the aura of the god and saints they are about, art counts, i.e. art becomes valuable *per se* – so to speak

---

48 Among the three branches of rhetoric defined by Aristotle, epideictic discourse is that which is devoted to praise and blame. In other words, it is this type of discourse that attributes value – or the lack thereof.

– through a form of auratic transmission. By dint of being about everything that counts art becomes more generally associated with what counts. Art's value-adding power, which we have seen artists are so eager to test and exert – and which often is confused with art's formative, transformative, or creative power, not to mention its value as 'crystallized work' – can thus indeed be described as resulting from art's specific and long-standing value-aboutness or proximity to what counts, from the fact that it has always been a means to value what counts – most often by simply pointing at, signaling, or being about what counts[49].

However, as we have seen, art being about what counts entails also being about how art is about what counts. Anyone who needs to evaluate art, i.e. to address the question of art's value – and this includes artists, individually or collectively, in the process of making art – has to answer this question: how does art achieve its task of being about what counts? More specifically, since what counts proper may be described as depending on various socio-historical and cultural conditions, the question that remains is, how does art achieve its aboutness?

6. Aboutness and the Power of Figurative Distance as Artistic Quality

This leads us back to the initial question about the relationship between art and money as exemplified by Boggs's paintings of – densely ornamented – dollar bills: what is the link between art and money? While artworks' reaching high prices or not and under what conditions – the so-called 'social magic' – truly is only part of the visible tip of the iceberg of the relationship of art and value, it seems that art and money are indirectly related, inasmuch as they are both in their own specific ways related to the question of value. However, while money as the 'universal equivalent' is a general value-measuring system or scale based on confidence or faith – what Boggs describes as an act of faith actually defines the *fiduciary* nature of money –, artworks present themselves as each in a singular way but all generally *about* value. This is the reason

---

[49] One should indeed here stress the element of *deixis* there is in *epideixis*.

why Boggs's trial for the reproduction of pound notes is irrelevant. His works are not reproductions *of* money but reflections *about* how money and art are differently related to value – or else his works could not be distinguished from their models – and hence they are about how art still foundationally is about what counts in a given social context in which it so happens that money seems to have imposed itself as the universal scale of value.

The question of aboutness is, what is the difference between a reproduction *of* a dollar bill – the motif for Boggs's prosecution – and a reflexive artwork *about* this dollar bill and what it stands for – money, possibly value? One is *of*, the other is *about*. One mimics and comes close, the other creates reflexive and figurative distance[50]. Whether the dollar bill is hand-drawn or not is secondary[51]. The difference between a real dollar bill and Boggs's dollar bills, in this respect, is similar to the difference between a box of Brillo and Warhol's *Brillo Boxes*: a box of Brillo is a box of Brillo possibly denoting Brillo pads, while *Brillo Boxes* are *about* boxes of Brillo, possibly about the pads they (do not) contain and everything they all may symbolize and refer to that may count. It so happens that Warhol's *Brillo Boxes* are handmade, silk-screened plywood facsimiles – which is not without consequences[52] – but as

---

50   I should here stress that *mimèsis* and *figuring* should not be seen as equivalent. Actually, I have tried to show that figuring or figuration – in the sense of making a figure of – may be described as an *enargeia*-generating pre-mimetic process of which *mimèsis* is but one possible referential development whose referentiality has prevailed in many artistic traditions and has tended to blur debates about the nature of art (see 'L'art comme Figuration. Pour une *mimèsis* non-mimétique', *Usages de la figure, régimes de la figuration*, ed. by Laura Marin and Anca Diaconou (Bucarest: Editura universitatii bucuresti, 2017), pp. 81-96.

51   In 1993, Boggs launched 'Project Pittsburgh' (Weschler, *Boggs*, pp. 124-31) which consisted in 'creating five million dollars of value out of nothing' (*ibid.*, p. 125) based on hundreds of laser-printed bills designed by himself – an operation Weschler described as 'an alchemical transformation likely to provoke the Internal Revenue Service every bit as much as the Secret Service' (*ibid.*, p. 125). The reference to alchemy, similar to many references to magic is here to account for Boggs's desire to create 'value out of nothing'. Indeed, art's power to create value out of nothing is what this article is all about.

52   On this question, on how the *Brillo Boxes* can be seen as trompe-l'œil of readymades and on the consequences of this, see Bertrand Rougé, 'Just Figuring: Or, The Endless End of Art. Readymades, Trompe-l'œil,

far as we are concerned here they could be real readymade boxes of Brillo to the same effect in a given artistic context, much as Boggs's dollar bills could be real dollar bills re- or de-contextualized so as to present themselves as really being *about* money and value. The handmade aspect of these artworks only draws our attention to this slight, fundamentally unnecessary but highly significant material and perceptual difference that signals the artwork as not a copy of some object but as something that distinguishes or distances itself from it in such a way that it designates itself as being somehow about this object and hinting there is something about it that counts.

Thus, a displacement or deliberate misplacement – what ancient rhetoricians called *translatio* – is enough to transform an everyday object into a powerful figure[53], exactly like the everyday denotation of the word 'honey' is transformed into being powerfully about something else (that counts) when it is effectively misplaced in 'Death, that hath suck'd the honey of thy breath, / Hath had no power yet upon thy beauty' (*Romeo and Juliet* III, 5). In Shakespeare's use of 'honey' the word is *used about something else* by being distanced from (a possible context for) its everyday use, and this distance – or *translatio* – is what creates the condition for the figure's aboutness. So indeed it goes with all art, as it always presents itself as more or less – and in different ways – distanced from what it is and what it is about[54].

Metaphors and Other Meta-Indiscernibles', in *The Philosophy of Arthur C. Danto* (The Library of Living Philosophers, vol. XXXIII), ed. by Randall E. Auxier and Lewis Edwin Hahn (Chicago: Open Court, 2013), pp. 279-305 (with a response by Arthur Danto, 'Reply to Bertrand Rougé', pp. 306-312).

[53] Duchamp perfectly understood this, although he does not seem to have perceived the rhetorical tradition behind it, when he anonymously described the artist's choice of a urinal for *Fountain*: 'He took an ordinary article of life, placed it so that its useful significance disappeared under the new title and point of view – *created a new thought* for that *object*' (*The Blind Man* 2 (1917), p. 5). On this question of readymades' rhetorical and figurative dimension, see Bertrand Rougé, 'La dislocation figurative. L'énergie de la Figuration contre la "fin de l'art"', *La Part de l'Œil*, 31, 'Force de figures: la figurabilité entre texte et image' (2017/2018), pp. 33-47.

[54] In 1964, Jasper Johns said something about his work that also closely resembles what a rhetorical *translatio* is all about – including its effect of *ostrannenie* –: 'I am concerned with a thing's not being what it was, with it becoming something other than what it is, with any moment in which one

As we have seen, being about what counts is relative in the sense that what counts changes with socio-historical conditions, and this is reflected in the great diversity of art's forms and subjects. Cometti focuses on this 'sociological' dimension, but I see it as the tip of the iceberg. Indeed, the 'sociological' relativity of what counts is not the determinant aspect of what art is. It is *art's being about it* that is. In other words, *art's being about what counts* – and being profoundly and diversely determined by being about what counts – may be a much more permanent ground for a *figurative* definition of art – as when Danto describes Lichtenstein's distinct use of Loran's diagrams as 'rhetorical'[55] and very aptly suggests that 'metaphors are minor works of art'[56]. Indeed, Danto justly insists on this point, 'To understand the artwork is to grasp the metaphor that is, I think, always there'[57], 'the structure of artworks is, or is very close to the structure of metaphors'[58]. However, I believe it is now possible to be more precise. I propose to reformulate this as: figurative distance is how artworks are and show themselves to be about what counts; figurative distance is the artistic quality that makes aboutness and hence art possible. This entails that describing the diversity of the figures used by art – not just metaphors – and their efficacy or *enargeia* in being about what counts is what constitutes the true analysis of art.

This leads to one last point. We have seen that art counts by dint of being about what counts and that how it achieves being about what counts – i.e. in the multiple ways it is figurative in a larger than strictly mimetic sense – is where art's strictly artistic quality resides and may be described and evaluated. This means that all other qualities usually defined as artistic qualities are not constitutive of art's aboutness but necessarily become part of what art is about – and that counts.

Beauty, for instance, has long been described as one of art's principal qualities, but from the perspective I have tried to articulate here beauty is not an *artistic* quality. Beauty is an aesthetic quality

---

    identifies a thing precisely and with the slipping away of that moment' (in Swenson).
55 Danto, *The Transfiguration of the Commonplace*, p. 147.
56 Ibid., p. 189.
57 Ibid., p. 172.
58 Ibid., p. 173.

that counts about what art is, in the many ways art can be about things that count – it tries to represent it, to reproduce it, to produce the same effects, to more or less analytically present what it identifies as its constituents, etc. How all this is done by art is artistic quality – and art does all this by creating multiple and complex forms of figurative distance. The same goes for all that exerts some sort of – real or imaginary – power, for being about what counts is being about what is powerful and makes its power felt by humans, to such an extent that, as in the case of beauty, all these powers art is about tend to be attributed to art itself – perhaps because art aims to exert its own figurative power by being about them.

Indeed, this paper began with the example of art and money and how this raised the question of value – especially the value that could be attributed to art through its association with money, the 'universal equivalent'. However, it may very well be that artists choose to create artworks about money because money is a form of power. For an artist in a relevant context to be able to create value comparable with or superior to the value of money is clearly a way to be about how art has the *figurative power to create* value. *Art's being about what counts actually is being about what has power to produce effects and make itself felt.*

Thus, art may have been described as having the power to transcend, to please, to seduce, to impress, to give life and to create illusion. But all these powers actually are related to all that art most usually is about that counts – and is perceived as having the power to make itself felt. The power to transcend is associated with art's being about religion, gods, and the sacred, and has, for instance, taken the typical form of the icon; the power to please and to seduce is related to its being about the forces of beauty and desire in human lives and has long been represented by the female nude; the power to impress is linked to its being about political power and social order and has typically led to many forms of monumentality; the power to metaphorically give life is linked to art's being about the forces of life and death and more generally of nature and has given rise to still lives, *vanitas*, landscapes, the quest for movement in the visual arts since the earliest cave paintings, all these calling for the power of illusion, itself derived from art's reflexively being about how it achieves its being about vibrant life.

This list is no doubt incomplete but it shows that major characteristics usually attributed to art actually are not qualities of art but *what art is about that counts because it has power* – real or imaginary, constant or conditional – which art is able to diversely mimic, reproduce or produce the effects of through *the power of figurative distance* – i.e. rhetorically[59].

7. Rhetoric v. Sociology: 'a modest ontology'?

To conclude, I wish to return to Cometti's views and see how they relate to those I have just tried to develop in relation to his interest in art and money. It seems to me that Cometti's analysis of art and money does not exhaust the subject of whether art can be defined. His sociological, historical or cultural perspective on how art functions and is acknowledged as art under a set of given circumstances, is an apt description of how things do work – sociologically, historically and culturally – in given contexts. However, it remains in doubt whether the overall correctness of this perspective – I have called it globally 'sociological' – justifies that all other perspectives on art, including ontological endeavors, should be abandoned[60]. Indeed, that there are changing conditions, purposes or definitions of art – including changing perceptions of what counts that art should be about – does not necessarily imply that the very idea of a common definition should be abandoned, for the common definition may very well include the sociological dimensions and may concern aspects of art, such as being about what counts, which are not structurally modified by the sociologically-determined evolutions of art's definitions and conditions – the invisible mass of the iceberg – however radical these changes may appear. For instance, do the radical

---

59 This rhetorical power can be described as *enargeia* (see Rougé, "'La (per così dire) energia delle figure'").
60 Heinich stresses the 'eminently sociological reality' of the paradigm of contemporary art's focus on discourses rather than objects as art-defining (Heinich, *Le Paradigme de l'art contemporain*, p. 90). She further describes contemporary art as 'une forme d'expression particulièrement en phase avec la sociologie [...] pragmatique' (*ibid.*, p. 115) and quotes Cometti (*Le Force d'un malentendu*, p. 218) to make her point.

artistic changes claimed by the modernists really entail that absolutely nothing has remained of previous artistic practices, as often hastily implied? Although Cometti often makes comparably radical claims based on such historical ruptures, he sometimes seems to be hesitant about them, as when he writes: 'le statut de l'art [...] est *peut-être* en train de se transformer sous nos yeux, de manière radicale'[61] – although this remark actually betrays his historicist hope that art's status is indeed undergoing a radical change. But do the radical changes in artworks' appearances or conditions of activation, including their famed 'dematerialization', necessarily imply that the 'definition' of art has changed? If by art we understand the visual arts, but also literature and music, then art in general is not in any way transformed by the introduction of multiples, abstraction, and dematerialization in the so-called visual arts, since these are characteristics that literature and music have shared for ages.

Cometti's conception of art is based on his appreciation of the state of art after the purist avant-gardes of the early 20th century epitomized by Kandinsky's 'interior necessity': 'A la nécessité intérieure, gage illusoire de la sublimité, répondent les pratiques contextuelles qui se sont imposées dans l'art au cours de ces dernières décennies'[62]. Cometti described a largely Cagean historical rupture whereby a nonhierarchical, experience-oriented, post-60s art of indeterminacy became based on triangular and open structures subject to varying contexts, as opposed to the binary pre-60s arts which, he believed, were stuck with a spectatorial theory of art whereby the beholder (subject) was engaged in a hierarchical face-to-face with the artist's work (object)[63]. This rupture with the past, in his mind, paved the way for what he deemed desirable evolutions: to get rid of the subject, 'rendre l'art et l'expérience esthétique au hasard et à la pluralité'[64].

The programmatic aspect of these remarks is not what interests me here. This analysis, it seems to me, is at the heart of Cometti's justification of his conception of art's *Eigenschaftslosigkeit*. It is

---

61 Cometti, *Le Force d'un malentendu*, p. 27 (my italics).
62 Cometti, *L'Art sans qualités*, p. 39.
63 Ibid., p. 70.
64 Ibid., pp. 48-50, 62.

this historical analysis of how the arts have entered a new era of subjectless – and often objectless – nonhierarchical and contextual indeterminacy, that leads him to assert that, 'il devient de plus en plus difficile d'attribuer aux œuvres d'art des propriétés essentielles nous autorisant à tracer des frontières'[65]. In other words, art cannot be essentially defined anymore – and, to a large extent, he means by this that it never could and never will be. The problem is that the historical grounds for this logical articulation – today's art has no qualities, hence it is impossible to ascribe to art any essential quality for all times – are frail.

Cometti, like Danto, chose to found his approach of art on what he sees as a major turning point in its history. While Danto centers his whole theory of the indiscernibles and of 'the end (of the history) of art' around Warhol's first exhibition of the *Brillo Boxes* in April 1964, Cometti's theory about the visual arts is based on a slightly longer period of change – from the 40s to the 70s – during which John Cage introduced indeterminacy in the production and reception of art, thus leading to the developments of Fluxus and the conceptualist views of art which overall seem to be Cometti's major artistic references[66].

The problem may be that, like Danto, he founds his philosophical reasoning about art on what he perceives as a historical rupture. This focus on rupture is very contextual. It is typical of modernism and of its avant-garde taste for the eradication of the past and the revolutionary elaboration of the new[67]. The problem is that this focus on historical ruptures predetermines the relativist historicism and sociologism of his philosophical conclusions. One way or another, foregrounding *change as radical* – which is the modernist stance – necessarily leads one to conclude that art either has ended (Danto) or cannot be defined, has no permanent

---

65   *Ibid.*, p. 68.
66   Cometti describes Cagean indeterminacy as akin to early-Kantian forms of the 18th-century, pre-Romantic sublime (Cometti, *L'Art sans qualités*, p. 15).
67   Cometti symptomatically chose to translate Peter Bürger's *Theory of the Avant-Garde* which defines the avant-garde as 'mettant radicalement en question l'institution art' (Peter Bürger, *Théorie de l'avant-garde*, trans. by Jean-Pierre Cometti (Paris: Questions théoriques, 2013), p. 170) and the ideology of aesthetic autonomy.

qualities, no essence (Cometti). Apart from the fact that such conclusions appear to be themselves contextually determined – by modernism or avant-gardism –, one may wonder whether they do not fall prey to a form of circular reasoning induced by the modernist claims: art must undergo radical change, hence art has come to an end (Danto) or has never existed as such but with various definitions under specific conditions in specific contexts (Cometti). Focusing on continuities rather than ruptures, while taking ruptures into account, should give different results – as I have tried to show here.

Cometti's standpoint being both Wittgensteinian and 'sociological' or historicist, allows him to see only those elements that support anti-essentialism, anti-foundationalism and the impossibility to define things like art that keep changing according to changing conditions. However, one need not fall into the trap of absolutizing all changes, even major changes, as *radical* changes. Cometti liked this rhetoric of radicality, which held his whole intellectual edifice together, but he also sometimes developed analyses that pragmatically relativized his radicality to the point of self-contradiction.

In his conclusion to *La Force d'un malentendu* – a book again largely devoted to a radical critique of ontological pursuits concerning art – he focused on the pragmatic necessity to be attentive not to artworks as objects but as defined by uses, by how they function and how they are contextually and interactively *activated* as art – which led him to conclude:

> C'est pourquoi il faudrait intégrer à notre vision des œuvres d'art [...] les *modus operandi* de celles-ci, en commençant par prendre en considération les conditions, forcément variables, de cette opérativité. Une vision plus attentive à cela n'aboutirait pas forcément à une condamnation sans réserve de l'ontologie, mais elle en modifierait considérablement le sens et la portée [...] On se méprend, dans les situations langagières, lorsqu'on concentre exclusivement son attention sur les mots. Ce sont, au contraire, les usages et les conditions pragmatiques qui en font partie qui entraînent les engrenages et permettent à la machine de ne pas tourner à vide. Il n'en va pas différemment pour l'art. L'être y est toujours solidaire d'un *faire* en deçà duquel il est vain de vouloir remonter. Ici aussi, vient un moment où la bêche se retourne. Une

ontologie qu'on pourrait appeler 'modeste' ne peut en être exclue: l'art et les œuvres ont leur mode d'existence propre [...] L'ontologie [...] est intégralement solidaire d'une anthropologie[68].

Strangely enough, this conclusion is entitled 'L'esthétique sans ontologie'... But the point I want to make is that what he describes here as artworks' *modus operandi*, as the changing pragmatic conditions of usage under which words acquire a different meaning or power is quite similar to what I have here described as the *rhetorical* power of art's figurative distance. And when a few years earlier Cometti wrote that 'Il peut certes paraître raisonnable de dire que la relation esthétique repose sur les ressources de plaisir et de compréhension liées à notre expérience de certains objets'[69], he seemed indeed to suggest that art provides the pleasure of understanding, which is precisely what Aristotle and Cicero described as the principal effect of metaphors. Perhaps, after all, the rhetorical quality of art's figurative distance outlives or transcends the more strictly sociohistorical vagaries of the arts and their institutions. Perhaps beneath the undeniable sociological workings of our cultures there is still room for a 'modest ontology' inspired by rhetoric.

References

Arasse, Daniel, *L'Annonciation italienne. Une histoire de perspective* (Paris: Hazan, 1999).
Bürger, Peter, *Théorie de l'avant-garde*, trans. by Jean-Pierre Cometti (Paris: Questions théoriques, 2013).
Cometti, Jean-Pierre, *L'Art sans qualités* (Tours: Farrago, 1999).
—, *La Force d'un malentendu. Essais sur l'art et la philosophie de l'art* (Paris: Questions théoriques, 2009).
—, *La Nouvelle aura. Économies de l'art et de la culture* (Paris: Questions théoriques, 2017).
—, *Conserver/restaurer: l'œuvre d'art à l'époque de sa préservation technique* (Paris: Gallimard, 2017).

---

68 Cometti, *Le Force d'un malentendu*, pp. 217-218.
69 Cometti, *L'Art sans qualités*, p. 68.

—, 'Onze thèses sur l'art et le marché de l'art', repr. in Cometti/Quintane (eds), pp. 12-14.

—, 'L'art riche. Faits et méfaits de la main invisible', in Cometti/Quintane (eds), pp. 78-98.

—, and Nathalie Quintane (eds), *L'Art et l'argent* (Paris: Editions Amsterdam, 2017).

Danto, Arthur C., *The Transfiguration of the Commonplace. A Philosophy of Art* (Cambridge: Harvard University Press, 1981).

—, 'Trompe-l'Œil and Transaction: The Art of Boggs', in *Embodied Meanings. Critical Essays and Aesthetic Meditations* (New York: Farrar, Straus & Giroux, 1994), pp. 104-111.

Dubuffet, Jean, *Asphyxiante culture* (Paris: Minuit, 2007).

Durkheim, Émile, *Les Formes élémentaires de la vie religieuse* (Paris: PUF, 1985).

Heinich, Nathalie, *Le Paradigme de l'art contemporain. Structures d'une révolution artistique* (Paris: Gallimard, 2014).

—, *Des valeurs. Une approche sociologique* (Paris: Gallimard, 2017).

Lahire, Bernard, *Ceci n'est pas qu'un tableau: essai sur l'art, la domination, la magie et le sacré* (Paris: La Découverte, 2015).

Maginnis, Hayden B. J., *The World of The Early Sienese Painter* (University Park: The Pennsylvania State UP, 2001).

Miller, John, 'Excremental Value: Piero Manzoni's *Merda d'artista*'. Tate, etc., 10 (summer 2007) <http://www.tate.org.uk/context-comment/articles/excremental-value> [accessed 29 January 2019]

Morgan, Tiernan, 'Damien Hirst's Shipwreck Fantasy Sinks in Venice', *Hyperallergic* (August 10, 2017) <https://hyperallergic.com/391158> [accessed 29 January 2019]

Rougé, Bertrand, 'Annonciation/Visitation: la distance ou l'étreinte. Vers une poétique picturale?', *Figures de l'art*, 16 ('Autour de Daniel Arasse') (Pau: PUP, 2009), pp. 81-110.

—, '"La (per così dire) energia delle figure". Transporter, figurer, ou l'*enargeia/energeia* des œuvres. Pour une énergétique de l'art', *Aisthesis: Pratiche, linguaggi et sapere dell'estetico*, 2 (Florence: Firenze UP, 2012), pp. 175-211. <http://www.fupress.net/index.php/aisthesis/article/view/10996/10416> [accessed 29 January 2019]

—, 'Just Figuring: Or, The Endless End of Art. Readymades, Trompe-l'œil, Metaphors and Other Meta-Indiscernibles', *The Philosophy of Arthur C. Danto* (The Library of Living Philosophers, vol. XXXIII), ed. by Randall E. Auxier and Lewis E. Hahn (Chicago: Open Court, 2013), pp. 279-305. (With a response by Arthur Danto, 'Reply to Bertrand Rougé', 306-312.)

—, 'Warhol, Duchamp, le geste ironique de l'art et le design comme rien. In-différence, inframince et *leftover* dans *Fountain* et les *Boîtes Brillo*', *Figures de l'art*, 35 (2017), pp. 213-234.

—, 'L'art comme Figuration. Pour une *mimèsis* non-mimétique', *Usages de la figure, régimes de la figuration*, ed. by Laura Marin and Anca Diaconou (Bucarest: Editura universitatii bucuresti, 2017), pp. 81-96.

—, 'La dislocation figurative. L'énergie de la Figuration contre la "fin de l'art"', *La Part de l'Œil*, 31, 'Force de figures: la figurabilité entre texte et image' (2017/2018), pp. 33-47.

Shell, Marc, 'Argent et art: la question de la représentation dans la finance et la culture', *Revue d'économie financière*, 22 (1992), pp. 207-221.

—, *Art & Money* (Chicago: Chicago University Press, 1995).

Swenson, Gene R., 'What is Pop Art?' (Part II). *Art News* (Feb. 1964), pp. 40-43, 62-66. (Interviews of Stephen Durkee, James Rosenquist, Jasper Johns, Tom Wesselmann, repr. in Mahsun, Carol Anne, *Pop Art. The Critical Dialogue*. Ann Arbor: U.M.I. Research Press, 1989, pp. 111-137).

Weschler, Lawrence, *Boggs. A Comedy of Values* (Chicago: University of Chicago Press, 1999).

Jean-Maurice Monnoyer

EXPOSITION AND INSTALLATION
Jean-Pierre Cometti Against the Commodification of Art Objects[1]

In the spring of 2016, just three months after Jean-Pierre Cometti's disappearance, his *La nouvelle Aura* appeared in print.[2] This monograph of eleven chapters was thus the last book Cometti was able to complete, and in truth it represents the culmination of a research trajectory at once *anti-essentialist*, *pragmatist*, and *contextualist*. To that trajectory are added some supplemental inflections, derived from what in Europe is called, after Theodor Adorno, 'critical theory'. Despite those remarkable inflections touching on the invasion of the market into the world of culture, one cannot say that Cometti's interest lies directly in the social theory of art. His anti-essentialist position proclaimed from the outset

> The objects and the practices that we elevate to the sublimity of works of art do not possess naturally, or by essence, any of the properties that we attribute to them: they are, in effect, without qualities.[3]

is in no way a simple adaptation of critical theory, nor a critique of the institutional conception of art of George Dickie. For Cometti it is a matter rather of a sort of anti-elitist credo ('who made you king', he asks[4]), a credo we might judge no less liberal than that of John Dewey, although Dewey's theses, of which Cometti has

---

1 Translated by Jerrold Levinson.
2 Jean-Pierre Cometti, *La nouvelle Aura. Économies de l'art et de la culture* (Paris, Questions théoriques, 2016).
3 *Ibid.*, p. 9.
4 *Ibid.*

defended the pertinence and renewal, are not always shared by him. However, this genre of presentation by reference to Dickie or Dewey does not convey much of the interest that the book arouses, and certainly, the nerve center of the book's problematic, which I will now examine, lies elsewhere. In what way has a practice of 'art-for-everyone' been instituted 'economically' on bases that Cometti finds suspect? What relations are there between the economy of 'installations' and the manifest renewal of expositions?

Cometti shows, with beautiful vehemence, that our contemporary art 'moment' overturns completely Walter Benjamin's forecast, set out in 1936 in 'The Work of Art in the Age of Mechanical Reproduction' – a rather long article appearing originally in French when the Revue of Max Horkheimer was published in Paris by the editor Alcan[5]. Benjamin's forecast signaled the end of that mode of art which, since Nelson Goodman, is called 'autographic', even though many artworks today are no longer on the order of inscriptions. Adorno wanted to defend a conception of art as autonomous ('art cannot be complicit in its own disappearance'), and did not think the 'demagicisation' (*Entzauberung*) of art advocated by Benjamin need issue in the pure and simple liquidation of art – an *Entkunstung*, in his coinage, and thus in an inverse fetishism of fascination with products[6]. Cometti overturns this opposition between Benjamin and Adorno in underlining the *usages* or *customs* of art. As we shall soon see, this overturning assumes another sense being given to those words, since for Cometti it is rather *allographic* art, and not *autographic* art, that has become 'auratic'. It is in fact outside the world of art as such, in the domain of prototypical luxury items and design objects, that the transformation of 'exchange-value' into 'art-value' has been effected. How is such a

---

5   See Walter Benjamin, *Ecrits français* (Paris: Gallimard, Folio Essais, n°418, 1991), pp. 177-248. I have indicated, in a long dossier, the preparatory work for that French edition of the text of the first version of the essay, joined by translation of a letter of Adorno dated 18 March 1936.
6   The center of Adorno's response consists in holding that autonomous art is not necessarily 'bourgeois', once it 'transcends itself through its own technology', such as happened with the new music of that time. Adorno denounced the effects of the massification of art, and judged that art proper was the only defense against the assaults of an increasingly over-planned and over-surveilled life.

permutation possible? We must begin by dwelling a moment on the use of this notion of 'art-value'.

Benjamin spoke only of a 'decline of the aura' (*Verfall der Aura*), pronouncing the decline of that magical, fervent, and reverential attitude we maintain in relation to the original where artworks are concerned, but without in any way endorsing the notion of an *end of art,* as propounded later by Arthur Danto in the sense of a 'historical' end of the narrative of art's evolution. Benjamin signaled only that what would follow the decline of the aura would be a tactile inversion of our approach to artworks, the result of their ubiquity and limitless reproducibility. In a first phase, reproductions of a work allow us to enter into greater *proximity* with the original. However, in a second phase, it is the *nature* or *substance* of the original that is under attack, whereby the original, through a technical transformation, is emancipated from its connection with ritual. The decline of that 'beautiful appearance' beloved of Hegel and of Goethe, which is at the root of this changed conception of a work of art, was destined, according to Benjamin, to open up a completely new *Spielraum* – a free and open play space, technically liberated from the *hic et nunc* or here and now that the 'unique' work of art, as such, retains. Benjamin was thinking of photomontage, collage, and cinema as likely agents of this transformation, which would inevitably result in a democratic 'socialization' of the conditions of viewing. Is it this new, liberated, play space, today multiplied even further, that would explain, a long time since the proclamations of McLuhan, Cometti's unexpected reference to Benjamin? Benjamin's thesis, brutally expressed in all its radicality, was directed against the authenticity and beauty of the original work, the aim being to tear down the veil – as if the work were enclosed in a transparent membrane made of space and time – a veil that Benjamin wished to destroy (*Zertrümmerung*)[7]. However, it is not that ultimately perceptual conception of our access to works that Cometti is here challenging.

Far from endeavoring to formulate more precisely what Benjamin's essay was trying to say about the aura surrounding

---

7   Walter Benjamin, *Das Kunstwerk in Zeitalter seiner technischen Reproduzierbarkeit* (Frankfurt am Main: Suhrkamp, 1975).

traditional artwork, Cometti maintains instead that a *new aura* attaches to contemporary works and performances. What he calls the 'aura of production' belongs, according to him, to the 'facture of works'[8] under certain conditions of exhibition and scenarization. But this aura, once manifested, installs in the space occupied by such works a sort of *Bannkreis*, or uncrossable magic circle, exercising on us a perfectly illusory attraction, and that, he explains, in virtue of the 'functioning of fetishist works of art'. Cometti designates, in rather generic fashion, contemporary art objects such as the recumbent effigies of Maurizio Cattelan (*All*, 2007), whose apparent luster is not imitation. Nine blocks of Carrera marble in effect enclose in their folds the vibrating patina of polished stone. This 'aura of production'

> avoids two major dangers: that of artificiality and that of naturalness. The aura, since a matter of art or that which we commonly take to be art, does not belong to any 'nature' of the object. Neither is it bound to the simple perception we have of it. *It belongs to the works themselves* insofar as they integrate the different factors, including the conditions of exhibition, that are there exemplified.[9]

Faced with such sculptures the veil posited by Benjamin is not torn asunder; instead, we find ourselves confronted by an installation whose immanent properties have been effectively swamped or overtaken by the auratic effect. Cometti endorses Benjamin's diagnosis of how 'exhibition value' has replaced 'cult value', but does not endorse the prognosis Benjamin bases on that.

It remains to elucidate the expression, recurrent in Cometti's discourse, of the 'functioning of fetishist art objects'. That is doubtless an apt phrase, if what Cometti says about art markets and prices is just, ever since artists like Damien Hirst and Takashi Murakami, to take two antithetical examples, and many others as well, broke with the public while at the same time flattering it, playing against the habitual consensus according to which the public is interested by what it sees and thinks it understands.

---

8   Cometti, *La nouvelle Aura*, p. 199.
9   *Ibid.*, p. 200 (italics added).

What is more, these artists have proclaimed loudly and clearly the *communicative opacity of art*. Separating art and life, they have kept the public at a distance, priding themselves on contemptuous estrangement in the face of the spontaneous reactions of spectators, critics, and art lovers. These artists willingly adopt behavior that is provocative and sometimes 'disruptive', as the publicists say, invoking the spirit of a place, manipulating both noble and ignoble materials, cadavers, animal mannequins, and things from the trash, because it is of little import to them what reception their productions receive. And not surprisingly, the public is denounced by them in its touristic wanderings.

Everything would seem possible, in effect, as lying behind the paradoxical reaction that such artists provoke: definitive rejection, exaltation, defamation, over-interpretation, under-interpretation, and so on. Something is happening, in effect, in contemporary art which defies any kind of accreditation of the sort of 'monstration'[10] – the word is Cometti's – it proposes, since it is a form of subversion from top to bottom of the idea of a museum. It is hardly forced to think that such productions have an *emetic aspect*, emptying art of all substance, encouraging sometimes a certain disgust, as if all spiritual food was to be refused, so much does the inspiration of certain of these works reside in a superlative and unrelenting negativism. It seems, therefore, in the pertinent and sensible diagnosis that Cometti offers of this recent evolution in art, that the artists in question have deliberately blocked all access to the 'content' of their works, because of the 'sumptuous and speculative' economy into which these fetishist objects are presumed to enter, through their *exhibition* and *insertion* at the heart of the dominant economic model. 'The curator and the artist [of today] are entrepreneurs'[11].

> That the spectator is thus 'assisted' does not signify that he is 'trapped'. What is in question [...] relates rather to the effectiveness of what we call *work, exhibition, installation,* and so on. That is to say, in the end, on the effectiveness of what we call *art*. In all that it is not a question of simple looking or of retinal capacity, but of

---

10 This word has no equivalent in English, but its meaning is something like *flagrant exhibitionism*, though not in the sexual sense.
11 Cometti, *La nouvelle Aura*, p. 208.

a much more complex and global *experience*, which mobilizes the most diverse powers we possess, and takes us far from a model of *contemplation* of works whose sublimity placed them at a spatial, temporal, and ontological remove. Immersion, interactivity, and proximity are substituted for that, thus implicating and involving the spectator in the work.[12]

Cometti's study is assuredly suggestive and merits examination. Despite the great generality of its discourse and its invocation of interactive experience, *La Nouvelle Aura* questions the social functioning and the 'activation' of the art of today. The justification of the reference, for me typically distorted, to the writings of Benjamin, will be investigated in due course.

1. Functioning and Dysfunctioning

Cometti's employment of the expression 'the functioning of fetishist art objects' is characteristic. But one wonders whether those objects function as fetishes or instead as 'postiches' or dummy symbols: that is, as fake objects, or else 'lesser objects' (*oggetti meno*) as proclaimed by Pistoletto in 1966. Another option is to describe them as *ficta*, in the manner of industrial totems of a new genre, often in appearance coarse and rough-hewn, like certain productions inspired by *arte povera*, which, however, had a contrary objective. Cometti nicely describes the rupture effected by such works with the status of object in its ontological dimension, and is why he is so concerned with Dada and Duchamp. Moreover, it is certain that in recent artistic production the minimalist impulse is seen as outdated, the avant-garde having been 'demoted'.

Above all, it is striking to consider how great an importance the concept of *functioning* assumes for Cometti and other art theorists, without truly reflecting on what that means, despite the very particular role the concept plays in Cometti's own system. One no longer wonders, reiterates Cometti, how works of art *function*. Their functioning, if that be admitted and as Goodman has described it – Cometti acknowledges to have been directly

---

12   *Ibid.*, p. 210.

inspired by him here – consists in a practical and symbolic activation which rests on a relationship of complicity with a receiving public[13]. At base, it is a matter of a kind of *affordance* that is supposed to correspond to a chosen mode of presentation, such as a particular lighting or a particular physical situating. But in the case of the 'fetishist art objects' that concern Cometti, what complicity is really required beyond a certain perplexity that we manifest in regarding them? If they are truly 'fetishized', further complicity is effectively banished. But Joseph Beuys claimed, of certain of his perversions of objects meant to thwart reception – think for instance of his suet-covered chair on which no one can sit – that they incarnated 'social sculptures'.

The English term 'it works' means, in the context of a controlled implementation, that symbols 'function' other than they do in normal activities of designation, and that they 'exemplify' other properties, in given cases, than those they literally denote (ones that Cometti denounces as 'immanent properties', which *de facto* would no longer be such). According to Goodman, recall, 'a sample exemplifies only those properties which it both possesses and makes reference to'. Why would the *functioning by activation* invoked by Cometti not be just as specific?

It is an issue, then, of an associative or participatory functioning, but not always an entirely pragmatic one, which is put in question by the art of the post-*avant-garde*. As the title of one of his books reminds us, Cometti is in search of what he calls, by name, 'factors of art'[14]. Only these *factors* are in reality supposed to be other than *truthmakers* serving to validate statements of the type 'this is a work of art' or 'this is not art', which we proffer unceasingly of objects that are proposed to us for judgment. These affirmations are perhaps just utterances, in which case it is possible that the ontological predicate 'to be a work of art' is not reducible to the declarative value that criticism accords it. No more, for example, than the status of Bach's *Mass in B minor* is reducible to the key that figures in its title, yet who could doubt that the Mass in B

---

13 Nelson Goodman, 'L'art en action', *Cahiers du Musee National d'Art Moderne*, 41 (1992), pp. 7-14.
14 Jean-Pierre Cometti, *Art et facteurs d'art. Ontologies friables* (Rennes: Presses Universitaires de Rennes, 2012).

minor is a work of art? This great piece of music, even in a wretched performance, 'functions' very well, beyond what philosophers might say of it, long after its first performance, and in each one of its subsequent performances. It is no longer simply a liturgical accompaniment. In the same way, a still life of Chardin is hardly less 'activated' by a regard that situates it firmly in the most static genre of painting there is, in virtue of its intentional power that has lost none of its original force.

As a reaction probably to the famous 'de-definition' of art of Harold Rosenberg, we have doubtless been witness for some years now to an 'over-definition' of art and a breaking wave of meta-artistic problematics, which put back in question the ontology of artworks, and not only those diverted from their functions, which works would no longer be anything but inappropriate supports of description. Cometti sees there a consequence of the 'politics of supply' on the art market. What is certain is that these works are sharply demarcated from the standardized run of paintings and sculptures.

However, this negative explanation is not sufficient. Many such works dysfunction terribly as regards their symbolic dimension or their relation to the medium they employ. They are no longer symbols articulated syntactically, as Goodman described that, but instead usurp the reality of the media that support them. Mediation 'virtualizes' the material reality of the vehicle. Cometti does not beat around the bushes concerning the *Punta della Dogana* museum in Venice for the Pinault collection[15]. And in fact the last multi-media exhibition of Damien Hirst in the sumptuous locales of the *Palazzo Grassi* seems to confirm Cometti's sentiment as a visitor to the *Punta della Dogana*.

One sees in the 2017 Hirst exhibition an assortment of heteroclite objects: seashells, statues, deformed monsters, all plunged in a bogus Atlantic Ocean. This grandiloquent and kitschy glorification, a mélange of Disney and Hollywood, with its departed ones, its drowned men, its mythological beings video-plasticized or reconstructed in an infantilized stereography, implies the use of an industrial software of the type *Catia*. This glorification is then parasitized, as regards its artistic status, by

---

15   *Ibid.*, p. 59.

the *process* of fabrication of the pieces – a parametric 3D device – which has the upper hand. The result is somewhat like a giant aquarium in which the public and society are overturned and submerged. So much for Hirst.

Cometti concludes: 'the *contemporary* has espoused the world of the *ultra-liberal*', as in the shopping malls of Abu Dhabi and certain luxury boutiques of airports'[16]. The advertising, publicity, and *merchandizing* of exhibitions of this contemporary sort no longer correspond to the specific functioning reserved for the products of art in their proper place. Even if certain artists precisely call for such 'placelessness', such installations are nonetheless deprived of all function. They are gigantic machines issuing from a decadent post-modernism, ones that necessitate a spectacular investment and a profusion of means, without a true 'implementation' in Goodman's sense.

> Under 'implementation' [...] I include all that goes into making a work work; and a work works [...] to the extent that it is understood, to the extent that what and how it symbolizes [...] is discerned and affects the way we organize and perceive a world.[17]

We must recognize that Damien Hirst is not concerned with this sort of cognitive integration: his 'world' is simply disfiguring (although figurative), recycling mythical symbols of antiquity through an eclectic plastic hysteria.

The question now is what this deflationary assessment contributes to reflection on contemporary art. It is difficult to defend the position labeled 'segregationist' in response to this loss of credit, since that would be limited to the scenography of the exhibition curator (one thinks of Harald Szeeman and the exhibition *When Attitudes Become Form*, which took place in 1969, whose repercussions were symptomatic, and which remains a notorious exception). Cometti, for his part, defends the position while criticizing its protocols, if finally rejecting its sense.

---

16   *Ibid.*, p. 63.
17   Nelson Goodman, *Of Mind and Other Matters* (Cambridge MA: Harvard University Press, 1984), p. 143.

We need here to note certain differences and to mark different stages, because not all the exhibitions that concern us are of the same facture. Account taken of the typical 'thingness' of installations in the first period of rupture with a decadent postmodernism – think of the large green corridor of Bruce Nauman (1970, Guggenheim Museum New York) or the black-and-white volume of Robert Irwin (1975, Museum of Contemporary Art, Chicago), prototypes of conceptual art at its peak, rigorous works materializing light in an anti-illusionistic optic, meticulously installed in their museums – it is difficult to say what separates the *mise en place* (putting in place) and the *mise en oeuvre* (putting into effect) of these electro-mimetic installations from what these installations concretely *are*. But when we consider the functioning of typical twenty-first century installations, things are quite otherwise: these installations no longer represent an artform in which works depend for their meaning or effect on their authorized presence in a defined space.

The majority of allographic artworks of today, presented through technological devices other than those that made of Carl Andre and Donald Judd veritable inventors and engineers, correspond rather to impulsive acts and takings of extreme positions, ones based on willful variations of customary exhibition procedures. They are what we might with justice label 'counter-exhibitions'.

It becomes in this case a delicate task – without a conceptual *definiendum* – to separate such productions from their public manifestation. The time of the art called 'segregationist' is probably over: the past fifty years have seen a decided change of décor and nature. According to Peter Osborne, we have entered a post-conceptual era[18]. Everything rests perhaps on a misunderstanding,

---

18   Peter Osborne, *Anywhere or Not at All: Philosophy of Contemporary Art* (London: Verso, 2013). Osborne's thesis is that the art called 'contemporary' prolongs conceptual art in its basic intuition, but which it radicalizes with a critical turn regarding *the manner in which the world is perceived*. This art 'post-conceptual' adopts, in contrast to conceptual art, an *anti-aesthetic stance*. The material forms employed greatly exceed those of earlier media. In place of the unique work of art we find a kind of distortion resting on the multi-instantiation of works, which escapes the idealization of the present. For Osborne the pivot moment was that of Josef Kosuth and Sol LeWitt in the 60's: since then, the artwork is no longer incarnated or embodied in a

in his view: Conceptual and Minimalist Art was a reaction to Pop Art, and the further deconceptualization of the art product in that vein has by now completely deprived the concept of art of an extension.

2. *Requestioning the question of art*

As I have written elsewhere, in order to corner his prey, in order to defuse his target and proceed to a certain 'anti-metaphysical' debunking, Cometti thinks there is never a need for, as Suetonius put it, a 'golden fishhook'; hermeneutic tools, even refined ones, seem no longer wanted. Chapters 4 and 6 of *La Nouvelle Aura* are devoted to showing that the Dadaist gesture and that of Duchamp remain more direct modes of assault on the old idol of Beauty. Cometti's deconstruction of artistic modernity appears more convincing than Osborne's, and leads almost inevitably to this 'restoration of the aura' evoked by Maurizio Ferraris on the subject of 'grand' conceptual art[19].

Far be it for me to say that Cometti is mistaken, since looked at historically there is a lot of truth in the idea that the resonance of the actions of Dada and Duchamp explains much about the recent evolution of art. But at base it is in interrogating the reflux of the avant-garde, the loss of the autonomy that is still claimed by the 'modern' artwork, that Cometti's account possesses its real value. Arguing that art must be 'without qualities', and refusing to art any essential attributions, he is led to the paradox of claiming the reality of 'that which *makes* art', *without art necessarily being*

---

particular place or site. No longer are works in a specific medium; instead, works become their own media. Inspired by Adorno and his notion of 'determinate negation', Osborne thinks that such works provide a model for reconstructing phenomena. One might retain from this reflection the dialectic between site and non-site, the site of depart from which matter is borrowed, and the non-site of arrival where that matter is re-installed. But that perspective, drawn from the writings of Robert Smithson, appears still uncertain.

19 Maurizio Ferraris, 'Naturalisation de l'esthetique et culturisation de l'art', in *Naturaliser l'esthetique? Questions et enjeux d'un programme philosophique*, ed. by Jacques Morizot (Rennes: Presses Universitaires de Rennes, 2014), p. 239.

what results from that. And the same goes for that 'auratization' of installation objects, recreating a sense of remoteness and strangeness around them[20]. Ferraris, for his part, is rather struck by an embrace of ugliness in such works, which is not the same thing.

The reprise of the aura coincides, for Cometti, with an analysis of that which makes it the case that there is 'art', while supposing that the 'modes of existence of works' should have conditions independent of the actions of artists. To which one might object that if there are no *artists* who act, then there is no *art*. The following passage nicely lays out the situation:

> Regarding the manners of being or existing that are in question, no distinction can be made between the *being* and the *manner* of being. That is why, where art is concerned, it is always preferable to put the matter otherwise and to say that what is at issue is not what art *is*, but what *makes* art, that is, the *art-makers* [...] One will then say that the *art-makers* are what make of a thing, in given conditions, and for a given time, a thing that 'makes art' – or in other words, that the thing exhibits a certain number of traits that distance it from its usual condition and that inscribe it in an autonomous field of related objects.[21]

Apart from the fact that this definition by default is strictly relational, it suffers from a certain indeterminateness, and diverts attention from the ontology of artworks such as the minimalist ones of Carl Andre consisting of rough wooden cubes of severe dimensions that one can reconstruct and reposition, because their parts, of untreated material, are not joined together but arranged in modular fashion. For such artists, only the work's structure counts, and its 'facture' – its handling or finish – is irrelevant. In many respects, such works are neither objects nor sculptures, but rather, tangible modes of occupation of space. The question of whether that which makes something *art* is that which *makes* something art is thus basically a kind of philosophical conundrum, and cannot serve as a Swiss Army knife for defusing or rendering irrelevant the psychological intentions of creators.

---

20   Cometti, *La Nouvelle Aura*, p. 19.
21   *Ibid.*, p. 152.

But the question is interesting, because it raises the issue of What Matters, or What Counts, for art, as if the *factum* thus described transformed our mode of access to the work – namely, perception – by dissolving it in so many contingent conditions of appearance, be they historical, contextual, social or scenographic. Now, if artistic seeing is *factive*, like all other visual behavior – since a work is manifestly exhibited in order to be seen, including a clause according to which one then sees something – this visual *relatum* can never constitute an artistic fact in itself, because Cometti denies to art any distinctive subject matter and any intrinsic properties. For him it is our Wittgensteinian *forms of life* that inform what our eyes see and what our ears hear, rendering them artistic or not. There is thus no artistic seeing which is in itself *factive*, nor any structuring of the medium to be interposed between the object and the spectator. It is rather the commissars of exhibitions who make something art, in making *mode of production* and *mode of presentation* coincide. The artist, for his part, produces only 'the immanent object [...] and does not produce what goes beyond that'[22].

From this radical position, Cometti himself offers a magnificent zeugma. In sum, what *makes* art does not make art *exist*, but nonetheless 'makes art', or constitutes the *fact* of art, in a *factice* way. (Compare the zeugma: 'I draw a sigh from my breast and a banknote from my wallet'.) One passes here from the artifactual to the virtual, from the processual to the artificial: the work is 'made' of what it is not. This 'mis-ontology' conveys rather well the effect of disenchantment on the public provoked by contemporary art, and from that point of view Cometti's examination is highly instructive, so numerous are the incongruously arranged installations that confront us. The mechanisms of exhibition and display are the correlative, according to Cometti, of the disintegration of the 'qualities proper to art'. But if one adopts that conception one should conclude that such qualities no longer enter into the social fact of art. Yet that conclusion is not drawn by Cometti, seeming to him too strong[23].

---

22 *Ibid.*, p. 156, note 15.
23 It is, however, a conclusion drawn by Fredric Jameson, in *Le Postmodernisme ou la logique culturelle du capitalism tardif*, trans. by Florence Nevoltry

While insisting on the mutations of the phenomenon that have contributed to the birth of the art we call contemporary, Cometti insists as well on the proliferation of the global demand for such art, similar to what Von Hayek had in mind when he spoke of the 'laxity of the market'. To think that the *auratisation* of the *Brillo Box* by 'three-dimensional' photographs should be taken literally, when they nevertheless spring from the ateliers of *The Factory*, where these photos were glued onto plywood cartons. It was always a question of putting up for sale real *factitious* objects, and not forgeries or counterfeits. Their *trademark* was no longer a mark of fabrication, and those boxes contained no scouring sponges. Cometti's analysis is admirable in dispelling the mirages of false appearance. Only it is no longer technologically a 'beautiful' appearance (what he calls a *technological aura*). It is now mere appearance, or *Schein* alone, to which the notion of aura applies, because it is neither an 'embodied meaning' nor a 'waking dream' in Danto's terms.

So we should not be satisfied to say of the first works of Jeff Koons, which were dedicated to Hoover vacuum cleaners under neon illumination, that they 'consecrated' the fetishization of that brand. The *making* of the artwork does not authorize us to transform the question of art into a question of mimetic indices. Cometti underlines what is a crucial point, that the 'unicity of the work of art' that Benjamin wished to explode goes hand in hand with a loss of transmissibility. Works of contemporary art are unmoored from their heritage, and thus subject to expiration, like financial instruments that change hands when the stock market collapses. But that does not imply that the *luxury value* of merchandise products would have been 'auratisized', as Danto gives us to understand and as Cometti imprudently concurs. It seems harder to counterfeit a Warhol, or a piece of metal with smoothly machined sides as in works of Judd, which attests to their authenticity. And if there is an effect of luster in certain reissued serigraphs of Warhol – with all due respect to those who think this form of serial art smacks of promotional pompousness – this would be through confrontation with the impalpability of the photographic 'flesh' that transports the 'causal' referent of the

(Paris: ENSBA, 2007).

photographic print to the terrain of exhibition. Thus there is a serious difficulty in thinking that the 'factors of art' or 'art-makers', if they are not actually constitutive of arthood, might nevertheless impose an *aura* on these very diverse pieces of contemporary art.

3. The matrix of installation

Concerned above all to account for the dramatic transformation we observe in contemporary art, Cometti begins his book by asking what role *installations* play in the post-conceptual evolution of art that ends up betraying those very productions. The concepts he puts in place to that end are rather original, though the description of examples at some crucial points are lacking. Cometti labels *transitivity* (in a non-logical sense) the fact that works are movable from place to place and subject to permutation, and depicts a cultural continuum in which churches, prisons, and factories facilitate this symbolic transport or transference of artworks to places not designed for them, which are all then subject, in a shared world, to the same transmutation. Every exhibition is for him an installation[24], so long as it answers to a visual paradigm that can be 'publicized'. Cometti denounces, for example, 'the manner in which art installs itself in vineyards, and beds down with fashion and luxury'[25]. Somewhat later, after having evoked a 'perplexity without remedy', Cometti reflects on the grammar of the word 'contemporary' and notes how much the intentions of artists explained in the informational cartels accompanying works contribute to 'mentalizing' the process leading to the realization of an installation. However, Cometti objects, an installation in fact consists, by its mode of being, not in a representation of the mercantile world in its destructive and consumerist flight forward, but rather, in an exemplification of a disconnected and neutralized present. His conclusion is that 'contemporary art' must simply denote a *regime of literality*.

---

24   Cometti, *La nouvelle Aura*, p. 41.
25   *Ibid.*, p. 46. There is an allusion here to the Chateau Lacoste near Aix-en-Provence, with its sculpture park.

This is what gives [contemporary art] a remarkable capacity for extension and ingestion that knows no *a priori* limits. Literality is here the counterpart of tautology. The aura [of contemporary art] issues from it paradoxically; it depends on the logic of a predicate ('contemporary') that can only be exemplified: the contemporary artwork exemplifies the predicate that designates it as such. In the expression, 'contemporary art', there is not, on the one hand, 'art', and on the other hand, 'contemporary'. The weight of these two terms is unequal, the predicate 'contemporary' being the primary determinant. A contemporary work is *not* a work that, for one reason or another, would 'satisfy' the predicate 'contemporary'. On the contrary, it is the fact of applying that predicate to it that makes it contemporary art, the entire question being that of establishing what conditions preside over its application, since it cannot really be a matter of qualifying 'properties', or only, as it were, after the fact or secondhand. Its particular and unprecedented grammar is difficult to explain, because we are habituated to conceiving of predicates in terms of properties capable of description [...] This, in part, is the error on which the majority of debates about contemporary art rest. Apart from the fact that the term does not apply to periods prior to World War II, or even to the decade of the 60's, such debates turn around properties which must, in one way or another, be shared by the objects that enter into the domain of application of the concept, at the risk of controversies without end. This apparently very legitimate logic – comforting though it may be – is probably ultimately to no avail. In reality, if one tries to hold oneself to strictly grammatical considerations, one is brought to recognize that it isn't the existence of properties of a certain type that condition the application of the predicate, but rather, that the usage of the predicate has for function to make of its bearer an *example* of itself.[26]

Intentionally blending here Wittgenstein's intuitions on *Sprachspielen* (language games) and *Beispielen* (examples), and adding to that those of Goodman on exemplification, which seem to me antinomic, Cometti imparts a significant import to this phase of his book. He is clearly targeting the 'paradigm' that Nathalie Heinich has sought to identify behind the common traits belonging to the diverse productions of contemporary art. However, the application of the predicate 'of itself' in the above

---

26 Ibid., p. 64.

quotation is not specified. This critical omission runs the risk of circularity, but it is one Cometti appears to accept. In practice, the art of installations might be defined as residing in a *modus operandi* that not only 'derealizes' objects – a tendency effectively already present in certain manifestations of *arte povera* – but also 'deobjectifies' or suspends the 'operatic' materiality of the physical properties their creators have invested them with, in what must be considered a truly frightful jargon.

One may certainly offer some examples in this vein. The heterotypical properties of these installations are in effect not grammatically expressible, as with the lead, felt, or paper utilized in them: they are not true subjects, in the sense of materials that might speak by themselves of other things. Cometti is not wrong to note the many 'difficulties' presented by such phenomena, but he neglects the research of Eddy Zemach on the 'wholes', or compositional complexes, which are surely in play in these installations. He prefers to invoke instead 'circuits of recognition' and 'contexts of interaction', but without telling us exactly what sort of work results from that, as if the resulting immanence was ultimately refractory to all analysis – which is not really the case.

One might think of those works of Jannis Kounellis that offer objects in an arrangement calculated to challenge the reality of their 'being there' – a 'being there' that is precisely transitory, but without affirming their 'presence' in the phenomenological sense of that term, as they are never 'presented' in the common world, and because these installations are fully dismantleable, being reinstalled elsewhere whenever necessary. One might think of those branches of firewood bundles from Mario Merz, which are, if nothing else, material instances of natural species of wood, arranged and displayed as the furnishings for a fire that has not yet taken place. The layout of these pieces is somewhat troubling, because of the instructions the artist has given on the accumulation of these bundles and on the balancing of the heap they constitute. Is a consumerist paradox being illustrated here, as certain critics would have it? I do not know, but evidently, we no longer have before us merely decorative products or simulacra.

As for in virtue of what such works are 'contemporary', the question appears henceforth without justification. The predicate remains available, but nothing practically constrains us to find the correct usage of the word, except to discredit a family of productions on the pretext that they do not call for a 'time' other than (that of) the state of affairs that they install[27]. The heart of the problem, for Cometti, resides in the apparent *contingency* of these assemblages: 'the fact that they are supposed to possess no specific physical and perceptual properties inclines us to so regard them'[28]. But the perceptual non-specificity of these works seems at least debatable in a number of cases.

A study by Julie Reiss[29], has defended the opposite point of view, initiating a series of publications that relaunch the debate. What is striking is that she insists on the fact that installations *photograph very badly*, and accordingly displays reluctance to engage with their documentary catalogues. Her thesis is that the loss of public space, under attack in many ways, is at the root of a different appeal to the spectator confronted with the occupying of space characteristic of an installation. But her definition of what constitutes such space occupancy is relative, and not cognitive in the sense of cognitive penetrability theorized by Susan Siegel[30].

More recently, Claire Bishop makes the same argument in her *Installation Art*[31]: Installations presuppose an *embodied viewer*, someone who can experience the tactile weight of the situation in which the installation is placed. Instead of presenting a *self-contained object*, the art of installation proposes a *specific location*, covering the space as a whole, into which the spectator penetrates. Bishop heralds a return to phenomenology, in light of the explicit

---

27   Ibid., p. 66.
28   Ibid.
29   Julie Reiss, *From Margin to Center: The Spaces of Installation Art* (Cambridge MA: MIT Press, 1999).
30   Susanna Siegel, *The Rationality of Perception* (Oxford: Oxford University Press, 2017). According to Dustin Stokes, Siegel has demonstrated how we 'see' that our audience does not listen to us when we give a talk, and has studied the effect of anxiety by which we avoid believing what our eyes show us. And in the case that concerns us her observation is decisive, since the link between the information provided and the epistemic response appears to reestablish itself, contra the automatic report of the *top-down effect*. Similarly, faced with an installation, what can we infer from it that would permit us to categorize the object, whether as an assemblage or otherwise?
31   Claire Bishop, *Installation Art* (London: Tate, 2005).

allegiance shown by Robert Morris and Carl Andre to Merleau-Ponty's *The Phenomenology of Perception*[32]. Acknowledging all that remains suspect in the subjectivity of the person who 'has' an experience, Bishop nonetheless develops her argument according to which the subject regarding an installation is at one and the same time centered and decentered, creating an antagonism for the *self-present viewing subject*.

This proves that the 'perplexity' of which Cometti speaks is in no way feigned. Where Michael Fried spoke of 'theatricality' or of 'presentness' – though there concerned with classical and modern works of art, and with the degree to which the subject is eclipsed by the work that absorbs him – the art of installations would like the spectator 'to be subjected, through his physical presence, to an experience of decentering'[33]. That the 'discrete' space of an installation is itself contiguous with the real world allows for a number of cultural and anthropological interpretations on which I prefer not to dwell. The multiplication of subject-centered worlds appears to me very unhealthy as well as wildly idealistic. It is enough for me to have shown here that the perceptual non-specificity claimed for installations can be questioned. There is indeed, behind the word 'contemporary', a horror of empty space, and despite rampant speculation on the prices of installation pieces, a refusal of the *commodification* of mundane objects into *objects of art*. Voila why Warhol has become a counter-example, foil, and bugbear for the creators of installations.

4. Aura-voir

In Cometti's thought there are no *artistic* properties that can be uncontentiously assigned to things, in contrast, without doubt, to aesthetic properties. (Though doubt might well be permitted there.) His book insists on the divorce that has been consummated between art and history, and not in space – between the space of the museum and the space of the common world. One reads also

---

[32] Maurice Merleau-Ponty, *The Phenomenology of Perception*, trans. by Colin Smith (London: Routledge, 1962).
[33] La *Nouvelle Aura*, p. 133.

this sentence: 'the mode of activation becomes the work'[34], which heightens the challenge to the idea of which it is the counterpart. For Cometti, there are two sorts of auras, *ephemeral* ones and *mediatic* ones. Goodman's heritage, in Cometti's eyes, should be reevaluated in light of Dewey's, whose notion of experience is richer and broader. But this terminological declension of the term 'aura' calls for interrogation by the multiplicity of its occurrences. One is reminded, evidently, of Goodman's disdainful 'au revoir' to the notion of *aura*, but today it seems that that lesson has been lost. Consider this passage, where the *hapax* [one-off event] of the 'aura-voir' surfaces in the text 'Art in Action':

> What are the reasons that militate in favor of the generally superior quality and force of direct interaction with works of art [as opposed to the attitude consisting in being content with the contemplation of reproductions]? It is sometimes said that the difference resides in the *aura* belonging to the original work, and which is absent from reproductions, copies, and commentaries. However, so long as the notion of aura fails to receive a clarification superior to that one finds in the dictionary – 'an emanation or subtle breath' – we will derive little profit from it. Aura should be interpreted, rather, as a complex phenomenon belonging to the history of a work, and as bound up with its allusions, associations, and other referential relations. This is, to be sure, a crude and inadequate description, but I cannot undertake to pursue the analysis here. For the time being, as far as aura is concerned, my last word shall be therefore 'aura-voir'.[35]

Observe that Goodman here understands aura precisely in the superstitious sense of *emanation*. Benjamin was clearly aware of that sense when speaking of the aura as a breath or *Atmen*, corresponding to the souls of deceased persons thought to inhabit the earliest daguerreotypes: 'There was an aura around them, a sort of medium', which corresponds well to that 'smoke without flame' from a verse of Stefan George cited by Benjamin in his *Short History of Photography* (1921)[36]. Goodman also underlines

---

34 Cometti, *La Nouvelle Aura*, p. 98.
35 Nelson Goodman, 'L'art en action'.
36 Walter Benjamin, 'Petite histoire de la photographie', trans. by André Gunthert, *Etudes photographiques*, tirage a part du no. 1, (1996), pp. 7-38 (for an English version, see Walter Benjamin, *Short History of Photography*,

the 'referential aspect' of photographs linked to the historicity of the photographic object without regard for the manner in which Benjamin studied the long exposure time required for the face of the philosopher Schelling to appear – that 'granitic' personage, according to Caroline Schlegel – who is then apprehended in a drastic immobility while it is the folds of his frock coat that impress most. Goodman's ironic rejection of aura is thus the fruit of a 'crude and inadequate description' that can only be taken at face value. What is certain is that Benjamin intended by the word to attest not to the historicity of the photograph but to its resistance to the *hic et nunc*, as if that 'here and now' was not as rigorously determinable as a point on a map in a geometric projection. It is that 'thanks to which reality has, so to speak, burned itself into the character of the image through and through'[37]. *The aura is thus indeed an 'aura-voir'*, at the punning level, or rather, what bids 'adieu' to the revival of the real in the semblance offered by the image.

That Benjamin has been thus caricatured is not surprising. For one, because philosophical theories are easily caricatured, for another, because the conception of resemblance held by Benjamin is the exact contrary of that held by Goodman, an affair of *formal matching* of properties for the latter, an *affiliation of essences*, often rather abstract and subtle, for the former. By the same token, one might observe that nowadays, twenty-five years after 'Art in Action', the relative discredit into which Goodman has fallen is the consequence of his irrealist nominalism, and that his irrealism is more 'unbridled' than that of all modal anti-realists combined. By comparison, Benjamin appears both more modest and more sober. If the postulation of the aura poses a problem for Goodman, deeply concerned with the refinement of a philosophical system, his own early systematization of appearance, built around imperceptible qualitative atoms, abstractions neutralizing the sensible given, is to my eyes entirely chimerical, and remains emblematic of a mereology without real grounding, a magnificent syntactic exploit. But it is one that leads us astray, and which perhaps explains

---

    Screen, 13, no 1 (1 March 1972), pp. 5–26 <https://doi.org/10.1093/screen/13.1.5> [accessed 20 January 2019]).
37 Benjamin, 'Petite histoire de la photographie', p. 7.

Goodman's subsequent turn toward philosophy of art[38]. The error of Goodman regarding photography underlined by John Kulvicki[39] brings out both the conceptual opposition between autographic and allographic, and the extent of doctrinal disagreement between Benjamin and Goodman.

Benjamin's notion of *aura* does not owe much to Ludwig Klages; there is nothing phantom-like about it, and it is perfectly clear that it derives rather directly from the application of the 'bichromatic gum' that allows for the first impressions of a photograph to present an image in blurred relief, which is just an artisanal trick of the trade. Through retouching *aura* was thus invented as a hypothetical designation that Benjamin recovered for another end. But the photographer might well object: 'The association of technical and sociological parameters – themselves hazardous – that Benjamin proposes fails to reflect any identifiable reality in the history of photography'[40]. This confirms the partly blind condemnation of Goodman, because Benjamin had invented that association. By analogy, what could only be a natural filiation for Benjamin, studying very different inscriptions and comparing their observable resemblances, would simply amount to anthropological trickery, in which the auratic effect has been confused with that of a temporal magnifying glass (*Zeitlupe*). Whence this assuredly enigmatic definition: 'the unique apparition of the faraway, however near it may be' (*einmalige Erscheinung einer Ferne, so nah sie sein mag*).

More charitably, one could translate *Erscheinung* by 'phenomenon' rather than 'apparition', and say that it is a matter of an in principle non-repeatable phenomenon wherein a distant thing fails to be apprehended – or has been lost, and must be exorcised – whatever enlargement or magnification of the image one effects. With the digitalization of images, what Benjamin says becomes patent, and acquires a divinatory flavor, because the basic aim of infographic work is to attain even greater finesse in the resolution of pixels. Think of Andreas Gursky's photograph of

---

38 I have taken the logic of Goodman's *La structure de l'apparence* seriously in Jean-Maurice Monnoyer, 'Lequel est le quale?', *Etudes de Philosophie*, 9-10 (2008-2011), pp. 311-332.
39 John Kulvicki, *Images* (Oxford: Routledge, 2014), notably pp. 100-107.
40 Gunthert, *Etudes photographiques*, p. 34

the banks of the Rhine (1999), 'the most expensive photo in the world' according to a recent sale, where all sense of 'faraway' has disappeared under an extremely suggestive forced lateralization. In this image the river shines more brightly than the sky with its unreal cloudlets, the grass is plusher than a silk carpet, as if the supernatural being of the Rhine (*Gott am Rhein*) was becoming homey and familiar to us. Voila Heidegger reinvented by his great-nephew! Being withdraws from the visual world, before what as it happens is the most polluted river in Europe, an obviously disingenuous withdrawal. Reality in 'high definition' becomes thus magical, since the diffraction effects of light are corrected, to the detriment of the actual referent and the informational content of the image, by the invocation of a superlative instance that outdoes or outstrips its model.

But it is precisely this contemporary sort of image, rather well described by Andrea Pinotti as a 'hyper-image', that the art of installations in some fashion discredits[41]. It is useful to repeat this, since for this artform in a number of cases an impenetrable and 'cold' element, such as a flux of photons, must be exhibited without distortion and physically realized, as in the neon sculptures of Bruce Nauman that rematerialize written inscriptions. But my aim here is not to attempt to describe Nauman's installations – luminous, filmic, or otherwise. Still, such works doubtless 'produced shock waves' in the 70's. They foreshadowed the advent of a perceptually 'occupied' space meant to rid us of images.

In this light one better understands how Jean-Pierre Cometti believed it just to evoke a *technological aura*, which from his pen emerges a curious lexical object. In its primary meaning for Cometti such an *aura* cannot be conferred on a thing – neither arbitrarily, nor artificially, nor metaphorically. In contrast to Rainer Rochlitz, who saw in the disenchantment of aura a mode of authoritarian interception of regard perverted by fixation on the 'hazy faraway' of memory, it seems to me that the desecration of aura announced by Benjamin finds in Cometti's hands a conceptually corrupt

---

41 Andrea Pinotti and Antonion Somaini, *Cultura Visuale, Immagini, Sguardi, Media, Dispositivi* (Torino: Piccola Biblioteca Einaudi, 2016). Though not without the post-modern risk of thinking that these iconic panoramas establish a new, sociologically transparent, order of things.

employment. Benjamin was obviously thinking of those Madonnas of Gérard David, or else those small landscapes of Joachim Patinir, which in their precision install a temporally inaccessible distance – the otherworldliness of Mary's mystical maternity or a nature of Edenic character – one that is definitively non-reproducible. But from another angle, if we wish to stop reveling in Benjamin, then to think, inversely, that *authenticity* consists in 'privileging' the present leads to misunderstanding, as Cometti believed and defended in his way, in a manner willingly contradictory[42].

Evidently, the relationship to history remains ambiguous throughout this discussion. But the defeat or decline of substantial art does not call for restoration of its *aura*. Goodman was conscious of mystification in the employment of the term; Cometti rather seeks a 'parasitic' characterization of the term so as to intercept it where it attempts to hide. Let me offer a concrete example, which should allow us to escape from the *aporia* that threatens. In the rolls of the Bibliotheque Nationale in the Rue de Richelieu one finds a citation of Proust meticulously copied out by Benjamin where the word, but not the concept, of aura appears explicitly. The narrator of *A la recherché du temps perdu* has gone out at night with his chauffeur to visit the porches of churches, orienting the headlights of the car so as to put in better relief the statues found there. The *aura* that emerges, as Proust labels it in *A l'ombre des jeunes filles en fleur*, is a phenomenon that makes itself known in the brief moment of illumination in which the statue is 'removed' from the edifice and brought 'nearer' the center of perception.

Rendering homage to Benjamin in *La Nouvelle Aura* Cometti has by no means produced an infertile work, but he has proceeded as an essayist, according to the rules of that genre, calling for a mosaic procedure by successive approaches not governed by a consistent overall schema. Cometti's nuanced reasoning and his estimable culture have prompted the preceding remarks, but they are surely not the only ones worth making.

In summary, I consider that Cometti's observations on the 'literal' spectator, to use his term, do not by any means treat contemporary art in an ignorant fashion, since in his text all

---

42 Jean-Pierre Cometti, *La Force d'un malentendu. Essais sur l'art et la philosophie de l'art* (Paris: Questions theoriques, 2009).

relevant critical perspectives are taken into consideration and given their due. It is a little as if we had already entered into an epoch in which commodified art (*l'art mercantilisé*) has become 'the opium of the people', to recall an expression of Max Raphael in Chapter 6 of his *Demands of Art*[43]. In the age of the videosphere, Raphael prophesized, all artistic expression will have become 'atavistic', and that is more or less what can be read between the lines of Cometti's last book, a very honest one. But it is also one that is despairingly grumpy and caustic, which was not the case of Cometti's idol, Robert Musil, and the author to whom he owes the expression 'art without qualities'.

For my part, I judge that the 'model' spectator to whom the artist of installations addresses himself, unlike Cometti's 'literal' spectator, is no longer a passive or a disillusioned contemplator: he is, instead, one possessed of a cognitive apparatus that enables him to make inferences and to conclude whether or not such installations truly participate in the disenchantment of the world.

References

Benjamin, Walter, *Ecrits français* (Paris: Gallimard, Folio Essais, n°418, 1991).
—, 'Petite histoire de la photographie', trans. by André Gunthert, *Etudes photographiques*, 1, (1996), pp. 7-38.
Bishop, Claire, *Installation Art* (London: Tate, 2005).
Cometti, Jean-Pierre, *Art et facteurs d'art. Ontologies friables* (Rennes: Presses Universitaires de Rennes, 2012).
—, *La force d'un malentendu. Essais sur l'art et la philosophie de l'art* (Paris: Questions theoriques, 2009)
—, *La nouvelle Aura. Économies de l'art et de la culture* (Paris, Questions théoriques, 2016).
Ferraris, Maurizio, 'Naturalisation de l'esthetique et culturisation de l'art', in *Naturaliser l'esthetique? Questions et enjeux d'un programme philosophique*, ed. by Jacques Morizot (Rennes: Presses Universitaires de Rennes, 2014).

---

43 Max Raphael, *The Demands of Art* (Princeton, N.J.: Princeton University Press, Bollingen series, LXXVIII, 1968), p. 183. (This sixth chapter was not translated in the French edition of the book issued by Klincksieck.)

Goodman, Nelson, 'L'art en action', *Cahiers du Musee National d'Art Moderne*, 41 (1992), pp. 7-14.
—, *Of Mind and Other Matters* (Cambridge MA: Harvard University Press, 1984).
Jameson, Fredric *Le Postmodernisme ou la logique culturelle du capitalism tardif*, trans. by Florence Nevoltry (Paris: ENSBA, 2007).
Kulvicki, John, *Images* (Oxford: Routledge, 2014).
Merleau-Ponty, Maurice, *The Phenomenology of Perception*, trans. by Colin Smith (London: Routledge, 1962).
Monnoyer, Jean-Maurice, 'Lequel est le quale?', *Etudes de Philosophie*, 9-10 (2008-2011), pp. 311-332.
Osborne, Peter, *Anywhere or Not at All: Philosophy of Contemporary Art* (London: Verso, 2013).
Pinotti, Andrea, and Antonion Somaini, *Cultura Visuale, Immagini, Sguardi, Media, Dispositivi* (Torino: Piccola Biblioteca Einaudi, 2016).
Raphael, Max, *The Demands of Art* (Princeton, N.J.: Princeton University Press, Bollingen series, LXXVIII, 1968).
Reiss, Julie, *From Margin to Center: The Spaces of Installation Art* (Cambridge MA: MIT Press, 1999).
Siegel, Susanna, *The Rationality of Perception* (Oxford: Oxford University Press, 2017).

MIMESIS GROUP
www.mimesis-group.com

MIMESIS INTERNATIONAL
www.mimesisinternational.com
info@mimesisinternational.com

MIMESIS EDIZIONI
www.mimesisedizioni.it
mimesis@mimesisedizioni.it

ÉDITIONS MIMÉSIS
www.editionsmimesis.fr
info@editionsmimesis.fr

MIMESIS COMMUNICATION
www.mim-c.net

MIMESIS EU
www.mim-eu.com

Printed by
Geca Industrie Grafiche – San Giuliano Milanese (MI)
June 2019